KNOWLEDGE AND EXPERIMENTAL REALISM
IN CONRAD, LAWRENCE, AND WOOLF

PATRICK J. WHITELEY

KNOWLEDGE
AND EXPERIMENTAL
REALISM IN CONRAD,
LAWRENCE,
AND
WOOLF

Louisiana State University Press
Baton Rouge and London

10   9   8   7   6   5   4   3   2   1

Designer: Laura Roubique Gleason
Typeface: Trump Mediaeval
Typesetter: G & S Typesetters, Inc.
Printer: Thomson-Shore, Inc.
Binder: John H. Dekker & Sons

The author is grateful to Viking Penguin, Inc., Laurence Pollinger, Ltd., and
the Estate of the late Mrs. Frieda Lawrence Ravagli for permission to quote
the whole of "The End, the Beginning," from *The Complete Poems of D. H.
Lawrence,* collected and edited by Vivian de Sola Pinto and F. Warren Roberts.
Copyright © 1954, 1971 by Angelo Ravagli and C. M. Weekly, Executors of the
Estate of Frieda Lawrence Ravagli.

LIBRARY OF CONGRESS CATALOGING-IN-PUBLICATION DATA

Whiteley, Patrick J., 1953–
    Knowledge and experimental realism in Conrad,
Lawrence, and Woolf.

    Bibliography: p.
    Includes index.
    1. English fiction—20th century—History and
criticism.   2. Realism in literature.   3. Experimental
fiction—Great Britain—History and criticism.
4. Knowledge, Theory of, in literature.   5. Conrad,
Joseph, 1857–1924—Criticism and interpretation.
6. Lawrence, D. H. (David Herbert), 1885–1930—
Criticism and interpretation.   7. Woolf, Virginia,
1882–1941—Criticism and interpretation.   I. Title.
PR888.R4W45   1987   823'.912'091   86-27721

ISBN 0-8071-1323-9

*Publication of this book has been assisted by a grant from the Andrew W.
Mellon Foundation.*

For my father and mother,
with love, for their indispensable
encouragement and support

CONTENTS

ACKNOWLEDGMENTS

My thanks go to Professor John B. Vickery, whose advice on this project helped me from beginning to end. His generous input may well have left me free to make my own mistakes, but it was always enlightening. The comments that Professors Steven Gould Axelrod and Marshall Van Deusen made on earlier versions of this essay kept me from making numerous wrong turns.

I owe much to Long Beach poet Gerald Locklin, a former teacher whose faith in my work far exceeded my understanding at crucial moments. My very special thanks go to Barbara Laughton not only for her constant moral support but for the critical acumen she brought to bear on her readings of this essay's early drafts.

KNOWLEDGE AND EXPERIMENTAL REALISM
IN CONRAD, LAWRENCE, AND WOOLF

INTRODUCTION

LITERARY REALISM AND
THE PROBLEM OF KNOWLEDGE

They said, "You have a blue guitar,
You do not play things as they are."

The man replied, "Things as they are
Are changed upon the blue guitar."

And they said then, "But play, you must,
A tune beyond us, yet ourselves,

A tune upon the blue guitar
Of things exactly as they are."

—Wallace Stevens
From "The Man with the Blue Guitar"

And then slowly they came to know that what they knew
might mean something different from what they had known
it was when they knew simply knew what it was.

—Gertrude Stein
Narration: Four Lectures

By now it is a commonplace that Joseph Conrad, D. H. Lawrence, and Virginia Woolf brought to the English novel some of
the most drastic transformations in its history. So drastic was
their experimentation that their works seemed to presage the
death of the novel altogether. Although he had James Joyce and
Wyndham Lewis immediately in mind, T. S. Eliot surely took
Conrad and Lawrence into account when in 1923 he suggested,
"The novel ended with Flaubert and with James. It is, I think,
because Mr. Joyce and Mr. Lewis, being 'in advance' of their
time, felt a conscious or probably unconscious dissatisfaction
with the form, that their novels are more formless than those of
a dozen clever writers who are unaware of its obsolescence."
For Yvor Winters the passing of fifteen years since the death of
Virginia Woolf had still not provided the distance sufficient for
discerning anything but a mortal blow to the novel when he
read her and her contemporaries' experimental fiction. In 1956

1

he pronounced, "The novel, for the most part an abortive form from its beginnings, is dying rapidly."[1]

It should be no surprise that Eliot later changed his mind; obviously, early twentieth-century experimental fiction, in the hands of major experimentalists like Conrad, Lawrence, and Woolf, served to render the novel at least as viable a conduit of human experience in our century as it was in the nineteenth. But in maintaining its viability it underwent changes that, even if they now seem less drastic than they did to contemporaneous readers, nonetheless are a lesson in the formal history of the English novel, especially as that form and history pertain to the complicated issue of literary realism.

To what extent do Conrad, Lawrence, and Woolf broaden our notion of literary realism? In what specific ways do they rely on or modify its norms? At what point in their experimentation do we discover literary realism's vanishing point? These are among the principal questions I want to examine in this study by analyzing these novelists' experimentation in the light of contemporaneous realistic epistemology. And however speculative my answers to these questions must necessarily be, I hope they will enhance our sense of what the early modern transformation of the English novel consisted of.

In using the insights of epistemology I assume from the beginning a valid analogy between philosophical and literary realism. Numberless critics have usefully called upon this analogy in order to discern the beginnings of the novel in England, finding in the seventeenth and eighteenth centuries a major shift in philosophical outlook conducive to the novel's growth. This shift in outlook, from scholastic to modern realism, radically changed the meaning of the word *reality*. No longer a set of universal forms, reality was now an expanse of particulars laid out before the senses.

The beginnings of modern realism and of the epistemology that most profoundly affected the course of the novel appear in the writings not of an empiricist, as my previous sentence would imply, but of a rationalist. In his *Discourse on Method*

---

1. T. S. Eliot, "*Ulysses,* Order, and Myth," in John W. Aldridge (ed.), *Critiques and Essays on Modern Fiction 1920–1951* (New York, 1952), 426; Yvor Winters, "Problems for the Modern Critic of Literature," *Hudson Review,* IX (1956), 386.

(1637), *Meditations* (1641), and *Principles of Philosophy* (1644), René Descartes revolutionized philosophy when he made the introspections of a solitary mind the ground for all knowledge, starting with the knowledge of one's own existence. His methodology required the ability to hold oneself apart from externality, by way of doubting its existence, in order to say, in that notorious and potentially solipsistic formulation, "I think; therefore I am." An essentially rationalist philosophy like Descartes' could not and did not care to prove the existence of an external reality through empiricist standards of verification. Instead Descartes appealed to his belief in a reasonable and merciful God in order to fortify his view that the external world indeed existed, thereby turning absolute doubt into absolute certainty. In the process he drove a wedge between the thinker and the objects of his knowledge, creating dualisms between subject and object, between the *res cogitans* and the *res extensa*. Because Descartes firmly believed in the existence of an external world despite the subject's dissociation from it, he has a central place at the beginnings of modern realism and, by analogy, in the rudiments of novelistic technique.

In the form in which it appears in eighteenth-century English literature, philosophical realism takes on the empiricist bent that John Locke lent to Descartes' dualistic epistemology. At this point the correspondence between philosophical and literary realism is clearest, especially as that correspondence is registered in the early English novel. For it is in the "new genre" that the primary features of modern realism are most apparent—in the emphasis on particulars, on the value of skepticism, on private experience, on particularized time schemes. The particularization of experience carried with it the particularization of character, which in turn invited psychological complexity. The novel's empiricist values made character more psychologically complex by proposing that character, a stable center of the self's experiences, could be discovered through a temporal series of observations. The empiricist assumption that nature is stable, and that time and space are transparent media for knowing it, allows for the fundamental concept of a repeatable experiment. Similarly, in the novel the rudimentary self was thought to remain stable, even if it seemed to recede behind realistic narrative's series of complex observations, which alone could promise eventually to uncover the self's essence. Its psychologizing of character is probably the feature of the realistic novel most profoundly and directly affected by its own empiricist biases.[2]

Where, though, does that leave Conrad, Lawrence, and Woolf? I suggest that it leaves them close to conventional literary realism's vanishing point, at a point where, if we want to see them as realistic novelists, we must update our sense of realistic epistemology by examining the possible analogies between their fiction and theories of knowledge espoused by figures such as Arthur Schopenhauer, William James, Edwin Holt, G. E. Moore, and Ludwig Wittgenstein.

My discussion of experimental realism in Conrad, Lawrence, and Woolf makes claims about both the literary history of the English novel and the formal limits of realistic representation; it involves, then, conceptually linked historical and paradigmatic observations. My historical claim is reinforced by the fact that even though Conrad, Lawrence, and Woolf cover a relatively brief period in the novel's history, their considerable stature has the power substantially to shape our sense of what the English novel as a whole offered between 1900 and 1941. Together they represent an era of profound doubt about the conventional realistic novel's assumptions and procedures. All three novelists have comparable interests in exploring the limits of realistic representation. And all three respond to the *Zeitgeist* of the late nineteenth and early twentieth centuries, to a spirit of profound doubt about cognition's efficacy. They doubted that philosophically realistic views of knowledge, which nineteenth-century positivism had tried to fortify, could ever explain how the mind comprehends the true nature of reality.[3] Further reinforcing the literary historical implications of

2. Kenneth MacLean, *John Locke and English Literature of the Eighteenth Century* (1936; rpr. New York, 1962); Ernest Lee Tuveson, *Imagination as a Means of Grace: Locke and the Aesthetics of Romanticism* (Berkeley, 1960); Ian Watt, *The Rise of the Novel: Studies in Defoe, Richardson and Fielding* (Berkeley, 1957); Eric Rothstein, *Systems of Order and Inquiry in Later Eighteenth-Century Fiction* (Berkeley, 1975); Harry Levin, "The Example of Cervantes," *Contexts of Criticism* (Cambridge, Mass., 1957), 79–96.

3. Among the works to which my discussion of this intellectual climate is indebted are Wylie Sypher, *Loss of the Self in Modern Literature and Art* (New York, 1962), Harold Kaplan, *The Passive Voice: An Approach to Modern Fic-*

my discussion are these novelists' points of similarity with their contemporaries, especially James Joyce and William Faulkner. As Richard Pearce has suggested, in Joyce's *Ulysses* (1922) and *Finnegans Wake* (1939) the encyclopedic narration does more than suppress the perspective-giving "frame" that realistic fiction often conceals as a way of seeming to be a transparent medium for representing reality; it shatters the frame with its aura of infinite plurisignificance. In Faulkner the interplay of perspectives chronically delays—and some have argued that it totally banishes—any hope that the mind can ever order its experience.[4] Thus, my historical claim is that, if we take conventional realism to mean an empiricist bent in the novel, Conrad, Lawrence, and Woolf make it gradually harder to persevere in the enterprise of realistic representation.

But the novel did not suddenly begin exploring its representational limits in the twentieth century, so my claim is also paradigmatic, having to do with the formal limits inherent in the novel's mimetic features. In fact, the novel is notoriously fond of looking in upon its own representational efforts. If the idea of the novel lends itself to any sort of paradigm at all, that paradigm is subversion; indeed, the novel is an inherently subversive genre. It began as a way of parodying established authors and genres in order to make literature seem to banish itself by opening out onto life. It did not take long for the English novel to attack its own epistemology, implicitly in Henry Fielding's *Shamela* (1741), explicitly in Laurence Sterne's *Tristram Shandy* (1759–1767). So although the term *experimental novel* has some historical validity in describing early modern fiction, it is in a larger sense a tautology. And so, ultimately, might the term *experimental realism* be a tautology, inasmuch as literary realism has traditionally been conceived of as an inherently experimental enterprise, imitating the natural sciences' experimental methodology. These are meaningful terms as long as we specify a historical context, namely, the tendency in major

---

tion (Athens, Ohio, 1966), and John A. Lester, Jr., *Journey Through Despair 1880–1914: Transformations in British Literary Culture* (Princeton, 1968).

4. Richard Pearce, "Enter the Frame," in Raymond Federman (ed.), *Surfiction: Fiction Now . . . and Tomorrow* (Chicago, 1975), 47–57; James Guetti, *The Limits of Metaphor: A Study of Melville, Conrad, and Faulkner* (Ithaca, N.Y., 1967).

early twentieth-century British novels to take sometimes radical departures from the norms of eighteenth- and nineteenth-century representations of reality and from representations of our powers of apprehending that reality.

Even if my discussion is as paradigmatic as it is historical, we still must anticipate some methodological questions about influence. Whenever we see a writer's direct contact with a philosopher—Conrad's knowledge of Schopenhauer, Lawrence's of Bertrand Russell and Trigant Burrow, or Woolf's of G. E. Moore—then the model of philosophy's relationship to literature seems straightforward enough. But even then it is problematic, for we must constantly remind ourselves that genuine artists do not start with a worked-out theory and then set their fictional worlds in motion according to it. In truth, the fiction becomes the philosophy; it does not follow it deductively. That is why D. H. Lawrence is so misunderstood whenever his best works are interpreted as the animation of preconceived ideas. Nothing could be further from the truth. Everything we know about his writing habits tells us that he used his fiction to test his ideas against "real" experience. And in *Women in Love* (1920) especially, he allowed his fiction to interrogate and subvert his ideas, leaving him with open questions. Even when we compare his discursive essays to his fiction we come up with often enriching inconsistencies. If his essays' formulations can be contradicted or modified by his novels, then how much more likely it is that others' discursive arguments can distort our sense of his fiction unless we sustain a healthy skepticism about allegedly direct and historically verifiable influences.

Recognizing the difficulties built into even historically verifiable influences, I will sometimes take recourse in comparing epistemological systems espoused by thinkers of whom these novelists have dubious and sometimes no direct knowledge. The direct contacts are worth noticing, even if they reveal the author's departures from their ideas. But I hold out for the possibility that a novelist's fiction can embody epistemological models of which he is not consciously aware. That is why I use the word *metatheory* to describe these novelists' ideas about knowledge and imagination. The word indicates a specific model of literature's relationship to philosophy, one that takes account of but is not restricted to direct and historically verifiable influences. I want to avoid the reductive view of philosophy's contact with literature that I just described in connection with Lawrence—a view to which strictly historical (not paradigmatic) accounts sometimes lead us.

The word *metatheory* is appropriate here for three reasons that will clarify the main outlines of my project's methodology and scope. The first is the simplest. My readings of theories of knowledge and imagination have their basis in fiction rather than in philosophical treatises, because my interest is primarily in the novel and secondarily in the history of ideas.

Second, especially as it pertains to the problem of imagination, my discussion does not aim to formulate a theory of how these novelists imagined when they wrote their fiction, nor does it aim to favor one explanation of how literary artists imagine over another. There are already a number of thought-provoking studies that take on this task. My enterprise differs from those, because I examine the way Conrad, Lawrence, and Woolf thought *about* knowledge and imagination, and show how their thoughts moved them to explore new ways of representing reality in the novel. They may be only imagining what imagination is. As far as I know, they did not imagine in any essentially different way than their predecessors did. If their works are qualitatively different, it is because they channeled their imaginative energy, as well as their powers of doubt, in different directions, mainly as a result of what they thought about cognition.

Third, whereas theories must meet the test of experience or at least logical argumentation, metatheories are, on an important level, incorrigible—or better, "noncorrigible." This does not mean that they meet no test at all. It means that they are validated in the context of the works from which they are inferred. A metatheory is noncorrigible to the extent that it cannot be proved through reference to the way the novelist, or anyone for that matter, actually knows or imagines the world. In the same way, any novel's "facts" are noncorrigible because they are tested against other elements within the fiction. Obviously, no one tries to verify how many children Moll Flanders had by consulting the public record. The truth about imagination itself is in the noncorrigibility of the mental image, since if I say I am imagining a winged horse, nothing counts as evidence that I am not imagining such a thing except my introspection.[5] So it is, too, with the novel's metatheories of epistemology. If we find logical inconsistencies, even in a metatheory within the same work, that is fiction's prerogative. It would require only the most blatant disrespect for a novel's artistic integrity if its success were judged by the standards of philosophical discourse.

In the last two reasons for using the word *metatheory* I implied a difference between the act of cognition and the act of writing; that is, the fictional embodiment of a thought about knowledge and imagination may have little or nothing to do with the act of cognition that initiated the fiction's composition. But it is not my intention to argue for the mutual independence of writing and thinking. It is one thing to say that writing can modify the character of knowledge and imagination; it is another to say that writing and thinking are independent efforts. If nothing counted as evidence of cognition except the experience of thinking itself, then it is questionable whether we could ever know that anyone but ourselves was capable of thinking. There would be no point in, and certainly no way of, discussing cognition's bearing on literature. Knowledge would be a closed book.

At the same time I reject the notion that writing and thinking are identical acts. While there is undoubtedly a profoundly important interaction between writing and thinking, so that within certain limits it is reasonable to suggest that writing, like language, is a mode of knowing, my discussion would take on a very different character if I worked on the assumption common in structuralist criticism and recent theories of composition that it is unreasonable to suspect a causal link between writing and the acts of cognition that precede it. For in this assumption is a covert attack on the imagination's efficacy. Denis Donoghue has lucidly described this attack:

> The imagination is a genuine ability. . . . The offensive element in Barthe's account of the subject as the wake of all the codes which constitute the "I" is the implication that the subject is merely the sum of his occasions. This figure does not allow any initiative to

5. My comments on the concept of noncorrigibility are indebted to Edward S. Casey, *Imagining: A Phenomenological Study* (Bloomington, 1976), 95.

the subject. But suppose the self were to be related to its codes as the future is related to the present; that is, let the imagination be taken to mean the act of a mind concerned to ensure the freedom of its future. . . . Grammatically, the imagination would correspond to the imperative mood, saying, "Let there be light, pleasure, joy, and freedom above all." . . . The future is not a beast in the jungle, lying in wait upon the present; it is still a realm of possibility, the code is not yet closed.[6]

My agreement with Donoghue's description explains why in the following chapters I use novelists' thoughts about their craft and sometimes describe the planning stages of their works in order to shed light on the metatheories of knowledge and imagination their works embody. I believe that their ideas, sometimes formulated in advance, do have some bearing on our interpretation of their works, but I leave room for my own doubts about whether initial formulations enter the fiction unscathed. I follow Lawrence's advice by trusting the novel and not the novelist.

I began this project with an interest in the imagination—what novelists thought about it, how they portrayed it, and how philosophy has portrayed it—but I soon discovered how impossible it was, especially in a study of these novelists, to keep the wider problem of knowledge out of the picture. The conventional novel, because of its complicity in philosophical realism, holds out for a clear distinction between what is known (or, more specifically, what is perceived) and what is imagined. It widens the gap between perception and imagination whenever its characters' introspections magnify the distinction between the two forms of cognition or whenever its omniscient narrators magnify the distinction that may not be apparent to the characters. But Conrad, Lawrence, and Woolf narrow that gap, and by doing so they make the problem of knowledge all the more central to an understanding of their works. The differences in their attitudes toward imagination notwithstanding, all three see it as inextricably bound to the laws governing cognition. For none of them can imagination transcend knowledge; it can only shape it. None of them claim for imagina-

6. Denis Donoghue, *The Sovereign Ghost: Studies in Imagination* (Berkeley, 1976), 70–71.

tion what Samuel Taylor Coleridge, Friedrich von Schelling, or Johann Gottlieb Fichte did.

If their attitudes toward imagination have just one point of agreement, it would be formulated in Wallace Stevens' argument that imagination must remain in contact with reality. Stevens wanted to cleanse the imagination of what he calls the romantic. I take him to mean that the imagination should not be held aloft, should not be parted from reality, much less held above it. When speaking about nineteenth-century positivism, which denigrated imagination, he says:

> About nobility I cannot be sure that the decline, not to say the disappearance of nobility[,] is anything more than a maladjustment between the imagination and reality. We have been a little insane about the truth. We have had an obsession. In its ultimate extension, the truth about which we have been insane will lead us to look beyond the truth to something in which the imagination will be the dominant complement. It is not only that the imagination adheres to reality, but, also, that reality adheres to imagination and that the interdependence is essential.[7]

Because they also perceive the bond between imagination and knowledge, Conrad, Lawrence, and Woolf doubt the capacity to doubt. Conrad doubts that the mind can inspect the distance between what is perceived and what is imagined. His narratives put a frame on reality, but these frames subvert the efficacy of both narration and knowledge; they put the subject at a hopelessly far distance from the object of his knowledge. For Lawrence, knowledge takes on its most pernicious cast when it leads us to the audacious belief that we can apprehend truth through intellectual debate, which leads the mind into self-interrogation and drives a wedge between the lies of the mind and the truth of the body. T. S. Eliot accused him of being incapable of doubting his own assertions. If we are unsympathetic with Lawrence's beliefs, it is easy to see his vision as an elaborate and untested projection of his imagination. If we are sympathetic with his beliefs, his unwillingness to subject his ideas to intellectual analysis is an asset, since they proclaim the value of an instinctual knowledge that rids intellectual

7. Wallace Stevens, *The Necessary Angel: Essays on Reality and the Imagination* (New York, 1951), 33.

knowledge of its pernicious and finally distorting character. Whatever we think of his beliefs, he was an artist, and it is as an artist, not as a philosopher, that he will be remembered. For Woolf, the imagination increases knowledge by allowing the mind to break away from its perspectival limits. As we shall see, her aim was to show us what is real. To do this, she broke away from the conventions of realistic fiction, which set a limit on what could be shown. She tried to make the barriers between individual minds permeable. Imagination, for her, is capacious knowledge.[8]

We certainly need to believe that we can sort out what we imagine from what we know, but imagination without knowledge is ludicrous. At the same time, knowledge without imagination yields no human meaning. A fact becomes a part of human consciousness when it finds a place within a network of desires and fears. By measuring their hopes and fears we find in these novelists a spectrum of responses to the imagination's relation to knowledge. Although the chapters usually follow the major works chronologically—from Conrad's *Lord Jim* (1900) to Woolf's *Between the Acts* (1941)—that chronology is not essential to my thesis. I refer to the growth of these novelists' ideas only occasionally, where growth is helpful in understanding their thinking. The essential thing is the range of responses, from Conrad's pessimism about whether knowledge and imagination have any efficacy to Woolf's qualified optimism. For Conrad, imagination embarrasses knowledge; it shows how hopeless the attempt to comprehend reality is. I argue, however, that a modicum of hope animated Conrad's literary activity. Woolf, by contrast, is more optimistic about the attempt to know and represent reality through imagination. She begins with a sense of knowledge's limits as defined in dualistic epistemology, and she comes to believe in the imagination's capacity to overcome, but not totally abolish, those limits. Lawrence is between Conrad and Woolf, but not because his attitudes are moderate. He stands between them because he is at once both intensely pessimistic and optimistic. He shares Conrad's suspicion that to worship at the altar of knowledge is to follow

8. Robert Kiely, *Beyond Egotism: The Fiction of James Joyce, Virginia Woolf, and D. H. Lawrence* (Cambridge, Mass., 1980), 184.

Western civilization to its doom. But the intensity of Lawrence's despair animates his faith—a faith that there is something beyond the mind that knowledge, as usually conceived, will not lead us toward, but that can redeem us. Insofar as it pertains to knowledge, his task is to change our habits of thought, not to abolish them. His faith is in a truth that is indistinguishable from imagination.

Throughout this discussion, we find ourselves coming back to three main issues: the quest for self-knowledge, the problem of knowing other minds, and the relationship of mind to matter and, its corollary, of mind to body. We address important related topics as well, but these three issues mark the chief points of comparison between philosophical and literary realism as well as between the conventional and the experimental in the English novel. These three issues have also served as my basis for deciding which of these novelists' works to discuss. Of course, one could discuss just about any novel in connection with these issues, but I have selected, from among the most significant works, those that these main issues would best serve to illuminate.

Self-knowledge, the first of the three main issues, is important because in their handling of it Conrad, Lawrence, and Woolf all cast doubt upon what in dualistic epistemology is the essential and initial step in the mind's comprehension of external reality: the capacity of the mind to inspect itself and thereby intuit the distance between subject and object and finally the difference between the imaginary and the real. In the work of all three novelists the individual loses his power to discover what is essentially himself, that core of the self which belongs only to him. In any attempt to draw a line between self and other, subject and object, he meets only frustration. As a consequence, the capacity to distinguish between subjective and objective experience, between the real and the imagined, diminishes. This consequence appears in all three novelists' works, but the failure of knowledge in the act of introspection takes on different forms.

For example, Conrad's *Nostromo* (1904) and *Under Western Eyes* (1911) illustrate especially well how introspection reveals only provisional knowledge that is indistinguishable from imagination. In the moment of introspection, instead of discovering a coherent self, the individual discovers only a set of incompatible masks. The self, then, is a set of provisional identities randomly assembled out of social experience. I suspect that, to Conrad's mind, there is a core of the self that holds these provisional identities together, but that center is unknowable. Introspection will not reveal it.

Lawrence's view of self-knowledge provides one explanation for introspection's failure to reveal the self to itself. In both his essays and novels, especially *The Rainbow* (1915) and *Women in Love,* introspection invents a false self instead of finding the true one. For Lawrence self-referential knowledge produces a schism between knowing and being, so that to know oneself is no longer to be oneself. The Cartesian *cogito* is impossible for Lawrence; being cannot be predicated on an act of introspection. The character of Gerald Crich in *Women in Love* is Lawrence's clearest illustration of these consequences of self-regard; he loses contact with both himself and others. The false self that his self-regard produces for him is an abstraction of the mechanization with which he identifies himself. *The Rainbow* chronicles similar attempts to predicate the self on its introspective knowledge, but Ursula's triumph at the end is her abandonment of the social self that her introspection created and that had mediated her experience of others. Stripped of her social self she can hurl herself unprotected into a world about which she has no certain knowledge. *Women in Love* explores the potential that just this abandonment of the false self opens to her—the capacity to *know* and to *be* simultaneously in her relationship with Birkin. To reach this plateau where knowing and being, self and other, subject and object are one requires the abandonment of the self-reflective quest for self-knowledge. To remain one with the blood, Lawrence implies, the mind must look outward toward the core of the self in the depths of others, for only through direct and absolute knowledge of another self can the individual find himself. That is because the concrete referent of each *I* is transindividual.

Similarly in Woolf the irreducible selfhood of one is continuous with the selfhood of all. In Lawrence that continuity is mediated by the blood; in Woolf it is mediated by the imagining mind her narrators voice in the major novels following *Jacob's*

Room (1922). Whether it is mind or blood, the monistic consequence is essentially the same: there is no solitary self because each is finally all. In Woolf, especially in *Mrs. Dalloway* (1925), *To the Lighthouse* (1927), *The Waves* (1931), and *Between the Acts*, the narrator voices the collective consciousness of the characters, and certain characters are allowed to comprehend that collective level of experience and thereby gain access to other minds directly. For Clarissa Dalloway introspection reveals not an isolated person but a level of experience all minds share. Self-knowledge, then, does not begin and end in a private moment of introspection. Identity is predicated not only on the individual's act of cognition but on others' cognitive acts as well. In *The Waves* the six main characters discover that the way to discover oneself is to assume the identities of those around one. Self-knowledge, for Woolf, is a collective effort.

For all three novelists the Cartesian *cogito* is inadequate. In Conrad, self-knowledge comes in a moment of introspection when the self discovers that it is a collection of provisional and incompatible identities. But this hardly qualifies as self-knowledge. The irreducible self at the center is an unfathomable cavern of darkness. In Lawrence the essential self is only a procession of various gods.[9] Finding the self means giving up hope that introspection can provide certain knowledge, accepting the unknown in oneself and in others, and being willing to give over to that unknown the way Conrad's Jim, Nostromo, and Razumov are too terrified to do. In Woolf the initial drive toward solitude in the quest for self-knowledge provides access to all minds, so that the self is at once isolated and involved, private and collective.

This revision of realistic epistemology's model of self-knowledge affects the shape of the realistic novel. It changes that shape principally by undercutting the novel's notorious capacity to plot psychological development in its characters.

Because the coherent and isolated self begins to disperse, Conrad, Lawrence, and Woolf lose their sense of that innermost, individual reference point toward which the signposts in a character's psychological development ordinarily point. The

9. D. H. Lawrence, "Benjamin Franklin," *Studies in Classic American Literature* (New York, 1964), 16.

self is no longer a linear configuration on which psychological events can be plotted so as to trace and reveal the development of the essential self at the center of its experiences. Instead, the self becomes more like a circle or halo of consciousness whose center and circumference are indeterminate. As we move from Conrad and Lawrence to Woolf, we see that the concern for representing consciousness itself displaces the representation of psychological development in characters. In Lawrence and Woolf the form their representation of consciousness takes conflicts with the empirical bases of those schools of modern psychology that are grounded in realistic epistemology. Even in Conrad, although he is adept in portraying psychological conflicts, we begin to see why psychological probings of characters must eventually become impossible if they continue on the level of complexity and ambiguity on which they operate in his major works: his probings into the self yield no center. Only Conrad's hope for finding a center provides his impetus for the psychological probing whose final goal is to discover a coherent self. And when in his later fiction—*Chance* (1913) and *Victory* (1915) in particular—he simplifies the problem of self-knowledge, his fiction becomes more conventional and less powerful.

For Lawrence, empirical psychology, though it fascinated him, was incompatible with his concept of blood-consciousness. This is mainly why *Sons and Lovers* (1913), with its ostensibly Freudian model, has met with such a mixture of critical response. The novel is problematic because, on one hand, it embodies a psychological character development that meets empiricist criteria for knowing other minds and for self-knowledge, and, on the other hand, it patterns Lawrence's emergent rival claims. In this and in his subsequent two novels, *The Rainbow* and *Women in Love*, psychological realism does not vanish from Lawrence's fiction, but his character portrayals follow patterns that take us further away from those of empirical psychology. In Woolf, the psychologically realistic has not disappeared either, but it is subordinated by her interest in representing consciousness itself, the particles of experience as they would enter nearly any mind: "Life is a luminous halo," she says, "a semi-transparent envelope surrounding us from the beginning of consciousness to the end." It is not the linear configuration more conducive to the conventions of eighteenth- and nineteenth-century psychological realism, "a series of gig-lamps symmetrically arranged."[10]

Just as they change the novel's alliance with dualistic epistemology by reformulating the quest for self-knowledge, so do Conrad, Lawrence, and Woolf break this alliance by revising the model for knowing other minds, which is the second of the three main issues we will address. Two main questions occupy us here: how narrators know characters and how characters know each other. In the first question we meet what at first glance is an exception to the parallel between philosophical and literary realism, for even in conventional realistic novels, omniscient narrators are allowed access to other minds that no person is ever allowed. Of course, even omniscient narrators share the limits real people have: they are bound by space and time because they can enter only one character at a time and their narrative medium is an unavoidably sequential one. Characters, though, having to make judgments on the basis of outward signs that mediate between one self and another, have only indirect knowledge of each other. Because the omniscient narrators can know selves directly, their knowledge is indubitable. We cannot doubt them because they are the criteria we use for judging what, in their world, is true and false. Incorrigible omniscient narrators are perhaps the last vestige of absolutism in a genre that is notoriously relativistic. Their authoritative voices preside over the characters of realistic fiction as though to ensure a common reference point for the array of perspectives that characterize the ambiguities of a realistic world. They represent what Robert Scholes and Robert Kellogg have called "authoritarian monism."[11]

The modern novel, especially since Henry James, has tended to disperse this authoritarian monism. James insisted that the omniscient voice be assigned perspectival limits. Whatever his reasons, they betrayed an uncertainty about the absolutism in the social and moral codes that the narrator traditionally voiced. The omniscient narrator in conventional realism voices the

10. Virginia Woolf, *Collected Essays* (3 vols.; London, 1966), II, 106.
11. Robert Scholes and Robert Kellogg, "The Concept of Omniscience," *The Nature of Narrative* (London, 1981), 272–82.

conscience of a society that is less relativistic than our three novelists are themselves. As the omniscient narrator began losing his capacity directly to know other minds (because of perspectival limits), it became harder within the limits of realistic epistemology to confer certainty upon the process of knowing other minds.

Here we find a parallel between philosophical and literary realism where there seemed to be none. Just as the conventional novel allowed direct knowledge of other minds in the cognitive relationship of the omniscient narrator to the characters, so has epistemological realism had to make a very broad assumption that other minds can be known at all. If I know I exist only because of my introspective power to observe my own act of thinking, then how can I be sure other persons are sentient? G. E. Moore, though himself a defender of realistic epistemology, could respond only by admitting that there is no definitive way of proving that other persons are sentient at all, let alone that their thoughts can be known, but he suggested that it is nonetheless reasonable to assume that other minds can be known.[12] Certainly any novelist would think so, even if he is a philosophical realist. In realistic novels the narrator's direct access to other minds embodies that certainty which, as far as their authors and narrators are concerned, requires no logical argumentation or empirical proof: other persons are sentient, and their thoughts can be known with as much certainty as there would be if their minds could be entered by an omniscient narrator.

The omniscient narrator's direct access to other minds is the literary analogue of philosophical realism's assumption that, although we have no direct access to other minds, it is reasonable and, thankfully, ordinary to act as though we had reliable knowledge of other minds. As the incorrigible voice of the omniscient narrator began to disappear in modern British fiction, so disappeared the literary embodiment of realistic epistemology's assumption that other minds can be directly known. The anxiety this disappearance produced was compensated for by the tendency in Lawrence and Woolf of the "authoritative mo-

12. G. E. Moore, "The Nature of Reality of Objects of Perception," *Philosophical Studies* (London, 1922), 57.

nism" reserved for incorrigible narrators to seep down to the level of the characters themselves, producing what we might call "intercharacter monism," a level of consciousness that provides characters with direct access to each other's minds.

This intercharacter monism is a logical implication of the consensus that Elizabeth Deeds Ermarth, in a brilliant recent study, has shown to be a fundamental assumption behind epistemological and literary realism. Ermarth's perspective is as refreshing as it is rigorously argued, since most inspections of literary realism's epistemology have pointed, as I often do here, to modern realism's emphasis on discordance and particularization, features that separate it from scholastic realism and that occasion the search for consensus in a world torn apart by doubt. The search for consensus in a world of apparent disjunction and dualism must assume from the beginning, Ermarth shows, that consensus is a reasonable expectation, even if its gratification is delayed. She emphasizes, for example, that Ian Watt's well-known comparison of literary realism's strategies to those of a jury is incomplete until we notice that the jury does not merely "verify a circumstantial view of life," but judges "whether or not a law has been broken." A jury measures its information against what it is certain is a universal law.[13]

Since Ermath's study is one that ought to have a lasting effect on our thinking about realism, I take the time to point out that we agree in the main and that our disagreements come from differences in emphasis. In my view conventional literary realism hides the consensus it must nevertheless assume from the beginning. At certain points Ermarth alerts us to this, for example, when she notes that true meetings of minds rarely appear in realistic novels or when she notes that realism's potential solipsisms are usually held away from our immediate attention.[14] Many times,though, she brings this consensus to the foreground, which of course helps us to see it, but the narrative conventions themselves push the union of perspectives out of our view. The frustrating search for order and certainty in a dualistic world is what makes conventional realism so gripping. Ermarth's foregrounding of the consensus leads to readings, es-

13. Elizabeth Deeds Ermarth, *Realism and Consensus in the English Novel* (Princeton, 1983), 33.
14. *Ibid.,* 80, 78.

pecially of the omniscient narrator, that mine will occasionally depart from. She sees the omniscient narrator as a collective consciousness whose bodily presence or spatiotemporal specificity would logically contradict realism's assumptions. This reading is both valid and useful until it brings her to discredit valuable critical tools that localize omniscient narrators, who inhabit sometimes implicitly defined temporal and spatial borders without banishing realistic assumptions. Realistic fiction's omniscient narrators often have *measured* advantages over the characters' perspectives because the conventional narrative wants to keep the collectivization of consciousness away from our immediate attention. At one point Ermarth's insistence that the omniscient narrator is totally disembodied leads her to dismiss certain conventional narrative distinctions like those which Dorrit Cohn has refined and which I occasionally rely on.[15]

These reservations notwithstanding, Ermarth's study, with its astonishingly cogent historical sweep, lays some groundwork for my observations, ending as it does at about the point in literary history where mine begins. She argues that in Henry James, and even more threateningly in Conrad, the subjectivization of the narrator impedes the consensus that realism needs in order to maintain its belief in the mind's ability to make sense of its experience. In this we are in complete agreement. The consensus in the backgrounds of James's and Conrad's fiction collapses. In Conrad, the doubt about the conceivability of overlapping minds creates chasms between self and other, within the self, and between the mind and externality, impelling him to erect extremely tenuous bridges. Lawrence and Woolf represent two responses to Conrad's view; both in their own ways invent forms of consensus, pushing their unifying constructs to the front of our attention, anxious that we should notice them. They push to the front what conventional realism was confident enough to leave in the background. Intercharacter monism principally augments this foregrounded unity.

In Conrad this intercharacter monism is only a potential,

---

15. Dorrit Cohn, *Transparent Minds: Narrative Modes for Presenting Consciousness in Fiction* (Princeton, 1978); Ermarth, *Realism and Consensus*, 73n.

just beyond the margins of his novels. It is not quite imaged because not quite imaginable. It is wrapped in a darkness that Conrad, like Lawrence, uses to represent the unknowable ground of human existence, even though for Conrad it threatens the very realm it grounds. Of the three novelists Conrad most laments the loss of a final, single reference point that would transform the chaos of daily experience by helping us see its underlying unity. Conrad lost hope that this unifying reference point could be found. Lawrence rejoices that the lens is shattered; he embraces the chaos that Western civilization wants to bring under its idea of order. For Lawrence, to be one with this darkness that grounds human existence is to turn the mind away from itself and back toward the body from which the mind arose before it became conscious of itself. The only satisfactory condition of the mind is beyond the point where it can inspect itself and therefore beyond the point where it can draw the distinction between imaginative vision and direct knowledge. At that point body and mind, one and all, participate in a monistic whole. Woolf pursues this end not through the body but through the mind, yet the search for monism in a dualistic world characterized by disjunction and isolation is essentially the same.

All three novelists reappropriate the authoritative monism formerly assigned only to omniscient narrators. And in doing so they reformulate the laws by which minds know each other. By placing his narrators within the frame of his novels, as Marlow is in *Heart of Darkness* (1902) and *Lord Jim*, Conrad inspects the limited access of one mind to another. *Heart of Darkness* is inconceivable as a tale narrated from an omniscient perspective because it is finally the story of narrative authority's disappearance. Kurtz cannot live to speak about his confrontation with the heart of darkness because it is the incomprehensible reality at the core of all experience. It is literally unspeakable. Marlow serves to emphasize the incomprehensibility; he can relate nothing to us but Kurtz's *reaction to* the confrontation. What actually goes on in Kurtz's mind is curiously slurred over, even though it had seemed to be the final destination of the narrative. For the same reasons, we can never have a final picture of Lord Jim: the omniscient narrator departs at the end of Chapter 4, and his stand-in, Marlow, cannot make a distinction between his perceptions of Jim and his imaginings about him. No "authoritarian monism" officiates the narrative except that monism out of which all things emanate and into which they ultimately collapse—the darkness. *Nostromo* exemplifies Conrad's experimental use of an omniscient narrator who retains his epistemological authority only by sustaining his ironical stance in relation to the characters. He gives the heart of darkness a voice. He is allied to the absolute darkness against which all human aspirations are absolutely pointless. His cynicism is the demoniac underside of the authority that the conventional omniscient narrator had in earlier fiction. Instead of voicing the social conscience, he implies that having a conscience—being human at all—is not worth the trouble. It is doubtful that Conrad could have continued to write fiction narrated from such an absolutely nihilistic perspective. With framed narrators, though, he can portray, as in Marlow, the interplay between perspectives, the view that human values are reasonable and the rival view the darkness embodies. The interplay allows him to entertain possibilities without committing himself absolutely to either extreme.

In contrast to Conrad, who almost always places his narrators within the frame of his fiction, Lawrence almost never does. "None of That" is a notable exception that we shall consider, but all of Lawrence's major works employ omniscient narrators. He modifies the authoritarian monism that characterizes earlier fiction, however, by positioning it at some deep but unspecified level within his characters rather than above them. It has been suggested that Lawrence retains conventional narrative techniques even while exploring unconventional topics and that therefore he loses control of point of view even in his greatest novels.[16] These "flaws," as *The Rainbow* and *Women in Love* show, are actually narrative innovations. They reappropriate narrative authority by shifting it from the level of the social conscience to the level of the individual conscience. Instead of standing above his characters and voicing the conscience of society, as the narrators do in Fielding, Jane Austen, W. M. Thackeray, and George Eliot, Lawrence's narrators are voices speaking out *against* society; they voice the conscience

16. Scholes and Kellogg, *The Nature of Narrative*, 278–79.

of the individual trapped in a morally corrupt society. This makes an enormous difference in the implied relationship between the narrator and the characters about whom—or better, in whom—he speaks.

Because in Lawrence the narrative voice is the conscience of the individual, it speaks as though seated within each character and not as though from on high, as in the stance of the *histor*. The ultimate reward for Lawrence's characters is to achieve the level of awareness from which the narrator speaks. When characters achieve this level of awareness, the distance between themselves and other characters and between the narrator and themselves vanishes. Thus, in *Women in Love*, when Birkin and Ursula achieve their consummation in "mystical-physical unity," the narrative passes out, as it were, and begins addressing the reader. The alternative would be for the narration to start talking about itself, its incapacity to make the interpenetration of selves in supreme knowledge present for the reader. The narrator cannot talk about Birkin and Ursula because, in these consummate moments that are both psychic and sexual, there is no more distance between the narrator and them than there is between Birkin and Ursula. Such moments are the narration's final destiny, and when it meets its destination, which is beyond language, there is nothing more to be said.

In Woolf also the "authoritarian monism" in *Mrs. Dalloway, To the Lighthouse, The Waves,* and *Between the Acts* drops its alliance with the social conscience. Instead of overseeing the characters, her narrator embodies their consciousnesses collectively. Although like any omniscient narrator she can be in only one mind at a time, the character of her narrative serves to dissolve the boundaries between one mind and another, so that she seems as though in one mind and in all at once. Like Lawrence's, Woolf's narrator can seem to retain a distance from her characters only for as long as they seem themselves to be at a distance from or inaccessible to each other. When Clarissa Dalloway, for example, in a private moment of heightened consciousness, recognizes her complicity in humanity's collective conscious experience, then her voice melds into the narrator's. *The Waves* takes this model of knowing other minds to its extreme. We are given the monologue of a narrator who enters six characters' minds and utters the words they are thinking, both consciously and unconsciously, but do not actually say. At the end, however, Bernard becomes the other characters in their absence and takes on the role of the narrator. He is at that moment an incarnation of the narrator and shares her direct knowledge of other minds. In Lawrence and Woolf, then, characters are afforded the direct access to each other's minds that would otherwise totally disappear when the omniscient narrator loses his authoritarian monism, as he does in Conrad.

The last of these three main questions is the mind-body and the mind-matter problem. This is not strictly an epistemological issue, as the first two are; but it is indispensable here because, in its treatment by Conrad, Lawrence, and Woolf, it indicates a distance between dualistic epistemology and the experimental features of their novels. Furthermore, because it addresses the question of what the mind is made up of and whether the mind can assert its powers over an alien externality, this issue implicates the subject-object question at the center of epistemological speculation.

Descartes' philosophy of dualistic interactionism sufficiently explains the exchanges between mind and matter in the realm of second causes, to which realistic fiction addresses itself. The *donné* of conventional realism allows characters and their surroundings about equal power over their surroundings as they have over the characters. Naturalistic fiction is a possible exception, since it gives primacy to determinants like environment (primarily in American naturalism) and heredity (in Continental naturalism). On these very grounds—the relentless pessimism—some critics have suggested that naturalism is not as realistic as it purports to be. The departures from dualistic interactionism that Conrad, Lawrence, and Woolf take assume radically different forms. Conrad and Woolf define two extremes: Conrad emphasizes matter and Woolf the mind. Both, in emphasizing one half of the dualism, entertain monistic views that fade the concept of interaction.

Among Conrad's works, no novel better illustrates the hegemony of matter over mind than *Nostromo* does. Here the belief that the mind's designs have any impact on externality is deflated into mere wishful thinking. For Conrad the mind is only a configuration of matter which presents itself with the illusion that it is a separate, efficacious, spiritual entity. The characters of *Nostromo* want to turn the silver of the mining enterprise into a spiritual force for guiding their society. They dramatize Conrad's belief that the mind tries to convert its surroundings into nonmaterial terms in order to control whatever it contacts. This fact must be faced: truth and power are in matter and material interests; mind and spirit are illusions.

That Woolf bases the monistic source of all experience on mind is especially clear in the final third of *To the Lighthouse*. There two synchronously, acausally, and formally related plots converge. Lily Briscoe's artistic rendering of the late Mrs. Ramsay's vision of reconciliation coincides exactly with James's and his father's approach to the lighthouse, which represents that reconciliation. Neither matter nor the mortality of the body—both of which pertain to the realm of extension—impedes the mind's power, the resources of Mrs. Ramsay and Lily. Similarly, no material impediments have any lasting power over the characters in *The Waves*, who achieve their ideal communal identity precisely when they are physically absent from one another.

At a certain point in Lawrence mind and matter and mind and body are indistinguishable. In the interest of advocating the superior power of the body, Lawrence encounters the same reversal that religious poets such as Thomas Traherne and Richard Crashaw do in portraying the redemptive power of the spirit: the pursuit of one interest to the exclusion of the other has the curious effect of converting the expression of the one into the terms of the other. The body is bodylike only for as long as we maintain the contrasting image of the mind; the mind is mindlike only for as long as we retain the image of the physical. Lawrence's initial and almost exclusive interest in analyzing and dramatizing the redeeming powers of the body becomes curiously spiritual in its rendering; his descriptions of sexual contacts seem more like representations of states of consciousness than of sexuality. Sometimes in spite of his intentions, the body in Lawrence takes on the attributes usually reserved for the mind. Consequently he puts us in a realm where the boundary line between mind and body, the realms of thought and sensation, is blurred.

Whereas Conrad and Woolf celebrate the triumphs, respectively, of matter over mind and of mind over matter, Lawrence renders the interaction ambiguous by dispersing the volitional powers of individual characters. This ambiguity about who is in charge, the individual or the transindividual blood that runs through him, looms especially large in *Women in Love*. Gerald illustrates the operation of the will, which like pernicious knowledge is individuated, admitting no ambiguity in the determination of agency. His will is modeled on dualistic interactionism. In Lawrence the will is finally the embodiment of a death wish because it isolates the self from the body that gives it life. The machine emblemizes man's *will*: it is predictable and consciously regulated. Gerald's commitment to the machine illustrates the power of his will.

But the power of the blood—the instinctual urges that, like blood-consciousness, are transindividual—is ambiguous. When it operates, as in the characters of Ursula and Birkin, there is no certainty about whom it belongs to or about where it will lead one. It must simply be listened to. It is the potential resource of any character who gives over to his instincts. In the leadership novels, specifically *Aaron's Rod* (1922), *Kangaroo* (1923), and *The Plumed Serpent* (1926), this transindividual power regulating the relationships of mind to body and to matter augments the principle of social coherence that in *Lady Chatterley's Lover* (1928) Lawrence calls "the democracy of touch." In *The Rainbow* and *Women in Love*, and to some extent in *Sons and Lovers*, this power is dramatized almost exclusively on the level of the individual, and therefore these novels serve to highlight more direct points of comparison with Conrad's and Woolf's novels. Furthermore, in *The Rainbow* and *Women in Love*, more than in any other of his novels, Lawrence pronouncedly introduces challenges to realistic narrative which he meets by employing innovations that are too often ignored or misunderstood.

At certain points the transindividual powers of the blood seem allied to the impulses of the narrator; for this Lawrence is often criticized. When these powers seem allied to the narrator's desires, the narrator seems to carry responsibility for the characters' actions, seeming to swerve their destinies with his own sleight of hand and, banishing their freedom, to animate the characters as though they were so many puppets.[17] This criticism fails to distinguish between the novelist and his nar-

17. Marguerite Beede Howe, *The Art of the Self in D. H. Lawrence* (Athens, Ohio, 1977), 69.

rators. When identified with Lawrence, his narrators, voicing the prerogatives of the blood and holding the pen at the same time, would seem to swerve the fiction to illustrate their convictions. But distinguished from Lawrence as they should be, the narrators speak, as though passive witnesses, from the deepest level of characters' awareness and are in no position willfully to determine their fates. Often, then, the criticism against Lawrence's narrative technique disguises objections to his ideas at the cost of ignoring his narrative innovations.

These three issues, then—self-knowledge, the problem of knowing other minds, and the interactions of mind with matter and the body—define the main epistemological concerns I address. With these and related topics in mind we will examine the fiction of Conrad, Lawrence, and Woolf, measuring the deviations from the parallel courses of literary and epistemological realism. This in turn will bring us to a more concrete understanding of how far the literary and philosophical parallel extends in guiding the interpretation of individual works and the larger generic history they steer. I hope to make some mark on our understanding not only of these novelists' experimentation but also of the realistic English novel's values and assumptions.

1

JOSEPH CONRAD

> When once the truth is grasped that one's own personality
> is only a ridiculous and aimless masquerade of something
> hopelessly unknown the attainment of serenity is not very
> far off. Then there remains nothing but the surrender to
> one's impulses, the fidelity to passing emotions which is
> perhaps a nearer approach to truth than any other philoso-
> phy of life. And why not? If we are "ever becoming—never
> being" then I would be a fool if I tried to become this thing
> rather than that; for I know well that I never will be any-
> thing. I would rather grasp the solid satisfaction of my
> wrong-headedness and shake my fist at the idiotic mystery
> of Heaven.
>
> > —Conrad
> > Letter to Edward Garnett

Appearance and Reality: *Heart of Darkness* and *Lord Jim*

The problematic interplay of appearances with their underlying
reality sinks its roots deeply in the realistic tradition of the
novel. For attending the novel's historical alliance with philosophical realism is the skepticism it shares with Descartes—a
skepticism whose epistemological formulation widens the distance between appearance and reality. When the power to doubt
external reality becomes the predicate for self-verification, both
identity and ontology become problematic. Out of this dilemma
arise the detailed systems of investigation that characterize
empirical inquiry. The classic literary formulation of this skepticism is Cervantes' *Don Quixote*.[1] As in Cervantes, in Conrad
reality is chronically tested and reappraised, for at any moment
what one takes as reality can be transformed into mere appearance. Knowledge becomes a preoccupation because the mind is

---

1. Levin, "The Example of Cervantes," *Contexts of Criticism*, 79–96.

in constant flux: it must continuously interrogate itself and its surroundings. This process can go on for as long as the mind hopes for a correspondence of appearance with reality.

Although for these reasons Conrad is rooted in the realistic tradition of fiction, my point is to examine those aspects of his experimental contributions to the novel that modify philosophical and literary realism's dualistic model of knowledge and imagination. At certain points Conrad arrests the interplay of appearance and reality, and of subject and object, and advances a monistic view of these categories that his fiction nearly, but not directly, embodies. The skepticism that he uses to test reality loses its momentum and undermines its own efficacy in distinguishing appearances from reality. Then the skepticism animating the tension between appearance and reality becomes itself interrogated through the application of skepticism to itself. Consequently, the distance between appearance and reality that skepticism opened actually closes, and reality collapses into appearances.

Conrad's thoughts about his craft help us begin to see how this process works. Although he spoke about the craft of fiction only rarely, in those passages Conrad betrays a concern about his capacity to make his readers believe in the reality of his fictional constructs. His primary way of operating is to emphasize sense experience, to provide the right appearances that can make the reader sure of the underlying reality. His preface to *The Nigger of the "Narcissus"* (1897) is the best evidence of his motives. Here the emphasis falls upon the artist's project of making the reader *see.* Phrases relating to sense experience carpet the whole preface. The artist's single-minded project is "to render the highest kind of justice to the visible universe," he says. In at least one respect this is surprising, for he implies an invisible universe that he elsewhere associates with the truth. Though the artist is certainly concerned to relate the truth, his primary task is to convey its appearances, to make the reader see as he saw and therefrom to infer the truth: "My task which I am trying to achieve is, by the power of the written word to make you hear, to make you feel—it is, before all, to make you *see.* That—and no more, and it is everything. If I succeed, you shall find there according to your deserts: encouragement, consolation, fear, charm—all you demand—and, perhaps, also that glimpse of truth for which you have forgotten to ask." By couching the relating of truth so far within sense experience, Conrad is not simply humbling himself. For his preoccupation with sense experience arises partly out of a deeply felt skepticism regarding the nature of reality and out of a distrust for the mind's capacity to organize appearances in such a way that they would augment the comprehension of reality. In the above passage, for example, he leaves the apprehension of truth up to the reader according to his deserts. The truth will be in the receiver of his messages, not in the sense data that seem to embody it.[2]

In his concern with rendering appearances, Conrad is not different from other artists of his generation. John A. Lester, Jr., in his study of Edwardian literature, abides by the generalization that "in regard to the immense significance of art to this generation . . . art's role was basically to be an outlet for the expression of subjective experience in a world which seemed to have capitulated utterly to 'exteriority.'" His citation of Arthur Symons indicates an important point of similarity to Conrad's symbolist and impressionist leanings. In an 1893 article on the decadent movement in literature, Symons states that the artist's quest is not directly to convey a "general truth," but "the very essence of truth." This would seem to contradict the emphasis upon appearance, but he defines this essence as "the truth of appearances to the senses, of the visible world to the eyes that see it." This formulation exactly conforms to Conrad's motives. It issues in a peculiar dualism between externality and the perceiving subject. The truth about the externality is in the subject, and yet it can be conveyed by nothing other than the externality.[3]

About Conrad's impressionism enough has been said else-

2. Joseph Conrad, Preface to The Nigger of the "Narcissus" (New York, 1963), 11, 13; Wilfred S. Dowden, Joseph Conrad: The Imaged Style (Nashville, 1970); J. Hillis Miller, Poets of Reality: Six Twentieth-Century Writers (Cambridge, Mass., 1965), 38–39; J. Hillis Miller, Fiction and Repetition (Cambridge, Mass., 1982), 37.

3. Lester, Journey Through Despair, 114–15; Arthur Symons, "Decadent Movement in Literature," Harper's New Monthly Magazine, LXXXVII (1893), 859.

where, but its connection to Conrad's view of knowledge is important.[4] Ford Madox Ford, Conrad's friend and sometimes his collaborator, has articulated the idea of impressionism in fiction even better than Conrad. As Ford describes it, impressionism requires a radical modification of narrative form. Whereas narrative ordinarily will relate an action from its inception to its completion, impressionism necessitates temporal dislocations, a technique familiar in Conrad as well as in Ford, whose *The Good Soldier* (1915) exemplifies the impulse to start in the middle of a story and weave the details gradually by moving backward and forward. This breakup of time, Ford insists, reproduces for the reader the impressions real life makes on him. If we see Mr. Slack building a greenhouse, he continues, our way of knowing the event is not the way we know it in conventional fiction: in real life we remember the event piecemeal, as its specifics touch upon seemingly unrelated and temporally scattered pictures. Speaking of himself and Conrad, Ford says: "We accepted without much protest the stigma: Impressionists that was thrown at us. In those days Impressionists were still considered to be bad people. . . . But we accepted the name because Life appearing to us much as the building of Mr. Slack's greenhouse comes back to you, we saw that Life did not narrate, but made impressions on our brains. We in turn, if we wished to produce on you an effect of life, must not narrate but render . . . impressions."[5]

In its impulse to reproduce the experience of reality, Conrad's impressionism is consistent with the intentions behind traditional literary realism, but its effects produce a schism. It reappropriates the mind's relation to externality, because the truth that lies behind appearances comes to reside mainly in the perceiver. The result is not, however, an idealistic view of knowledge; externality is not simply the projection of the mind. The truth about the appearances, however, is in the mind. Since this is the case, Conrad subordinates the chains of causes and effects informing the events outside to the mind and emphasizes the mind's attempt to interpret those events. For Con-

4. Joseph Warren Beach, *The Twentieth Century Novel: Studies in Technique* (New York, 1932), 259–60.

5. Ford Madox Ford, *Joseph Conrad: A Personal Remembrance* (London, 1924), 182. Last marks of ellipsis are in the original.

rad the question is rudimentary—not so much how things happen, but what happens, less what one knows than how one knows.

The frame device, as Conrad uses it, is central to this shift in emphasis. The meaning of an experience, when it is related by a framing narrative, is implanted in the narrator's interpretation of it and not strictly in the experience itself. Jefferson Hunter's study, *Edwardian Fiction*, takes into account the popularity of the frame device in the lesser known fiction of this period. The frame device has a long literary history well before Conrad, but even Hunter admits that Conrad's employment of it is unique.[6]

Conrad uses the frame device with varying effects: it often serves to confound the narration's attempts to embody reality as it is rather than as it is seen. The device's more obvious effects are conveyed in *Nostromo* (1904), when Captain Mitchell writes his history of Costaguana. Here the effects are obvious because the omniscient narrator, who cites Mitchell's history, is at the same time very anxious to indicate how insipid it really is. It is, he says, "a more or less stereotyped relation of the 'historical events.'"[7] Much of the problem with the narration is that its writer is not one of the novel's great minds, and yet the narrative is so internally consistent that potential visitors to Costaguana, we are asked to believe, would take it as the truth. The novel's reader knows it is not the truth, because it simplifies the enormous complexities which he has seen informing the silver mining enterprise. Conrad purposefully inserts this narrative toward the end of the novel, where its distortions are best laid bare. It is left to Monygham to relate the accurate view: "There is no peace and no rest in the development of material interests" (*N*, 419). But Monygham's observation drifts away with the wind; the lie will be set in print, immortalized.[8]

If all Conrad's exposures of the tendency of narratives to miss the central point were as transparent as this one, the prob-

6. Jefferson Hunter, *Edwardian Fiction* (Cambridge, Mass., 1982), 28–34.

7. Joseph Conrad, *Nostromo* (Baltimore, 1963), 239. Subsequent page references to this novel (hereinafter cited parenthetically as *N*) are to this Penguin edition.

8. Edward W. Said, "Record and Reality," in John Unterecker (ed.), *Approaches to the Twentieth-Century Novel* (New York, 1965), 109.

lem would not be as interesting as it is, and perhaps the problem would be so transparent that it would cease to be a problem at all. It is when Conrad seduces us into believing in the truth of a narrative and then pulls the carpet out from under his narrator that the problem becomes important and interesting. We are left, then, with the same problem that Erving Goffman describes in his illuminating study of the rules governing our organization of experience: "One is left with the embarrassing methodological fact that the announcement of constitutive rules seems an open-ended game that any number can play forever. . . . One is left, then, with the structural similarity between everyday life—neglecting for a moment the possibility that no satisfactory catalog might be possible of what to include therein—and the various 'worlds' of make-believe but no way of knowing how this relationship should modify our view of everyday life."[9]

Something like this is at the heart of *Lord Jim* (1900), where our strongest impressions of Jim come through Marlow's narration of his conversations with him and of his thoughts about him. His perspicacity almost throughout should convince us that he is a reliable narrator. When Marlow quotes the proverb "onlookers see most of the game,"[10] we should be ready to see, from his own example, why they do. The onlooker can maintain the detachment necessary for interpreting experiences that those involved, like Jim, cannot maintain. And yet Marlow's frequent interrogations of himself in his attempts to understand Jim undercut his epistemological authority: "I don't pretend I understood him. The views he let me have of himself were like those glimpses through the shifting rents in a thick fog—bits of vivid and vanishing detail, giving no connected idea of the general aspect of a country. They fed one's curiosity without satisfying it; they were no good for purposes of orientation. Upon the whole he was misleading" (*LJ*, 62–63). It is easier to rely on a narrator with a healthy skepticism about his subject, but Marlow is not often in control of the direction his

9. Erving Goffman, *Frame Analysis: An Essay on the Organization of Experience* (San Francisco, 1974), 6.

10. Joseph Conrad, *Lord Jim* (New York, 1949), 171. Subsequent page references to this novel (hereinafter cited parenthetically as *LJ*) are to this Penguin edition.

skepticism should take. He cannot channel it in appropriate directions because he often loses sight of what the appropriate direction is: "He swayed me. I own to it" (*LJ*, 75). It does not help Marlow, in pleading for Jim, to admit that like Jim he recognizes no essential difference between truth and illusion (*LJ*, 170). Jim's enigmatic character at times makes Marlow wonder whether the Jim he sees is a real person at all; and when he indicates his central mediating role in making Jim present for the reader, he comes close to suggesting that Jim is his own invention: "He existed for me, and after all it is only through me that he exists for you" (*LJ*, 171). Neither Conrad's nor Marlow's point is to make us doubt Jim's existence, but we are asked to recognize that the border between the true and the fictional is not as sharp as we might expect. It is the framing device that helps us see the borderline's faintness as a realistic depiction of knowledge's limits. Without a narrator within the narration, Jim's romantic aspirations, which in Marlow's account sometimes make Jim seem only an imaginary character in a fairy tale, would become not just a problem of knowledge (as realistically conceived) but a literary convention.

One reason Conrad employs the frame device is to dramatize that the truth of an experience is immanent not in its appearances but in the mind that is interpreting the appearances of the experience. An omniscient narrator can ordinarily be expected to get at the kernel of the experience. A narrator framed by the fiction, however, must work with the appearances and cannot, if he is a realistic character, break down the boundaries governing his perspective. Even if he could reach the final kernel of his experience, though, it would not yield the truth. For as Marlow says in *Heart of Darkness* (1902), "[T]he meaning of an episode was not inside like a kernel but outside, enveloping the tale which brought it out only as a glow brings out a haze, in the likeness of one of these misty halos that sometimes are made visible by the spectral illumination of moonshine."[11] The truth of an episode is in its circumference, its external appearances. What is true is what is seen, but what is even truer is

---

11. Joseph Conrad, *Heart of Darkness* (New York, 1973), 8. Subsequent page references to this novel (hereinafter cited parenthetically as *HD*) are to this Penguin edition.

how it is seen—by a subject who is farther from the kernel than the appearances are. Thus, Conrad takes keen interest in rendering the visible universe in framed tales whose outermost limits (its readers) register the truth.

If the truth of an experience is in the narration of its appearances, then language takes on a different role in Conrad. As the mind looks in upon itself in order to discover the truth of its sensations, language begins to lose its referentiality. As the mind does, so must language begin to interrogate itself, searching for internal consistencies rather than its consistency with what it can only try to represent. I am not the first to notice how Conrad's language begins to lose its referentiality.[12] This characteristic of his language has a connection with the wider problem of appearances and reality. His language's capacity to refer to reality collapses whenever language takes on the illusory status of appearances. Before we examine some specific places in the texts where language collapses, we take note of a few instances where his fiction explicitly examines language's failure.

To see Conrad interrogating language's role is not simply to have the problem explained to us; it is to see the problem at work. It is to see language talking about itself because it has lost its power to refer to the experiences external to it. In his own proficiency in at least three languages, Conrad must have shared the same suspicions about language that the English translator has in *Under Western Eyes* (1911).[13] As a teacher of languages, the translator, who is also the narrator here, has spent so much of his life talking about language—its governing laws, its systems of order—that it occurs to him that language is opaque; it does not allow the reality beyond it to shine through but instead becomes the final object of its own inten-

12. Guetti, *The Limits of Metaphor*, 119–20; Werner Senn, *Conrad's Narrative Voice* (N.p., 1980); Royal Roussel, *The Metaphysics of Darkness: A Study in the Unity and Development of Conrad's Fiction* (Baltimore, 1971), 102; C. B. Cox, *Joseph Conrad: The Modern Imagination* (Totowa, N.J., 1974), 7–8; Peter J. Glassman, *Language and Being: Joseph Conrad and the Literature of Personality* (New York, 1976). Contrast these to F. R. Leavis, *The Great Tradition* (London, 1948), 219.

13. Joseph Conrad to Edward Garnett, September 16, 1899, in Edward Garnett (ed.), *Letters from Joseph Conrad 1895–1924* (Indianapolis, 1928), 155.

tions: "To a teacher of languages there comes a time when the world is but a place of many words and man appears a mere talking animal not much more wonderful than a parrot."[14] This suspicion of language's artificiality occurs not only to the western narrator of *Under Western Eyes* but also to Tekla, the woman most devoted to the Russian revolutionist Ivanovitch. It finally dawns on her that his ideology is a web of internally consistent but meaningless words. The most trying part of her devotion to him is not the physical hardship of writing down his words in a cold, bare room where she is forbidden even to look at him because her "unintelligent look of expectation" happens to bother him. Rather, it is the astounding inconsistency between what he says and what he does. This is a man with a cultish devotion to women, yet he treats her like his slave, and a disloyal one at that. When she transcribes his essays, the distance between his words and their meaning looms forth: "The trying part of it was to have the secret of the composition laid bare before her; to see the great author of the revolutionary gospels grope for words as if he were in the dark as to what he meant to say" (*UWE*, 128). Ivanovitch's trouble is in reacquainting his words with his truest intentions—the intentions his actions convey better.

But the translator's problems with language are more crucial and harder to see through than Ivanovitch's. Since the whole novel is narrated by the translator, and since all we know about the Russian character is filtered through him, the meaning depends on the narrator's capacity to make his language as transparent as possible. Where it becomes opaque, the novel takes on a baffling, if enriching, complexity.

Not only must we rely on the translator's language, but we must also rely on his interpretation of Razumov's journal. For the better part of *Under Western Eyes*, he has never met Razumov, but relies on his journal entries. The translator's suspicions about his capacity to render the meaning of the journal undoubtedly help his credibility. Like Marlow in *Lord Jim*, he has a healthy skepticism, and the very fact that he relies on a

14. Joseph Conrad, *Under Western Eyes* (New York, 1979), 11. Subsequent page references to this novel (hereinafter cited parenthetically as *UWE*) are to this Penguin edition.

written document fortifies the authenticity of his enterprise. After a certain point, however, his suspicions work against his credibility. When he questions the directness of Razumov's document and therefore falls back upon his own assumptions about what he calls "the Russian character," then we are left to decide for ourselves whether the narrator is speaking about his own assumptions or about Razumov's true character.

One brief example shows how this works. At one point the translator directs our attention to his summarizing tendencies in interpreting the journal: "The thoughts in themselves were so numerous—they were like the thoughts of most human beings, few and simple—but they cannot be reproduced here in all their exclamatory repetitions" (*UWE*, 28). By itself, this is perfectly understandable. But when he indicates in the same breath the time lapse between the impressions and the narration of them, his summarizing tendencies are hard to interpret: he says that Razumov's thoughts "must have been graven as if with a steel tool . . . since he was able to write his relations with such fullness and precision a good many months afterward" (*UWE*, 28). How can the translator and narrator test the fullness and precision? What counts as precision except his ability to string together the tortuous details? There is no certain way of telling. This would not be an important problem except that the translator constantly reminds us of the limitations of his western eyes.

Worth noticing in connection with Razumov's journal is the difference between Conrad's use of written documents and the use to which eighteenth-century fiction put them. The early novel conventionally relied on written documents to fortify the narrator's epistemological authority. One almost forgets that *Moll Flanders* (1722) relies on an editor who merely cleans up the language in Moll's written report of her life. The reason one forgets is important: the editor departs after his prefatory note because his interpretation of the document is not a problem. Like Defoe, Richardson, in both *Pamela* (1740) and *Clarissa* (1747–1748), relies on an editor who orders the novels' letters. Although this order has no small part in the way we interpret the letters, the interpretation is not a problem for the editor, even if it might be for the reader. The mood of certainty increased by the early novel's use of written documents is deflated in Conrad's use of Razumov's journal in *Under Western Eyes*. Here, as in his special use of the frame device, Conrad's experimental interest in the novel modifies our expectations of how and how much language can grasp the nature of external reality.

When the narrator of *Under Western Eyes* interrogates language explicitly, we are led to believe that his problems in interpretation are at least as great as the reader's. At other moments, though, when language collapses into itself, the reader is presented with a more perplexing task than the narrator has, which happens in two notable moments in Marlow's narration, once in *Heart of Darkness* and again in *Lord Jim*. In the latter, at one point when Marlow visits Patusan, Jewel relies on him to sum up Jim's character. She has devoted herself to Jim by this time, and her future depends on knowing what Jim was like before he came to Patusan. Marlow's view is especially important to her because he is the emissary from the "outside world" from which Jim arrived. Jewel wants the unqualified summary of his character that both Marlow and the reader have been groping for. At this moment Marlow recognizes language's falsifying character. Instead of reflecting reality, he sees, language partakes in its misleading appearances. As though momentarily peering through the crevices of the appearances language upholds, Marlow stares into a horrifying abyss:

> For a moment I had a view of a world that seemed to wear a vast and dismal aspect of disorder, while, in truth, thanks to our unwearied efforts, it is as sunny an arrangement of small conveniences as the mind of man can conceive. But still—it was only a moment: I went back into my shell directly. One *must*—don't you know?—though I seemed to have lost all of my words in the chaos of dark thoughts I had contemplated for a second or two beyond the pale. These came back, too, very soon, for words also belong to the sheltering conception of light and order which is our refuge. (*LJ*, 236)

His solution in addressing Jewel is to lie. Words cannot contain the horror he has glimpsed, so he will report to her that Jim is the truest man he has ever known. To tell the truth, he says, is an "enterprise for a dream" (*LJ*, 239). His response creates greater problems for the reader than it does for Marlow because it damages the credibility of the rest of his narrative. If he can

lie to her, he can lie to us. Even granted that the special problems involving Jewel would try anyone's attempt to tell the
truth, Marlow's reasons for lying go beyond her particular situation and involve language itself.

An even more evocative instance when language fails Marlow appears near the end of *Heart of Darkness*. Here the project
of relating the qualities of the visible universe comes to an enigmatic halt. The chaos at the heart of all human action is like
the "dismal aspect of disorder" that Marlow confronts when he
speaks to Jewel in *Lord Jim*. Only here it is the culmination of
the whole narrative. When Marlow looks over Kurtz's shoulder
and confronts the heart of darkness, the realm of appearances
disappears. The visible universe disappears because the lights
go out, and we are left only with Kurtz's whisper:

> "Did he live his life again in every detail of desire, temptation, and
> surrender during that supreme moment of complete knowledge?
> He cried in a whisper at some image, at some vision—he cried out
> twice, a cry that was no more than a breath—
>   "'The horror! The horror!'" (*HD*, 99–100)

Marlow can only wonder whether in this moment Kurtz reviewed his life or responded to some presence, for neither his
nor Kurtz's utterances can specify the horror. The expression of
Kurtz's "complete knowledge" is completely evasive. No one
can shed light on the heart of darkness, so the report that there
is darkness is the only fact that can be imaged. We can know
that the report was only a breath, that it was a sound verging on
silence, but that is all. What is horrible is that there is no knowable reality, and if it cannot be known, it cannot be spoken.[15]

On the basis of what we have seen in Conrad's use of impressionism, the frame device, and language, we begin to see how
Conrad subverts the ordinary model of appearance and reality.
The rendering of the visible universe, the frame device's way of
appropriating the meaning of experience to its narration (insofar as that meaning can be comprehended), and language's way
of fortifying the surface of reality and failing to penetrate to its
core—these features, in the last analysis, are ways of avoiding
the imageless reality below the surface of art and life. By calling
these features techniques of evasion, I am not calling Conrad's

15. Guetti, *The Limits of Metaphor*, 65–66.

integrity into question; rather, these evasions are Conrad's way of admitting his terror. The ultimate terror he suspects is that at the center of human experience is only a void. By at least trying to suggest that void, Conrad depicts knowledge's failure to apprehend the nature of reality, which is to be feared not only because it is unknown, but also because it threatens human experience's continuance. We are concerned first, however, with how Conrad subverts the usual formulation of appearance's relation to reality.

If the visible universe and our way of describing and thinking about it have to do with a realm of appearance beneath which reality lies, then we can at least hold out for the possibility that our knowledge and sensations are ultimately grounded. The longer we investigate appearances, the more likely that our search will be rewarded. The more we test our knowledge, the sharper it will be. Our skepticism might be rewarded. In Conrad, however, it is otherwise. The more he tests appearances, the further away from reality he moves. Nor is the answer in ceasing to test appearances, for as we have seen in *Heart of Darkness*, the reward for penetrating to the core is the absence of all sensation, of all appearances, and therefore of all meaning, since meaning is in the realm of appearances, which paradoxically disappear. Meaning disappears when language fails, and language fails when its hopes for embodying reality are crushed beneath the horror.

If, as Conrad suggests, reality is the absence of appearances, then we have to readjust our sense of appearance's relation to reality. At the point where appearances no longer indicate reality (because they disappear), appearance and reality lose their relationship to one another completely. If reality is the total absence of appearance, then it becomes pointless to say that appearances are the appearances of anything except themselves. They continue to be genuine appearances only for as long as Conrad can hope they will lead him beyond themselves. Then the direction of Conrad's skepticism changes, and instead of interrogating the nature of reality, it interrogates itself and then collapses under the pressure. My subsequent discussion of Conrad concerns both his reappropriation of appearance's relation to reality and his skepticism's inward turning, which produces an infinitely regressive struggle to fortify the efficacy

of cognition. The problems of imagination's relation to perception, of the mind's relation to matter, and finally of the grounds
for self-knowledge serve to indicate, in Conrad's special handling of them, why his novels must veer away from epistemological dualism's model of knowledge and imagination.

Imagination and Perception: *Lord Jim*

If perception cannot acquaint the mind with the imageless reality beyond human experience, then the best that it can do is to
put us in touch with appearances. Perception, as it works in
Conrad, does not penetrate the façade of appearances. It can
provide the mind with at best provisional interpretations of
appearances, not by penetrating them but by ordering them.
When the appearances are ordered, they seem truest because
they imitate the deepest truth's anticipated consistency. As
we shall see, however, the most internally consistent appearances are liable at any moment to break apart, leaving the mind
with unresolved, disjunctive impressions of both itself and its
surroundings.

In using the word *perception* here, I mean to indicate a certain kind of knowledge—knowledge as it pertains to appearances, impressions, and sense experience. Since at this point we
are dealing with a form of knowledge that cannot penetrate to
the core of reality, we are concerned with those instances in
Conrad's fiction where the struggle is not finally, as it is in
Heart of Darkness, to meet the ground of experience, but
rather where the struggle is to order the impressions given
through perception. Perception's relation to imagination is important here, because in Conrad, whenever the mind recognizes
that its perceptions are not grounded in reality, then perception
itself collapses into imagination, and the mental image becomes the final object of knowledge. When that happens, then
all human experience takes on the fleeting characteristics of
imaginative experience. This causal chain underscores the
meaning of *Lord Jim.*

It is worth noting here certain points of similarity between
Conrad's portrayal of knowledge's limits and the theories espoused in contemporaneous philosophy. Particularly in the phi-
losophies of William James and Henri Bergson, for all their im-

portant differences, the final object of knowledge came to be regarded as the sensations themselves in perceptual experience. For others, like F. H. Bradley and John McTaggart, who held out for human knowledge's capacity to penetrate the façade of reality, positing an ideal realm was the only reasonable alternative. But Conrad was never an idealist; although he believed in a reality beyond perception, he gave up hoping it could ever be known. An important document that summarizes the philosophical climate of this period in Conrad's life, specifically in the first ten years of the century, is the first chapter of George Santayana's *Winds of Doctrine* (1913), "The Intellectual Temper of the Age." As Santayana explains it, not without obvious bias against them, contemporaneous theories of knowledge ultimately lead to solipsism and idealism:

> Immediate feeling, pure experience, is the only reality, the only *fact*: if notions which do not reproduce it fully as it flows are still called true (and they evidently ought not to be) it is only in a pragmatic sense of the word, in that while they present a false and heterogeneous image of reality they are not practically misleading. . . . The world, being a feeling, must be felt to be known, and then the world and the knowledge of it are identical. . . . Life, like the porcupine when not ruffled by practical alarms, can let its fretful quills subside. . . . And such indeed is the inevitable goal of the malicious theory of knowledge.

This summary indicates a trend of which Conrad is a part. Yet if we go back to our definition of perception and imagination, we can see the important difference that kept Conrad away from the idealistic conclusions to which Santayana believes such a theory of knowledge ultimately leads one. As long as Conrad holds perception apart from imagination, perception's efficacy in approaching reality, by comparison with imagination's, is fortified.[16]

But insofar as the ultimate object of knowledge is the mental image, perception collapses into imagination and conducts

16. William James, *The Principles of Psychology* (New York, 1950); Henri Bergson, *Time and Free Will: An Essay on the Immediate Data of Consciousness*, trans. F. L. Pogson (London, 1910); F. H. Bradley, *Appearance and Reality: A Metaphysical Essay* (1930; rpr. London, 1966); John McTaggart, *The Nature of Existence* (2 vols.; Cambridge, 1921); George Santayana, *Winds of Doctrine* (New York, 1913), 12–13; Kaplan, *The Passive Voice*, 8.

the mind back to itself rather than outward toward reality. As Robert R. Ehman formulates the epistemological problem of imagination and perception, "The notion that the imaginary is intrinsically indistinguishable from a real object of perception arises in large part from assuming that an image is a final object in its own right." Ehman argues that the mental image *is* a relation to its object: "The relation of the image to its object," he says, "is . . . always internal to the image."[17] If Ehman asserts that the image is the relation to the object, it is because he works on the assumption that the mind can comprehend the object of the image and then compare the two and have the difference between perceiving and imagining laid out before it. He does not hold that the mental image is the final object of knowledge (it is rather the relation to it), so that in this he differs from Conrad. I bring Ehman into the discussion to indicate the consequence of Conrad's way of making perception overlap imagination by making the mental image knowledge's final object. Imagination's complicity in perception fortifies its epistemological authority, even if it finally embarrasses knowledge.

Perhaps this is why Conrad puts so much stock in the imagination, even though elsewhere he denigrates it. When he suggests, "On ne communique pas la realité poignante des illusions," he implies, as he does elsewhere (*HD*, 39), that the dream sensation of an experience cannot be revealed to others; others take the imaginary experience as reality because nothing internal to the presentation exposes its imaginary status. That the truth is embedded in the imaginary militates against a skeptical appraisal of its imaginary status. If there can be as much truth in the imaginary as there is in the perceived, then how can the two categories of knowledge be separated? At one point in his *Personal Record*, he puts this much stock in the imagination: "Only in men's imagination does every truth find an effective and undeniable existence. Imagination, not invention, is the supreme master of art as of life. An imaginative and exact rendering of authentic memories may serve worthily that spirit of piety towards all things human which sanctions the conceptions of a writer of tales, and the emotions of the man

17. Robert R. Ehman, "Imagination, Dream, and the World of Perception," *Journal of Existentialism*, V (1964), 391.

reviewing his own experience." Mainly this belief in imagination, I suspect, solidified Conrad's commitment to his artistic tasks. As he says elsewhere, "in truth every novelist must begin by creating for himself a world, great or little, in which he can honestly believe."[18]

If for Conrad perception and imagination are the same thing, then one could reasonably ask why they should be examined as though they were separate. The fact of the matter is that Conrad often holds these two categories of mentation apart as a way of interrogating the reality of his fictional worlds and his characters' condition in those worlds. A perfectly conventional impulse behind realistic fiction, his putting mind and world in dualistic opposition communicates the reality of his fictional world, which his characters test, organize, but often fail to know. In interrogating its reality, perhaps Conrad hopes more and more to believe in that fictional world, but on that we can only speculate. The important point is that in portraying his characters' failure to comprehend their world, Conrad exhibits that world's existence seemingly independent of consciousness and thereby advances a philosophically realistic model of knowledge. Conrad's place in the literary history of realism is special because of what he suggests rather than because of what he directly exposes; just beyond the margins of his greatest achievements is the epistemological monism that Lawrence and Woolf more directly incorporate in their fiction, though neither of them gives over to it completely.

If Conrad could give up the task of comprehending the imageless reality beyond human knowledge, if he could settle for the truth of imagination, then the mind that his model advances would have an unproblematic and confluent relation to externality. The world would be an extension of the mind, and the dualistic model would have no place in his description of knowledge. But the fact is that Conrad could never settle for this view. He clung to a belief, however terrifying, in an externality beyond human comprehension. What makes him stand out is the intensity of his fear regarding the mind's alienation

18. Georges Jean-Aubry (ed.), *Lettres Françaises* (Paris, 1930), 34; Joseph Conrad, *Personal Record* (New York, 1926), 25; Joseph Conrad, "Books," in Walter F. Wright (ed.), *Joseph Conrad on Fiction* (Lincoln, 1964), 79.

from its surroundings—an intensity that encouraged him to turn the mind back around to itself in hopes of making the mind the ground of its own being, autonomous.

That is why Conrad's fiction is populated with characters who try to make their own minds the basis for their own existence and why perhaps he gives moral sanction to lying as often as he does. In his excellent introduction to the Modern Library edition of *Nostromo*, Robert Penn Warren has examined what he calls the "true lie" motif in Conrad.[19] We recall Marlow's important lie to Jewel, which is morally sanctioned because Jim's true character cannot be known, and if it could it could not be spoken. The same is true in regard to Marlow's lie to Kurtz's fiancée in *Heart of Darkness*: "The heavens do not fall for such a trifle. Would they have fallen, I wonder, if I had rendered Kurtz that justice which was his due? . . . I could not tell her. It would have been too dark—too dark altogether . . ." (*HD*, 111). Here Marlow speaks as though justice could have been done in relating Kurtz's disintegration, when everything we know (or better, everything we do not know) makes it hard to imagine what he would tell her. Similarly, when he justifies his lying to Jewel in *Lord Jim*, Marlow speaks as though he would have been believed if he had told the truth, when the fact is that he probably would not. How can he convince Jewel that the outside world has forgotten about Jim? For in this is the Cretan paradox that his very presence before her indicates that the outside world has not forgotten Jim. "I belonged," he reflects, "to this Unknown that might claim Jim for its own at any moment" (*LJ*, 232).

Just as lies are built into language, imagination is built into perception. Whenever Conrad lays before us the distinction between what is imagined and what is perceived, we have a relatively unproblematic view of what is real. The distinction is laid out especially clearly in the early part of *Lord Jim*, when the omniscient narrator takes responsibility for giving Jim's background. The omniscient perspective affords a clarity to this distinction that Marlow, when he takes over the narrative, only rarely achieves. Presumably this is because the omniscient view is not subject to the same limits to which Marlow's view is subject.

19. Robert Penn Warren, Introduction to *Nostromo* (New York, 1951).

From the omniscient perspective, the distance between what is imagined and what is perceived is widest. We discover, for example, that Jim's abstractions in regard to the seaman's code are an extension of his imaginative grasp of the world. They are fed on light literature that embodies only the surface of reality. A water clerk like Jim "must have Ability in the abstract and demonstrate it practically" (*LJ*, 9); that is, the abstraction must be translated into action. But Jim's abstract ability remains abstract. He holds himself apart from action because he wants his imaginative self-image to be autonomous, untouched by reality. Early in his career he is faced with the danger of a collision during a gale. The bow-man of the cutter, "a boy with a face like a girl's" (*LJ*, 13), prevents the collision while Jim considers jumping overboard. The captain observes him and lightly admonishes him, suggesting that next time he would know better than to contemplate such an act. Thus, Jim's self-image is an untested possibility.

Even more revealing than the incident itself is Jim's interpretation of it. He does not apply what he has learned about himself when, on the *Patna*, he succumbs to fear. What Jim takes from the earlier incident is not the practical knowledge of his latent cowardice but rather the intimation of heroism. He believes that next time he will be equipped with a knowledge that will not only help him avoid making the same mistake but that renders him superior in heroic stature to those around him who acted. Simply put, he convinces himself that in the earlier incident his mates were so busy taking heroic action that they failed to abstract from the experience the knowledge Jim was able to abstract by virtue of his position beyond the margin of their actions. Precisely *because* he held himself apart, he is, in his view, superior to the others. When the gale is over, he can reflect: "He had enlarged his knowledge more than those who had done the work. When all men flinched, then—he felt sure—he alone would know how to deal with the spurious menace of wind and seas. . . . He could detect no trace of emotion in himself, and the final effect of a staggering event was that, unnoticed and apart from the noisy crown of boys, he exulted with fresh certitude in his avidity for adventure, and in a sense of many-sided courage" (*LJ*, 13).

Jim's propensity for abstraction is reinforced by his inability to see beyond appearances and through to the underlying reality. Appearances for him are an opaque shield upheld by his imaginative grasp of the world. The omniscient narrator passes the distinction between appearance and reality over Jim's head and thereby shapes the reader's understanding of Jim's disjunctive relationship to his surroundings. Jim's perceptions are one with his imaginings, and the narrator lets us know how factitious his perceptions are: "[H]is thoughts would be full of valorous deeds: he loved these dreams and the success of his imaginary achievements. They were the best parts of life, its secret truth, its hidden reality" (*LJ*, 22).

It is precisely this inability to distinguish his perceptions from his imaginings that informs Jim's negligence on the *Patna*. Just before the collision of the *Patna* we see him staring at a map rather than at the real water before him. For Jim there is an exact correspondence between the map and the course of the ship: "He was so pleased with the idea [of his abstract heroism] that he smiled, keeping perfunctorily his eyes ahead; and when he happened to glance back he saw the white streak of the wake drawn as straight by the ship's keel upon the sea as the black line drawn by the pencil upon the chart" (*LJ*, 22). This correspondence obtains because as long as one does not look below the serene surface of the real water, the perspective is foreshortened (it lacks depth) just like the map's image of the area. Only on the surface can one see the ship's keel "as the black line drawn by the pencil upon the chart"; the real depth is something the map cannot embody in three dimensions. For Jim, not to see beyond the map is to take the image of the water for its reality. The map is the imagination's tool for planning action, and as long as the water is serene, it is adequate. Its limitation, unknown to Jim, is its inability to present anything but a frontal image of the real ocean; it cannot reveal the ocean's threat. Yet it is precisely this frontal image that Jim takes as an adequate perception.

When Marlow takes responsibility for the narrative, he is caught in some of these same limitations. Jim is an enigma to Marlow precisely because he cannot make any certain distinction between what he perceives Jim to be and what he imagines him to be. Jim thus becomes an issue for Marlow because Marlow's self-image is implicated in the project of knowing Jim. At this point the distinction between what is perceived and what is imagined is uncertain. Marlow cannot decide whether Jim's behavior during and after his trial is an attempt to escape or to confront the facts of his earlier behavior. Wherever Jim travels, he finds evidence (in others' suspicions) for his cowardly act in abandoning the pilgrims. The evidence, since Jim finds it everywhere, seems omnipresent, so that to run from one place to another could also be interpreted as an attempt to find the evidence wherever it is: "It might have been a f[l]ight and it might have been a mode of combat" (*LJ*, 151), Marlow suggests.[20] The part of Marlow that wants the facts to be faced wants to interpret Jim's running as an attempt to confront them. Here as elsewhere, it is impossible to tell where Marlow's imagining begins and his perception leaves off.

Stein's advice only complicates matters.[21] According to him, man suffers from a debilitating cleavage between what he is and what he wants to be. In terms of perception and imagination, what man is is what is perceived, and what he wants to be is what he imagines. Man's concern with the question of how to be indicates that he is nature's exile, that what he imagines is not what he perceives. The butterfly, Stein says, can simply be. Its imagination does not interrogate, because it has none: "'This magnificent butterfly finds a little heap of dirt and sits still on it; but man will never on his heap of mud keep still. . . . He wants to be a saint, and he wants to be a devil—and every time he shuts his eyes he sees himself as a very fine fellow—so fine as he can never be. . . . In a dream. . .'" (*LJ*, 162–63). Man lives according to an imagined self-image, and in so living, he experiences a chronic tension between what he is and what he wants to be, between what he perceives and what he imagines. He can either cease to want to be and instead be what he simply is, which would be equivalent to seeing without imagining; or he can be only what he wants to be, equivalent to imagining without perceiving. The question is not, as Stein

20. *Fight* appears in the Penguin edition, *flight* in the Doubleday uniform edition. The latter obviously makes more sense.

21. Bruce Johnson, *Conrad's Models of Mind* (Minneapolis, 1971), 60; Roussel, *The Metaphysics of Darkness*, 95–96. Contrast these to Eloise Knapp Hay, "Conrad Between Sartre and Socrates," *Modern Language Quarterly*, XXXIV (1973), 85–97.

would have it, either/or. Neither road is open to the exclusion of the other, for the same reason that imagination can never be finally bracketed off from perception; imagination is, once again, built into the laws governing human cognition. Stein recommends that we submit to our dreams: "'A man that is born falls into a dream like a man who falls into the sea. If he tries to climb out into the air as inexperienced people endeavour to do, he drowns—*nicht wahr?* . . . No! I tell you! The way is to the destructive element submit yourself, and with the exertions of your hands and feet in the water make the deep, deep sea keep you up'" (*LJ*, 163). To climb out of the water would be to see oneself and one's world without imagination, something Stein does not recommend. And the "exertions of your hands and feet in the water" are not intended to take the dreamer out of the water, only to "make the deep, deep sea keep you up." The exertions represent the effort to make human actions consistent with imaginative contemplation, as Jim's actions obviously have not been. To cease to act would be to fall so deep within the dream that the dreamer would die; to exert himself in the water is to reunite action with contemplation.

On the basis of this observation, Stein recommends that Jim not crawl out of his heroic ideal, but continue living it in a place where his actions can be consistent with his imaginings. He recommends Patusan because it presents to Jim "a totally new set of conditions for his imaginative faculty to work upon" (*LJ*, 167). Alien and virtually unknown, Patusan is the perfect escape hatch from a world where Jim's contemplation and action are divorced from each other.

Jim's moving to Patusan translates contemplation into action and perception into imagination. The threshold to Patusan is appropriately suggested by Jim's falling asleep after he escapes from Rajah Allang's stockade by leaping over a high barrier and landing in the muddy sand. Whether he actually sleeps is suggestively ambiguous: "Then as a sort of happy thought the notion came to him that he would go to sleep. He will have it that he *did* actually go to sleep; that he slept—perhaps for twenty seconds, or only for one second" (*LJ*, 193). Waking and sleeping are as confused as perception and imagination.

The romance motifs that enter the narrative at this point, along with some jarring discontinuities in the early part of the story, advance the dreamlike quality of the narrative. The central romance motif is connected to the ring that Stein gave Jim in order to identify him as a friend of Doramin. The disjointed character of the narrative here produces a phantasmagoric effect. For example, we are told of Jim's wandering halfway across the settlement, looking "out of all semblance to a human being," "a flying terror" (*LJ*, 194), and then he is suddenly and for a moment unaccountably pushed down. After a short delay we are able to recognize that Jim is being held up by two of Doramin's men.

On Patusan, finally, Jim earns respect, so that "his word decided everything" (*LJ*, 204). For a period of time his experience and his imagination are one, so that, as in Yeats's metaphor, "the moon and the sunlight seem / One inextricable beam."[22] Even Marlow falls under the spell. When he visits Patusan, he observes that "there is something haunting in the light of the moon. . . . It is to our sunshine, which—say what you like—is all we have to live by, what the echo is to the sound: misleading and confusing whether the note be mocking or sad. It robs all forms of matter—which, after all, is our domain—from their substance, and gives a sinister reality to shadows alone" (*LJ*, 187). Marlow suspects a sinister reality because he has one foot in the sunlit world apart from Patusan. But Jim does not suspect anything; his skepticism has been set aside for the free play of his imagination. He so much loses his skepticism that he becomes subject to the renegade Brown. Jim's imagination makes him more suggestible to the similarities among men than to their differences. What perception pulls apart imagination melds. That is why it is so easy for Brown to make Jim identify with him. Jim sees himself in Brown, the outsider, and in seeing himself in an outsider, he unwittingly tears the social fabric among the Bugis people into which he has woven himself.[23]

Jim reads Brown's circumstances as reflections of his own because he has grown so accustomed to seeing the world as the mirror of his mind. Brown lands on Patusan because he is flee-

22. W. B. Yeats, "The Tower," *Collected Poems* (New York, 1950), 193–94.
23. Morton Dauwen Zabel, *Craft and Character: Texts, Methods, and Vocation in Modern Fiction* (New York, 1957), 82.

ing retribution for his having stolen the very boat he arrives on; Jim, on the other hand, has never felt sufficiently punished for his own crime. Brown makes Jim feel as much a foreigner to Patusan as he is. He argues that since they are both intruding white men, neither has more right than the other to land there. Unlike Brown, though, Jim has earned his place; yet he is too gullible at this point to recognize that important difference. When Brown recognizes Jim's fear, he exposes his own, and thereby tightens Jim's bond with him: "'I've lived—and so did you though you talk as if you were one of those people that should have wings so as to go about without touching the dirty earth. Well—it is dirty. I haven't got any wings. I am here because I was afraid once in my life'" (LJ, 288).

Then Brown delivers the final blow. He asks Jim whether he realizes that when a man is concerned with his very survival he can be brought to risk the lives of others—"three, thirty, three hundred people" (LJ, 291). At this point, however much Jim has wanted to break his ties to the outside world that Brown represents, he cannot turn Brown away. To do so and make him face almost certain starvation would be to turn his back on his racial identity, which has at this moment a Kiplingesque intensity. Brown presents two alternatives: "'Either bring your infernal crowd along or let us go out and starve in the open sea, by God! You have been white once, for all your tall talk of this being your own people and you being one with them'" (LJ, 287).

When Jim stakes his reputation on the racial identity of Brown, he ignores his stature in Patusan society and substitutes for one appearance another that contradicts it. In identifying with Brown, he lets his imaginatively sustained identity be subverted by an even more factitious one. Even if Jim's Patusan identity, which has been supported by his actions, conforms to his imaginative self-image, it is nonetheless more substantial than his identity with Brown. If Brown is a true representative of the white races, as Jim seems to believe, then identifying with him can do nothing to uphold Jim's moral integrity. Because he believes in Brown, Jim lets him land and then depart peacefully, but when Cornelius betrays Jim, delivering a message to Brown persuading him to attack Dain Waris' guards, Jim's credibility with the people is shattered. In letting Brown leave, Jim has betrayed the Bugis people and reenacted his abandonment of the pilgrims on the *Patna*.

The ending of *Lord Jim*, however, has a significant ambiguity that is at the heart of the epistemological problem that Jim, Marlow, and the reader share—the problem of making a distinction between what is perceived and what is imagined. This ambiguity helps explain why there is so much disagreement among this novel's commentators, some of whom argue that in the last analysis Jim reverses his earlier abnegation of responsibility and others of whom argue that he simply persists in it.[24] To argue for one interpretation to the exclusion of the other, though, is to ignore the meaning of the ambiguity, for it is impossible finally to decide whether Jim's failure reverses itself or persists. It is impossible for the reader to tell because it is impossible for either Marlow or anyone else to tell. When he presents himself to Doramin and faces certain death, Jim at the same moment defects from Jewel. If he remains true to his word to Jewel and abides by her, he will not have the public heroic stature he would privately have with her. His leaving her can thus be reasonably interpreted as a defection from his word for the sake of maintaining his imaginative heroic stature: " 'Nothing can touch me,' he said in a last flicker of superb egoism" (*LJ*, 310).

Yet the concluding drama has Marlow's imagination stamped on it. Once again we have no certain way of telling where his imagination begins and his perceptions leave off. In his letter to a "privileged reader," Marlow says: "The story of the last events you shall find enclosed here. You must admit that it is romantic beyond the wildest dreams of his boyhood, and yet there is to my mind a sort of profound and terrifying logic in it, as if it were our imagination alone that could set loose upon us the might of an overwhelming destiny" (*LJ*, 258). The remainder of the story is in this letter to a "privileged reader," but no reader is privileged enough to have an exact account of how heroic Jim finally was. Marlow becomes Jim's voice now that Jim has failed to record a message about his final experiences (*LJ*, 256). In the third-to-last and penultimate paragraphs we are left

24. Roussel, *The Metaphysics of Darkness*, 98; Dowden, *The Imaged Style*, 70; Miller, *Fiction and Repetition*, 35. Contrast their reading and mine to Ian Watt's in *Conrad in the Nineteenth Century* (Berkeley, 1979), 352.

with two contradictory images of Jim. The first perhaps conforms to Marlow's imagination: "Not in the wildest days of his boyish visions could he have seen the alluring shape of such an extraordinary success! For it may very well be that in the short moment of his last proud and unflinching glance, he had beheld the face of that opportunity which, like an Eastern bride, had come veiled to his side." Marlow's perception, characterized by skepticism, tells us another story: "But we can see him" he says, "an obscure conqueror of fame, tearing himself out of the arms of a jealous love at the sign, at the call of his exalted egoism. He goes away from a living woman to celebrate his pitiless wedding with a shadowy ideal of conduct" (*LJ*, 313). The first description enforces the image of marriage; the second presents the image of divorce. The truth of the ambiguity is in its never resolving itself; correctly interpreted, it generates two opposite meanings. "We ought to know," Marlow says, but we do not: "Who knows? He is gone, inscrutable at heart."

Lord Jim concludes by making the categories of perception and imagination reversible, implying that the final object of knowledge is the mental image of a reality that can never be directly comprehended, but must be faced. In *Heart of Darkness*, to face reality is to stop thinking—to stop perceiving and imagining. In *Lord Jim*, to face reality is to try to make its appearances cohere; as long as they cohere, as in an unproblematic narrative (which *Lord Jim* is not), then appearances can seem true. But whenever the perceptions break apart into unresolvable disunity, then the mind must face the cracks in the façade—cracks that betray the mind's factitious activity and its metaphysical inferiority to the world it truly lives in.

Mind and Matter: *Nostromo*

So far we have recognized that for Conrad perception is at best a frantic attempt to organize sense experience, that sense experience, in effect, bottoms out when its basis in reality founders, and that therefore it becomes an extension of the imagination. If the mind cannot hope to apprehend the nature of reality, then it cannot hope to have any real effect upon it; the mind can rearrange the appearances, but that is not the same thing as exerting power over reality. Once Cartesian skepticism has turned back upon itself by recognizing its inefficacy in testing the ground of experience, the mind discovers its total inability to exert power over its surroundings. Any sense of the mind's powers in Conrad is only an illusion. He strays from Descartes' model of dualistic interactionism, which allows for both the material world's power over the mind and the mind's power over the world, and advances instead the view that the mind is wholly subject to externality and can exert no power over it. When perception and imagination fold into one another, the mind's power is as much an illusion as knowledge is. Our concluding discussion of *Nostromo* is about how the mind fails and why its power is illusory.

For Descartes' dualistic interactionism Conrad substitutes Santayana's epiphenomenalism, which holds that the mind is wholly subject to external forces. In Santayana's words, the mind is only "a lyric cry in the midst of business."[25] Although Santayana identifies epiphenomenalism as a materialist view of mind (since matter becomes the foundation for all human action), to identify Conrad's view as epiphenomenalist is not necessarily to call him a materialist, as Jeremy Hawthorn does.[26] Conrad certainly doubted that human action could affect the world, but he intensely hoped that it would, and his hope underwrites his artistry: to create a fictional world in which he could honestly believe was to lay out before him the grounds for that hope.

Conrad believed that consciousness is born from the material world, however incompatible they ultimately are. The mind is a configuration of matter "in progress": in a letter to Edward Garnett he says that *"all matter"* is "only that . . . through which the various vibrations of waves (electricity, heat, sound, light, etc.) are propagated, thus giving birth to our sensations— then emotions—then thought."[27] It gives him no comfort that the material world is the mind's grounding, because he indicates in the same sentence matter's "inconceivable tenuity,"

25. Santayana, *Winds of Doctrine,* 7; Jerome A. Shaffer, *Philosophy of Mind* (Englewood Cliffs, N.J., 1968), 39–40.

26. Jeremy Hawthorn's use of the term *materialism* is both Marxist and philosophical in *Joseph Conrad: Language and Fictional Self-Consciousness* (London, 1979), 57.

27. Garnett (ed.), *Letters,* 143.

which comes from its unpredictable way of changing its appearances. The mind can never feel securely grounded in a world
whose rules can change at any moment.

In a letter to R. B. Cunninghame Graham, Conrad advances
his "knitting machine" metaphor as a way of explaining the
appalling logic governing the mind's relation to its material
source. The knitting machine, he says, is the creative principle
of the world. Everything created by this machine is held in constant threat because it is all subject to the annihilation of
which the creative principle itself is the agent. Nor has any
mind the power to challenge this threat. "You cannot by any
special lubrication make embroidery with a knitting machine.
And the most withering thought is that the infamous thing has
made itself: made itself without thought, without conscience,
without foresight, without eyes, without heart. It is a tragic accident,—and it has happened. You can't interfere with it." Although there is no avoiding this threat, there is a way of making
it worse, of intensifying its claims. By being conscious at all,
the mind grounds itself in the source of its destruction, and by
being conscious of the threat, the mind aggravates its problem.
Conrad describes this situation in another letter: "What makes
mankind tragic is not that they are the victims of nature, it is
that they are conscious of it. To be part of the animal kingdom
under the conditions of this earth is very well—but as soon as
you know of your slavery the pain, the anger, the strife—the
tragedy begins. We can't return to nature, since we can't change
our place in it."[28]

Edward Said has drawn a parallel between Conrad's knitting-
machine metaphor and Schopenhauer's *principium individuationis.* Schopenhauer's view is worth noticing here because it
establishes a bridge between Conrad's metaphysical speculations in his discursive writing and his metaphorical examination of this view in his fiction. The *principium individuationis*
(principle of individuation) transforms the creative force's will
into time and space, where it is evidenced. But in so transform-
ing it, it converts it into terms which are metaphysically antag-

28. Joseph Conrad to R. B. Cunninghame Graham, December 20, 1897, and
January 31, 1898, in G[eorges] Jean-Aubry, *Joseph Conrad: Life and Letters*
(2 vols.; Garden City, N.Y., 1927), I, 216, 224.

onistic to the essential nature of the originating will. As Schopenhauer describes it in *The World as Will and Idea* (1883), "the will as a thing-in-itself lies outside the province of the principle of sufficient reason in all its forms, and is consequently completely groundless, although all its manifestations are entirely subordinated to the principle of sufficient reason." The manifestations he speaks of are equivalent in Conrad to material reality's appearances, which are given to perception and imagination but which are always subordinated to the underlying reality.[29]

Corollary to the *principium individuationis* is a view of human action for which work is Conrad's favorite metaphor. Just as the apprehension of the creative will changes, depending on whether the will is inside or outside of time, so does the power of the mind change, depending on whether it is caught up in the task or viewing the task from an external perspective. This understanding is at the heart of Conrad's view of work and of the mind's status in relation to action. Schopenhauer describes the dual perception of human action in these terms: "[T]he strange fact [is] that every one believes himself *a priori* to be perfectly free, even in his individual actions, and thinks that at every moment he can commence another manner of life, which just means that he can become another person. But *a posteriori*, through experience, he finds to his astonishment that he is not free, but subjected to necessity."[30] Similarly in Conrad's fiction, work viewed from the outside reveals a slavery that the mind caught in the task takes as freedom itself, for the mind cannot see, as those on the outside do, that it exerts no power over its surroundings. Outsiders, Marlow says, see most of the game: freedom is the illusion, slavery the fact.

Both *Heart of Darkness* and *Nostromo* exhibit the mind's slavery in this way. In *Heart of Darkness* Conrad conveys this double view of work by shifting the reader's perspective from the inside to the outside. When Marlow realizes that the steamer on which he is about to take his journey needs repair,

29. Edward W. Said, *Joseph Conrad and the Fiction of Autobiography* (Cambridge, Mass., 1966), 139; Johnson, *Conrad's Models of Mind*, 42–51; Arthur Schopenhauer, *The World as Will and Idea*, trans. R. B. Haldane (1883; rpr. [3 vols.] London, 1950), I, 146.

30. Schopenhauer, *The World as Will and Idea*, I, 147.

he consoles himself in the work: "I had expended enough hard work on her to make me love her. . . . I don't like work—no man does—but I like what is in work, the chance to find yourself. Your own reality—for yourself, not for others—what no other man can ever know. They can only see the mere show, and never can tell you what it really means" (HD, 41). But Marlow is perspicacious enough to consider, and to afford to the reader, an outside view of this same effort to find oneself. This second view comes when the chief accountant, from whom Marlow first hears Kurtz's name, wins Marlow's respect for his painstaking attention to detail in both his work and his appearance, even though he is isolated from his own civilization. In the midst of the jungle he bends over his books, "making correct entries of perfectly correct transactions," while "fifty feet below the doorstep I could see the still tree-tops of the grove of death" (HD, 28), where the starving slaves had withdrawn to die. This ironic detail points out the inefficacy of the chief accountant's efforts. After Marlow confronts the heart of darkness, work appears overtly as slavery when he sees the people's active devotion to the "sepulchral city," civilization's outpost on the rim of darkness, transform itself into the most laughable drudgery: "They were intruders whose knowledge of life was to me an irritating pretense, because I felt so sure they could not possibly know the things I knew. . . . I had no particular desire to enlighten them, but I had some difficulty in restraining myself from laughing in their faces, so full of stupid importance" (HD, 102). The people's activity becomes laughable because, given what he has seen beneath the surface of commitment, Marlow knows they have fallen into mechanistic, involuntary movements that reduce them to the status of automatons and render them, according to Bergson's definition of humor, the object of a supreme joke.

This same ironic attitude is maintained throughout Nostromo because the omniscient narrator stands apart from his characters' activities. From his perspective they blunder into slavery. As long as the Costaguanan mining project is a means to an end, as it is viewed by its principal organizers, then the illusion of the mind's power over matter can be sustained.[31]

31. Johnson, Conrad's Models of Mind, 122; Miller, Poets of Reality, 49–50.

Then the mine is the material means to an ideal end, and as long as the ideal runs ahead of the material means, it can seem to lead it, to mold it according to the mind's designs.

Perhaps of all the characters, Emilia Gould, the wife of Charles, the mine's strongest leading force, upholds ideals that are tainted least by material interests. In her commitment to the enterprise Emilia is not totally blinded; she witnesses, after all, the building of the roads that mar the landscape and the disappearance of the waterfall she had immortalized on her canvas (*N*, 93). Nonetheless she clutches at the *idea* of the mine, convinced of the mind's hegemony over matter. In this she is the spiritual kin of Natalia in *Under Western Eyes*, the patient believer who serves her brother's memory as Emilia serves Charles. Her status as a woman in Conrad's fiction makes her ineffectual, but at least she is not victimized by her ideals the way male characters with the same motives are. Her ideal in her commitment to the mine is to shed a guiding light through Costaguana—a light that would organize human action and lend it meaning beyond itself. This would be the ray of hope that Charles' father, who had closed down the mine, completely lost. "God looked wrathfully at these countries," he observes, "or else He would let some ray of hope fall through a rift in the appalling darkness of intrigue, bloodshed, and crime that hung over the Queen of Continents" (*N*, 81). In her hope to make the mine a spiritually uplifting enterprise, Emilia tries to ignore the materialistic underpinnings of the silver itself: "[S]he had laid her unmercenary hands, with an eagerness that made them tremble, upon the first silver ingot turned out still warm from the mould; and by her imaginative estimate of its power she endowed that lump of metal with a justificative conception, as though it were not a mere fact, but something far-reaching and impalpable, like the true expression of an emotion or the emergence of a principle" (*N*, 99).

At the transporting of the first silver ingots, this ideal adequately directs the enterprise by augmenting social cohesion. There is a lull in the usual violence because even the outlaws, revolutionaries, deserters, and Hernandez's famous bandits, who Charles feared would rob the first fruits, in fact rally around the project. They provide both practical and moral support by working as guards. Just as Emilia had wanted, the San Tomé mine—"an institution, a rallying-point for everything in the province that needed order and stability to live" (N, 101)—supplants the spiritual power that only religious order had held in Costaguana. The task of building the railroad, like the working of the mine which follows, carries the redemptive power of a religious conviction: "the survey of the track was like the tracing of the path of life," and the work's force "would be almost as strong as a faith" (N, 46).

Charles shares with Emilia the desire to bring order to Sulaco. Their vision actually becomes the bedrock of their marriage, which gives the mine the power to make or break it. But Charles' interests in taking over his father's mine arise from unsuspected psychological motives. His father was terrified of the political turmoil that opening the mine would create, and he forbade Charles to live with him in Sulaco because he feared its people. While Charles and his father are separated, Charles' imagination has time to invent a new motive for taking over the mine. His reopening of the mine would be, for him, a reversal of what he considers his father's moral failure: "It hurt Charles Gould to feel that never more, by no effort of will, would he be able to think of his father in the same way he used to think of him when the poor man was alive. His breathing image was no longer in his power. This consideration, closely affecting his own identity, filled his breast with a mournful and angry desire for action. . . . The mine had been the cause of an absurd moral disaster; its working must be a serious and moral success" (N, 66). In one stroke he hopes to prove his own moral virility and overcome his father's failure of nerve by proving it was unnecessary.[32] The more intricate his motives, however, the further away from the truth Charles is led. The truth is that the enterprise is not advanced by his designs; his designs in the end are the slave of material interests.

The detached and ironic omniscient narrator of Nostromo registers the makings of this reversal well before anyone else notices them. There is, for example, the suspicious suggestion that the last political revolt, which had catapulted Ribiera to power, was at least partly financed by the San Tomé Mine Administration (N, 107). The social coherence that the project has brought to Sulaco is, when viewed ironically, mere slavery,

32. Johnson, Conrad's Models of Mind, 107; H. M. Daleski, Joseph Conrad: The Way of Dispossession (London, 1977), 124–25.

no more clearly apparent than when we see Nostromo riding through the village at dawn to awaken the miners who are late for work by dragging them out of their homes at gunpoint (*N*, 89–90). In one of his most coldly ironic moods, the narrator indicates that in Sulaco there are few unemployment problems. In a colony of slaves, one supposes so. Even by this point, then, we see a disparity between the original design and the actual outcome. The humane desire to lend a sense of purpose to an aimless South American country becomes, in practice, a form of slavery.

When the ideal begins fading, the mine's materiality takes over. What was the material vehicle to an ideal destination becomes an end in itself. It assumes control over everyone. Emilia recognizes the confusion of means and ends earlier than does Charles. It is she who first raises the question of how far they will go in saving the mine from their political rivals, the Monterists:

> "Ah, if one only knew how far you mean to go," said his wife, inwardly trembling, but in an almost playful tone.
> "Any distance, any length of course," was the answer, in a matter-of-fact tone, which caused Mrs. Gould to make another effort to repress a shudder. (*N*, 179)

His answer is matter-of-fact because he does not see through the situation; he does not recognize, as Emilia shudders to do, that the enterprise has taken him by the hand. He is the follower, not the leader. Where before the Goulds' attachment to the project had helped keep them together, now it begins to drive a wedge between them. All Charles' attention goes toward advancing the project rather than toward Emilia, who is beginning to lose faith in it. As Decoud later perceptively writes in his letter to his sister, "The little woman has discovered that he lives for the mine rather than for her. . . . Mrs. Gould's mission is to save him from the effects of that cold and overmastering passion which she dreads more than if it were an infatuation for another woman" (*N*, 207).

The reason she fears his entrapment by the mine is clear by the time Charles takes desperate measures to save it from the Monterists, who want to assume political power and nationalize the mine. When he escorts the dying Don José, his wife, and Antonia to the refugee camp for their safekeeping, it dawns on him that the mine must be saved for its own sake, no longer for the sake of the ideal, which has all but disappeared. He recognizes his complicity with Hernandez the bandit; now, he sees, he is on the bandit's level, and the mine which he controlled has forced him into this position: "In his determined purpose he held the mine, and the indomitable bandit held the Campo by the same precarious tenure. They were equals before the lawlessness of the land. It was impossible to disentangle one's activity from its debasing contacts. A close-meshed net of crime and corruption lay upon the whole country" (N, 300).

When Charles recognizes that the mine is no longer the adequate material means to his ideal end, that it is an end in itself, he still does not give it over. Instead of seeing it as a material interest, he sees it as itself the idea, and so its material underpinnings are pushed out of his awareness. As Royal Roussel describes this point in the action, the mine "has become imbued with a spiritual quality which allies it to the nature of consciousness itself."[33] Although Charles always saw the mine as a spiritual and intellectual force, he also acknowledged its material side as the means to an end. Now that the mine may be taken away from him, however, he wants to hold on to it only for the sake of possessing it. The ideal has vanished, and possessing the mine has become a self-justifying cause.

The main clue to Charles' appropriation of the mine to the realm of mental, specifically imaginative, experience is his willingness to let everything else change except the mine. Denis Donoghue's formulation of the distinction between imagination and perception clarifies this relationship. Since perception, he says, leans toward an external world, "it has no design upon objects except to sense their presence, their relation to other objects and to the mind." It assumes objects' underlying stability because it "acknowledges that objects have another life in which they are not perceived, though they may be deemed to await perception." Perception assumes the essential stability of externality; if externality were unstable, then it would be hopeless for the mind ever to make sense of it. If the mind registers discontinuity when it is perceiving, it assumes the discontinuity is in the subject rather than the object. When the mind is ready to perceive, it is more willing to change itself in

33. Roussel, *The Metaphysics of Darkness,* 117.

order to maintain its faith in the continuity than it is to accept the discontinuity of the external world. In imagination, by contrast, the mind "is prepared, if feeling requires it, to see everything change except itself."[34] Since Donoghue's formulation is consistent with Conrad's sense of the distinction between perception and imagination, the distinction, insofar as Conrad upholds it, gives us a clue to how the mine tests Charles' mental powers.

Because Charles is willing to see everything change but the mine, he is no longer, in effect, perceiving the mine; he unwittingly imagines it. He has turned the mine into the predicate for his mind's efficacy. He would prefer the mine "shattered into small bits" (N, 303) than have it fall into the Monterists' hands, because it matters less whether the mine actually exists (imagination does not require its objects' actual existence) than whether he or the Monterists take possession of it. He goes as far as instructing Don Pepé to dynamite the mine if an attack upon it seems likely to succeed. But no tactic works. Charles must face the fact that his mine is an object in space, not an idea, and that it will ultimately be guided by the principles of material interest rather than by his thoughts. In *Nostromo* no mental construct has any lasting effect. Mind takes matter's lead.

If Charles had taken a more skeptical view of his interest in the mine, then, one would think, he could have maintained a more lasting control over both himself and his mine. He might then have recognized that he was confusing the standards for material and imaginative interests. If he could see through himself, one believes, he might have assumed greater control. One of Decoud's principal roles in *Nostromo*, though, is to indicate the inefficacy of skepticism. Decoud is repeatedly called one of life's dilettantes, precisely because he prides himself on his detachment from human experience, a detachment that Charles cannot maintain. "Martin Decoud . . . imagined himself to derive an artistic pleasure from watching the picturesque extreme of wrong-headedness into which an honest, almost sacred, conviction may drive a man. . . . [He and Father Corbelán] got on well together, as if each had felt respectively that a masterful conviction, as well as utter scepticism, may lead a man very far

34. Donoghue, *The Sovereign Ghost*, 45.

on the by-paths of political action" (N, 172–73). Decoud is not just skeptical; he is self-consciously so, which makes a difference, because his ultimate failure is not, strictly, in his capacity to maintain his skepticism, but in his inability to test his skepticism's limits—to be, in effect, skeptical of his skeptical self-image.

Well before he spiritually collapses on Isabel Island, Decoud's limits appear. His romantic interest in Antonia challenges his power to detach himself from human interests: "Decoud had often felt his familiar habit of ironic thought fall shattered against Antonia's gravity. . . . He was very far from thinking Antonia ordinary, whatever verdict his scepticism might have pronounced upon himself" (N, 166). Additionally, his agreeing to help Nostromo hide the silver ingots on the island indicates his complicity in human designs. Albert J. Guerard has made the interesting speculation that there is a difference between Decoud as he acts and Decoud as the narrator characterizes him. "To put matters bluntly," Guerard says, "Conrad may be condemning Decoud for a withdrawal and skepticism more radical than Decoud ever shows; which are, in fact, Conrad's own."[35] This charge may be judged true on the evidence of what I have described. Perhaps Decoud is less skeptical in his actions than he is when the narrator is thinking about him because thinking allows for more detachment from one's surroundings than acting does. One acts skeptical by changing commitments from one thing to another. Thought, on the other hand, invites withdrawal. The narrator can be more skeptical than Decoud in his actions because the narrator can stand apart from the characters in a way that no character within the novel can. Action sustains the illusions that Decoud thinks he can see through, and according to the narrator, "In our activity alone do we find the sustaining illusion of an independent existence as against the whole scheme of things of which we form a helpless part" (N, 409).

When he is on Placid Gulf with Nostromo, Charles consciously looks for some indication that he is acting or moving at all. He may be skeptical, but he is not a cardboard character; he must maintain some sense of purpose. The water is so dark and still that he must put his hand in it to make sure he is mov-

35. Albert J. Guerard, *Conrad the Novelist* (Cambridge, Mass., 1958), 199.

ing. Although the collision on Placid Gulf might have brought him and Nostromo together in the project of saving the ingots from Sotillo, it does not. That far Charles will not go. The two men are torn apart psychologically and then physically: "There was no bond of conviction, of common idea; they were merely two adventurers pursuing each his own adventure, involved in the same imminence of deadly peril" (N, 247).

This peril is figured in the darkness that brackets them off from the light, from the world of human bonds, and from the light of knowledge and imagination. In the darkness, both of them confront the vacuity at the center of human experience. Decoud has gathered his sense of purpose, ironically, from the very gesture of skepticism. He upholds himself through his power of detachment. But what happens to his effort to withdraw from the world when the world effectively withdraws from him? Placid Gulf denies the sensational world in which Decoud has been a dilettante. Suddenly his latent need for involvement in his surroundings comes alive, but even his attachment to Antonia is rendered pointless. Its meaning dissolves in the darkness: "Even his passionate devotion to Antonia into which he had worked himself up out of the depths of his skepticism had lost all appearance of reality. For a moment he was the prey of an extremely languid but not unpleasant indifference" (N, 224).

Decoud's skepticism is dealt its final blow when we recognize that "he, too, was in the toils of an imaginative existence" (N, 223). Not only are his commitments illusions, but so are his efforts to withdraw from them. The mind cannot exert the power necessary for it to withdraw from its surroundings. Nor does solitude on the island, where he waits for Nostromo's return, supply the detachment he has lost hope of. Instead, the solitude makes skepticism all the more ludicrous:

> Solitude from mere outward condition of existence becomes very swiftly a state of soul in which the affectations of irony and skepticism have no place. It takes possession of the mind, and drives forth the thought into the exile of utter unbelief. . . . Decoud caught himself entertaining a doubt of his own individuality. It had merged into the world of cloud and water, of natural forces and forms of nature. In our activity alone do we find the sustaining illusion of an independent existence as against the whole scheme of things of which we form a helpless part. (N, 408–409)

He doubts his very individuality, because the Cartesian model fails. For Decoud it is not "I think; therefore I am"; it is "I think; therefore I am nothing." He cannot make a distinction between the acts and the intentions of his awareness. The objects can go on without him, but he cannot go on without them; his mind is a slave to the objects of its knowledge.

Decoud now lacks the faith-giving imagination that renders discrete events as a meaningful trajectory of coherent human action. He relies instead on the truth of his disconnected sensations and hence cannot sustain hope that someone will take him back into the community and restore his sense of belonging and therefore of himself. His Placid Gulf adventure has opened before him a vast gap in experience that he cannot bridge; the universe has become "a succession of incomprehensible images" (N, 409). No longer do the sensations he wholly relied on tell him any truth. To imitate truth, the appearances would have to cohere, but now they no longer add up. He hangs by a "cord of silence," then, which he wishes would snap if only to make a noise. His "intellectual audacity" forces him to be swallowed in "the immense indifference of things" (N, 412). To think is to fail. His suicide is a foregone conclusion.

Conrad embarrasses the mind by confronting it with its more enduring material source in order to reappropriate its relation to externality. In these moments the interplay between mind and world is arrested, for basically the same reason that the tensions between appearance and reality and between perception and imagination were arrested. The dual tension can continue for only as long as the mind is on relatively equal footing with its surroundings. When the mind collapses under the pressure of the objects of its knowledge, then dualism verges on monism. Conrad's place in the history of the realistic novel is especially important here because he puts this monism just beyond his fiction's range and thereby challenges its foundation in philosophical realism.

Self-Knowledge: *Nostromo* and *Under Western Eyes*

As it is metaphorically advanced in the tradition of realistic fiction, even the Cartesian formula for establishing self-knowledge renders identity problematic. In the novel's usual formulation of the quest for self-knowledge, the self is an orphan in a hostile world that tells it little or nothing about its identity. In classic examples like Fielding's *Tom Jones* (1749), Austen's *Emma* (1816), or Dickens' *Great Expectations* (1861), the self pushes its origins away or has them taken away by accidental circumstances. It loses itself and then looks for itself. This formula is predicated upon a disjunction of subject and object, for only when externality is appraised from a safe distance and in a gesture of skepticism does the self arrive at a sense of its own meaning, purpose, or identity. The formula also assumes the possibility that the self can surmount its act of knowing and in the end can apprehend the distance between illusion and reality—between what it had thought and what really is. Although in the novel the quest for self-knowledge often enough ends in uncertainty, realistic fiction ordinarily holds out for the possibility that the quest can end, that stability in the self is a reasonable expectation.[36]

In Conrad this model falters. Self-knowledge can never be rewarded, because the mind can neither distance itself from what it knows nor surmount its acts of knowing. And just as the mind cannot maintain an ironic detachment from its surroundings or from human actions, so it cannot stand outside itself or maintain a self-detachment that would finally make the self the object of its own knowledge. Granted that the Cartesian model renders identity problematic, Conrad makes the problem not only difficult but, in the end, hopeless. His modification of the Cartesian formula creates a schism in the realistic norms of his own fiction that undercuts that model's hopes for ever achieving self-knowledge. To show how this works, we examine Nostromo as well as Razumov, in *Under Western Eyes*.

The titular hero of *Nostromo* does not appear, curiously enough, until about a quarter of the way into the novel. Until that point the reader is confronted with a tumult of details whose relationship to the hero it is impossible to discern. As one critic has suggested, the reader wades through a chaos of details with the hope that when Nostromo finally appears he will lend focus and order to the diverse strands of the plot.

36. Guetti, *The Limits of Metaphor*, 176.

Although his appearance puts these strands in some order, through his complicity in the Gould Concession, it does so in a curious manner. First of all, it is questionable whether in the usual sense this novel is primarily about Nostromo at all. One could make a case for his centrality, but doing so would require more support than immediately comes to mind. Decoud, Charles and Emilia Gould, and Monygham all vie for the reader's attention, but they do not serve to shed light on Nostromo's character as clearly as, for example, Marlow and Stein serve to shed light on Jim's (insofar as light can be shed on it). It is as though in *Nostromo* Conrad had given up the project of finding his principal character's center, his final meaning.

Conrad reverses the adventure of self-discovery in Nostromo's case. Nostromo begins with an unproblematic sense of himself and ends in confusion; he starts by thinking he knows who he is and ends by discovering what he is not. At the point where he enters the narrative, the meaning of the silver enterprise is clear to everyone involved. Nostromo's identity is as unproblematic as the silver's purpose in Sulaco because his identity is caught up in it. The narrator establishes the connection between the two in a pattern of imagery wrought with the visual impressions of silver.[37] Like a mirror of the community's desires, the silver in its association with Nostromo makes others' knowledge the adequate basis for his sense of self. As long as the Sulacoan community controls the silver, it can provide Nostromo with an unproblematic self-image. Nostromo's name means "our man," because his identity is predicated on Sulaco's sense of purpose, which is stabilized by its grip on the Gould Concession.[38]

The silver's complicity in Nostromo's heroic identity is nowhere clearer than in the memorable scene that closes Part I. Surrounded by silver—silver buttons, a silver cord and tassels, and silver plates on his headstall and saddle (*N*, 113)—Nostromo confronts Morenita, his lover. If we can judge by the way he treats her in this scene, the most significant part of their relationship is others' knowledge of his cavalier attitude toward

37. Dowden, *The Imaged Style*, 94–102.
38. Conrad to Cunninghame Graham, October 31, 1904, in Jean-Aubry, *Life and Letters*, I, 338.

her. When she asks for a love token, he responds by telling her he does not love her, publicly humiliating her "in the wide circle formed round the generous, the terrible, the inconstant Capatez de Cargadores" (N, 116). To further the impression of his bravado, he hands her a knife, not in order for her to stab him as she wants to, but for a purpose almost as dramatic in its rendering—in order to cut the silver buttons from his coat in lieu of a gift. The silver is the best she can hope for; to give himself is to give her his silver.

Even if Decoud cannot see through himself, he can see through Nostromo, who eventually volunteers to help him hide the silver ingots on Isabel Island across Placid Gulf. Decoud believes Nostromo's motive is only "to be well spoken of" (N, 208), and there is certainly some truth in his statement. Nostromo's sense of self is so caught up in the silver that to save the silver is to save himself by fortifying his reputation. But there is a complication: in order to fortify his reputation with the people, he must undercut the self-image he has sustained as a member in spirit of the Viola family. Here he faces something like Jim's predicament when Brown challenges his identity by questioning his allegiances.

Teresa Viola tests Nostromo's loyalty to the family by asking him to find a priest in her dying hour rather than depart for his mission. When he refuses to look for a priest, he has changed from the man he had been, and Viola recognizes that: "Get riches at least for once, you indispensable, admired Gian' Battista, to whom the peace of a dying woman is less than the praise of people who have given you a silly name—and nothing besides—in exchange for your soul and body" (N, 215). The identity supported by his place in the Viola family proves less compelling than the one sustained by his role in the silver enterprise. The logic behind his self-knowledge makes his identity stronger the more widely it is known. "It concerns me," he tells Teresa, "to keep on being what I am: every day alike" (N, 213). The public sphere offers more stability to his self-image than the private sphere of the Violas.

Nostromo is "our man" because he is not his own man. On Placid Gulf, just as Decoud learns that his skepticism is an inadequate basis for his self-image, so does Nostromo learn that his reputation is an inadequate foundation for his personal identity. After he lands the silver on Great Isabel, he is as if re-born: "He stood . . . with the lost air of a man just born into the world. . . . Then, in the suddenly steadied glance fixed upon nothing from under a thoughtful frown, appeared the man" (*N*, 340). We recall that Decoud's gaze fell on a world that trapped him on all sides and from which he could not detach him-self. But Nostromo's gaze falls on nothing, and he by contrast searches for anything to which he can attach himself. His gaze is fixed on nothing because public support for his heroic stature is gone; all that is left is the man, potentially any man, but no man in particular—a man without qualities. At this moment he recognizes that he has not been in control of the actions that supported his heroic self-image. He beholds "all his world without faith and courage. He had been betrayed!" (*N*, 345). He has been betrayed into serving what are ultimately material in-terests. Now he is faced with contradictory self-images: is he a selfless hero or a wealthmonger?

The political turmoil back in Sulaco only complicates matters. Instead of getting the hero's welcome he deserves, he is practically ignored,because the Sulacoan population is too caught up in the impending arrival of Sotillo and the Monterists. He might as well have been hiding the ingots for his own bene-fit. And he will. When the people begin to recognize the silver as an ultimately materialist concern, Nostromo recognizes him-self as a materialist and his identity changes completely. When he left Sulaco for his mission, he was the center of attention; now when he returns, he must hide himself. The gap between his past and his present makes his identity discontinuous. Now his past seems like "a flattering dream come suddenly to an end," and he is left with a schism at the heart of his identity: "it was not in keeping" (*N*, 342).

During his visit to Monygham, whom he mistakenly counts among those who have let him down, Nostromo acts as if he wished Sotillo would believe he had landed the silver on Great Isabel, even though if Sotillo were to know the silver's location, it would surely be lost. His seemingly perverse impulse to have Sotillo know, however, betrays a desire to be recognized, at any cost, as the agent of his own actions. Now he is morally iso-lated; since he can trust no one with the knowledge of the in-gots' real location (least of all Monygham, who is not known for his ability to hold up under interrogation), Sulaco's future rests entirely on his shoulders. There is no code of ethics for him, especially now that his self is divided. If his identity can lose stability, then so can the codes of behavior. Jim faced the same instability when he tried to follow the ethical codes of two societies, Patusan's and the seaman's codes, and had the psychological need to identify with both societies. When the codes make opposite demands, then the self faces a crisis of identity that can only be solved by choosing one code over the other. Nostromo chooses the codes appropriate for material interests, now that Sulaco clings to the mine for its own sake. He decides not to tell anyone where the ingots are and to sell them secretly for his own profit. This is a different Nostromo, and that is probably why from now on he takes various names but is no longer called Nostromo.

Like his identity, Nostromo's allegiances are now divided: one part is devoted to the stolen silver and the other to Sulaco. His romantic allegiances are divided along these same lines. His betrothal to Linda Viola is only the consequence of her father's assumptions about Nostromo's interest—assumptions which were, significantly, guided by Teresa's dying wishes. His commitment to Linda corresponds to his no longer viable public self, the self devoted to Sulaco. Linda even looks like Teresa, and more than once her voice reminds Nostromo of Teresa, who haunts his conscience by reminding him of the tenuousness of his public self. His heart, though, is with Linda's sister, Giselle. Only to Giselle does he confess his possession of the ingots, and she upholds his materialist self-image. Now Nostromo assumes Decoud's skepticism.

It is fitting that Nostromo should die as the consequence of mistaken identity. Viola shoots him, thinking he is the lover Giselle was forbidden to see. Nostromo has such a vivid sense of his surroundings that to the end he cannot set himself apart and posit an identity independent of them: "he could not imagine himself dead. He was possessed too strongly by the sense of his own existence, a thing of infinite duration in its changes, to grasp the notion of finality" (N, 431). There is no finality in him because there is no stable identity; it partakes in the changes that characterize the seemingly infinite duration of his existence. Only when he stops breathing can his real identity be revealed, but even for those who are allowed to know what he has become, there is only a set of unresolved selves.

The plot of Razumov's adventure in self-knowledge, in *Under Western Eyes*, follows a pattern different from Nostromo's, but it ends in the same ambiguity. Whereas Nostromo begins in certainty and ends baffled, Razumov from beginning to end tries out various identities but never finds the right one. At the end, the modicum of stability he finds after his confession is not so much a resolution of the problem of self-knowledge as it is a surrender to the impossibility of ever knowing for certain who he really is and to whom he belongs. It was in a mood of resignation to an "as-if" identity that Conrad once wrote to Edward Garnett:

> When once the truth is grasped that one's own personality is only a ridiculous and aimless masquerade of something hopelessly unknown the attainment of serenity is not very far off. Then there remains nothing but the surrender to one's impulses, the fidelity to passing emotions which is perhaps a nearer approach to truth than any other philosophy of life. And why not? If we are "ever becoming—never being" then I would be a fool if I tried to become this thing rather than that; for I know well that I never will be anything. I would rather grasp the solid satisfaction of my wrong-headedness and shake my fist at the idiotic mystery of Heaven.[39]

The prerequisite for this resignation is to avoid introspection, and it is hard to believe Conrad maintained this stance. In *The Secret Agent* (1907), the French agent Verloc has a problematic identity: what he is to his wife, her brother, and her mother is not what he is to himself. Self-knowledge does not become nearly as much of a problem for him as it is for those he lives and works among because he is surrounded by people who believe that things do not "bear much looking into." Neither the unsuspecting Chief Inspector Heat nor Verloc's wife is perspicacious enough to see beneath his mask.

In *Under Western Eyes*, however, the problem of identity becomes the center of the drama because everyone around Razumov is suspicious, if not always perceptive, and because Razumov himself chronically tests the grounds of his identity.

39. Garnett (ed.), *Letters*, 46.

The political instability of the Russian autocracy just before the revolution aggravates the problem of Razumov's self-knowledge, much as Sulacoan political instability disrupted Nostromo's quest. For Razumov, the political climate is more disruptive, because in the autocracy he finds the parentage he had never known when he is given to suspect that he is the illegitimate child of Prince K. He is never assured that Prince K is his father, and the uncertainty invites his abstract notion of his parentage as the whole Russian nation, specifically its aristocratic history, so that the revolution threatens not only his country but the image of his parentage and the stability of his identity: "His closest parentage was defined in the statement that he was a Russian. Whatever good he expected from life would be given to or withheld from his hopes by that connexion alone. This immense parentage suffered from the throes of internal dissensions, and he shrank mentally from the fray as a good-natured man may shrink from taking definite sides in a violent family quarrel" (*UWE*, 17). After he meets Prince K, his identity with the autocracy is stronger, but still abstract enough to be challenged. Before he meets him, it is even more subject to revision.

A conscientious university student, Razumov tries to write a patriotic, prize-winning essay. He wants to be recognized in order to fill a void at the center of his identity. Here, as in other parts of the novel, the act of writing is central to the quest for self-knowledge. When the revolutionist Haldin bursts in upon him, however, Razumov miscarries his attempt to write and thereby stabilize his identity. Haldin has just assassinated an important autocratic figure, and Razumov knows it; so the best explanation for his impulse to save Haldin by carrying a message to Ziemianitch is the intensity of their contact. Uppermost in Razumov's mind is the desire simply to be rid of Haldin, even if it means helping him escape, but perhaps because of the vagueness of Razumov's contact with the autocracy, his gestures toward helping Haldin escape reveal more complex undercurrents. When he finds Ziemianitch in a drunken stupor, the anger which motivates him to beat the man into insensibility betrays his commitments to Haldin, to be true to his word, and, by extension, to his hidden revolutionist impulses.

Razumov's suppressed commitment to Haldin comes back to haunt him. Even though he steps over a phantom image of

Haldin to prove to himself his power to inform on Haldin, when Razumov returns to his room the revolutionist exerts an even stronger power over him. Haldin's physical presence "seemed to have less substance than its own phantom walked over by Razumov in the street white with snow" (*UWE*, 53). Haldin's spirit, which is a projection of Razumov's desire for commitment to him, takes on a life of its own. By converting Haldin into a phantom of his imagination, Razumov makes him a part of himself, of his very consciousness. Razumov then can no longer posit his own identity without implicating Haldin in the process, and Haldin's remark only intensifies his hold on the young man: "They can kill my body, but they cannot exile my soul from this world" (*UWE*, 55).

When he informs on Haldin, Razumov maintains the revolutionist part of his identity by not telling Prince K about Ziemianitch. His ostensible motive is to spare Ziemianitch a cruel flogging for his role in the plot to aid Haldin's escape, but his real motive is his revolutionist self-image. Yet Razumov commits himself to the autocracy, too, by consenting to spy on the revolutionists in Geneva. Like Nostromo in abiding by his wider reputation rather than by his private and, he thinks, less stable self-image as a member of the Viola family, Razumov sides with the autocracy because of his misguided belief in its stability. By posing as a revolutionist in Geneva, Razumov can have it both ways: he can seem to serve the revolutionists and put Haldin's ghost to rest, and at the same time he can actually serve the autocracy.

By taking a sham identity, Razumov lives in the illusion that he knows who he really is. His whole identity was spurious before, but now he has a consciously upheld sham identity, against which the validity of his autocratic identity can be tested. His adventure in Geneva reverses the terms of his quest in Russia: in Russia he put himself forth so that others could see who he was; in Geneva he puts himself forth in order to hide who he is.

If the sham and the real selves could be held apart as easily as Razumov thinks they can, then he could go on with self-knowledge more certain than he ever had. Just as perception collapses into imagination, though, so does the real self collapse into the sham self. If the two identities were compatible in a single self, then Razumov would have the internal coherence that would stabilize his identity, but they are not. To serve the revolutionists is to betray the autocracy, and to serve the autocracy is to betray Haldin's spirit. Razumov cannot keep the two commitments apart; they are mutually contradictory and yet they are somehow held together in him by a bond he cannot apprehend. At some deep level Razumov is one self, but he cannot know that unified self because he cannot penetrate the disjunctive façades.

In hoping to penetrate the contradictory self-images and lay bare the core of his identity, Razumov exhibits a perverse desire to have the revolutionists see through his mask. On one level, he does not want to be seen through, for seeing through his revolutionist identity would endanger his autocratic self. He fears visiting Madame de S, famed for her "inspired penetration" (*UWE*, 180); but when certain of Madame de S's murmurs indicate that she is favorably impressed with him, he is revolted. If she is favorably impressed, she has not, after all, penetrated the façade. Razumov's reaction indicates his deeper wish to be discovered: "The fantastic absurdity of it revolted him because it seemed to outrage his ruined hopes with the vision of a mock-career" (*UWE*, 186).

This desire to be discovered is even more intense in Razumov's dealings with Sophia Antovna, perhaps the most committed revolutionist in the novel. Possibly because she is the most committed, she most believes in Razumov's devotion to the revolutionists. In him she sees the true spirit of revolt. When he senses her credulity, his impulse to expose himself almost makes him lose control. During their long and treacherous conversation outside the Château Borel, Razumov insinuates the hypocrisy in Ivanovitch's feminism and in his designs for social reform. He comes closer than ever to betraying his autocratic loyalties: "It was weakness; it was this disease of perversity overcoming his will. Was this the way to meet speeches which certainly contained the promise of future confidences from that woman who apparently had a great store of secret knowledge and so much influence? Why give her this puzzling impression?" (*UWE*, 212). Razumov cannot see through himself; he cannot interpret his own motives for exposing himself. Because he cannot see through himself, he wants others to see through him.

The bizarre logic governing these impulses to disguise and reveal himself comes to an ironic climax when Madame de S reveals a letter informing her of Ziemianitch's suicide. The letter threatens Razumov, since if the full story about Ziemianitch were known, Razumov's complicity in aiding Haldin's escape would fortify the revolutionist identity from which he wants to break away. He would rather see himself as a sham revolutionist than as a real one; as long as he artificially upholds the one identity, he is in full control of the "real" autocratic one. The distance between his mock self and his real self will tell him, perhaps, who he is. The letter, however, does not reveal the truth. It indicates instead that Ziemianitch committed suicide out of remorse for having failed to save Haldin, and the man who first beat him is thought to have been some "police hound in disguise." Madame de S's faulty account becomes a model of how consistent lies can take on the aura of truth: "Such were the last words of the woman revolutionist in this conversation, keeping so close to the truth, departing from it so far in the verisimilitude of thoughts and conclusions as to give one the notion of the invincible nature of human error, a glimpse into the utmost depths of self-deception" (*UWE*, 235).

Now that Razumov feels safe, now that he knows more about himself than others do about him, he feels detached from everyone. He becomes like a god overseeing the activities of a world apart from him. This stance accounts for his "neutral pity" for Ziemianitch at this point—pity "such as one may feel for an unconscious multitude, a great people seen from above—like a community of crawling ants working out its destiny" (*UWE*, 237).

When he prepared for his mission in Geneva, Razumov's actions were "a waking act." They prepared him for a dream in which the only fear was "of awakening at the end." When his revolutionist and autocratic identities cannot be held apart any longer, however, his life becomes both "a dream and a fear" (*UWE*, 262). The Geneva experience welds imagination to reality. Similarly, the mask that hides Razumov makes him see what he could not otherwise have seen. His sham identity conducts him into Natalia's life: he falls in love with Haldin's sister. It is mainly his love for her that blurs the distinction between his two selves; the intensity of his love penetrates to the core of his identity—a core neither wholly revolutionist nor wholly autocratic. His identity, he finds, is an imageless core of darkness.

When all attempts fail to lay bare that core of himself, Razumov breaks under the pressure. He goes out at midnight, the same time he went out and betrayed Haldin, as though to reverse his allegiances. He confesses first to Natalia, then to Laspara, but he cannot erase what he has been. Laspara points out to him the hard truth—perhaps the hard lie?—that "Confession or no confession, you are a police spy!" (*UWE,* 303). Razumov's love for Natalia tells him, though, that even his identity as a police spy is bogus; Laspara has only substituted one false image for another.

Razumov suffers the penalty for his sham identity. He thought by living a sham existence he could maintain his autonomy, that he could be the source of his own self-image. But he cannot set himself apart from his surroundings. To know himself is to know others, not to hold them at a distance. Appropriately, then, he ends his journal with the poignant observation, "I am independent—and therefore perdition is my lot" (*UWE,* 298). For his attempt to isolate himself, Razumov is rewarded with Nikita's deafening blow to the head. Even if he is released from the burden of establishing a separate identity, his inability to hear another voice is a silent reminder of his audacity.

Self-knowledge holds Conrad's interest because he suspects that beneath the surface of disjunctive self-images lies a coherent self in the depths of each individual. Unless he could at least suspect a coherent self, the quest for self-knowledge would have no point, and the disjunctive, surface identities of Nostromo and Razumov would not hold for Conrad the dramatic interest they have. If the self had no irreducible concrete referent, then there would be no dramatic interest in the attempt to penetrate the surface identities that hide it. Even though Conrad intuits this concrete referent, he still loses hope that it can ever be comprehended. By dashing his characters' hopes that they will ever find it, he arrests the drama of the self's interaction with others, for where their hopes end his novels end. If Nostromo or Razumov were to apprehend himself, he would see either nothing at all—an internal landscape corresponding to the heart of darkness—or he would see that the concrete referent of one self is identical to the concrete referent of other selves, so that one is all and the self is back where it began, futilely trying to detach itself from others in order to find itself. This discovery of shared identities does not appear in Conrad's fiction explicitly; it is just beyond his narratives' margins. Such a discovery does appear in the fiction of Lawrence and Woolf, and it appears as the consequence of their realizing, as Conrad does, that knowing oneself is no less problematic than knowing external reality. Lawrence and Woolf bring directly into their fiction the solutions that in Conrad are just beyond the world he represents when he brings cognition, and realistic narrative with it, to an impasse.

2

D. H. LAWRENCE

If there were not an utter and absolute dark
of silence and sheer oblivion
at the core of everything,
how terrible the sun would be,
how ghastly it would be to strike a match, and make a light.

But the very sun himself is pivoted
upon the core of pure oblivion,
so is a candle, even as a match.

And if there were not an absolute, utter forgetting
and a ceasing to know, a perfect ceasing to know
and a silent, sheer cessation of all awareness
how terrible life would be!
how terrible it would be to think and know, to have
  consciousness!

But dipped, once dipped in dark oblivion
the soul has peace, inward and lovely peace.

—Lawrence
"The End, the Beginning"

Lawrence and Dualism

For both Conrad and Lawrence, the hidden core of the self
and the hidden core of the external world are one. Self and
other, then, at their furthest depths, are monistically related.
Although Conrad recognizes the darkness, the reality beyond
human comprehension, he shuns it because it threatens the accustomed order that upholds civilized life. His fiction, too, recognizes the darkness, but Conrad knows that the darkness is
beyond the representational powers of his fiction. To write fiction at all is to shed some light on the darkness, disperse it a
little, and lay an orderly path for knowledge and imagination.

The darkness Conrad flees Lawrence embraces. In both
Conrad and Lawrence, knowledge and imagination uphold a
transitory dual interaction between self and other. As long as
cognition upholds the self, predicating existence on its introspection, it draws a line around the self and between subject

and object. For both Conrad and Lawrence this state is only temporary; cognition fails. Conrad hangs on to knowledge and to the imagination, which collapses into knowledge, because there is nothing else to do. For Lawrence, however, ceasing to know is a moral imperative: better to perish in the darkness than continue in the light, because the horror at the core of existence is a horror only for the mind. The darkness crushes only the mind's pernicious hopes to control willfully the blood, which is the foundation of all life. To continue in the light is the real horror for Lawrence because the cost is the mind's fatal alienation from the blood.

Lawrence's fiction tries to embrace the darkness too, whereas Conrad's fiction can only circle and approach the darkness. It keeps one foot in the light by relying on middle terms between reader and darkness—mediating devices such as the framed narration. Conrad presents the darkness as a fathomless absence, because his indirect presentation of it necessarily renders the darkness a vacancy at the center of everything. But Lawrence, in embracing the darkness, tries to present it directly, without mediating terms and as a presence rather than an absence. To embrace the darkness is to crumble the mediating terms between self and other. Only then can the dark core of the self intermingle with the darkness at the heart of others. Our attention here is on the problems Lawrence confronts and the techniques he uses in bringing a model of direct knowledge into the purview of realistic fiction. By direct knowledge I mean an unmediated and monistic relationship between subject and object. This form of knowledge allows for no doubt, unlike Cartesian epistemology, because to know directly is no longer to have the critical distance that would provide the leverage for doubt.[1]

No reader can overlook the interest Lawrence showed in a whole universe of dualities, the central one the male-female duality. Nonetheless, at the center of his vision is a resolution, a metaphysical and epistemological monism that his essays and novels formulate, even if inconsistently. The principal reason for the inconsistency is that he is required to employ the

1. Norman Malcom, "Direct Perception," Knowledge and Certainty: Essays and Lectures (Ithaca, N.Y., 1975), 73–95.

very cogitation he disparages. Using the thinking process cuts Lawrence in half. He distrusts cognition because it threatens self-reflection and thereby creates a dualism between self and world and within the self. As long as the mind is alienated from the blood in the act of looking in on itself, it is wedged between the self and everything with which the self requires contact, including the blood. Only if the mind is reunited with the blood can it effect an unmediated contact with other selves. This is the basis for Lawrence's concept of "blood-consciousness," which he describes in a letter to Bertrand Russell:

> [T]here is a blood-consciousness which exists in us independently of the ordinary mental consciousness, which depends on the eye as its source or connector. There is the blood-consciousness, with the sexual connection holding the same relation as the eye, in seeing, holds to the mental consciousness. . . . And the tragedy of this our life, and of your life, is that the mental and nerve consciousness exerts a tyranny over the blood-consciousness and that your will has gone completely over to the mental consciousness, and is engaged in the destruction of your blood-being or blood-consciousness, the final liberating of the one, which is only death in result.[2]

Lawrence's concept of blood-consciousness, because it calls for the establishment of an unmediated connection between subject and object, is a monistic epistemological model. He never presented himself as an advocate of epistemological monism. As far as he is concerned, rendering blood-consciousness in terms of a rational theory would perpetuate the very dualism that it is otherwise the effect of his thinking to overcome.

Thus one would search far and wide in vain for sustained philosophical aptitude in Lawrence's essays. To put matters bluntly, as an essayist compared to thinkers like William James and Bertrand Russell, Lawrence is irredeemable. His discourse is often undisciplined and self-contradictory, but there is no point in hailing or condemning Lawrence by any but artistic criteria. If his inner conflicts impair his discursive essays and reasoning, they make an astonishing contribution to the his-

---

2. Harry T. Moore (ed.), *The Collected Letters of D. H. Lawrence* (2 vols.; New York, 1962), I, 393. Subsequent page references to this edition are hereinafter cited parenthetically as *CL*.

tory of the English novel. Before we examine how, rather than why, his discursive reasoning falters, we need to inspect closely his thoughts about cognition.

In Lawrence, truly to know is to be directly connected with the object of knowledge. His tendency to set knowledge up in opposition to being presents the illusion that he is a thorough-going dualist: "KNOWING and BEING are opposite, antagonistic states. The more you know, exactly, the less you *are*. The more you *are*, in being, the less you know."[3] But in this instance Lawrence is not speaking about blood-knowledge. He is referring to mental knowledge, whose dualistic implications, for him, account for the self's alienation from the true ground of its being. His and Conrad's suspicion of knowledge have a common root. Schopenhauer, whom they both read with admiration, voices that suspicion in terms remarkably similar to Lawrence's. For Schopenhauer, having an idea of something necessarily divorces the knower from the object of knowledge: "this idea," he says, "just because it is *my* idea, cannot be identical with what is known." Knowledge connects us only with ideas, which are the distillation of the thing, not the thing itself. Even attempts at self-knowledge will not bridge this gap, for as Schopenhauer puts it, since the idea or image of the self presented to the self in introspection "falls within my *knowing* consciousness, it is already a reflex of my nature, something different from this itself." Hence, "knowledge is only a secondary property of our being." Lawrence having read Schopenhauer about 1905, this is too close an account of knowledge for us not to suspect that his almost always pejorative uses of the words *idea* and *image* derive from it.[4]

Nevertheless, Lawrence saw a genuine place for knowledge in the human condition. As Birkin says in the "Class-Room" chapter of *Women in Love*, consciousness comes to man "willy-nilly," and the question is not how to be rid of it, but what to do with it. Elsewhere Lawrence says, "*To know* is a force, like any

3. D. H. Lawrence, *Studies in Classic American Literature* (New York, 1964), 113.
4. Schopenhauer, *The World as Will and Idea*, I, 151; Emile Delavenay discusses Lawrence's reading at this period in *D. H. Lawrence: The Man and His Work*, trans. Katharine M. Delavenay (London, 1972), Chap. III.

other force. Knowledge is only one of the conditions of this force, as combustion is one of the conditions of heat."[5]

In his discursive writings, where we see him thinking analytically, Lawrence is at a loss to articulate the monistic view of the world that he conveys in his most intuitive moments, when he is thinking *through* his fictional characters. The *Study of Thomas Hardy* perhaps best exhibits Lawrence's reliance upon opposition for conducting his arguments. His switching back and forth between dualistic and monistic pictures of the world sometimes leads him into contradiction or least away from clear expression. This can happen in single paragraphs. At one point Lawrence begins a paragraph asserting the essential wholeness of the cosmos, suggesting that at its origin the universe was homogeneous. Then he changes his mind, as though to demonstrate that just by having thought about the monistic character of the world he destroyed his vision of it: "There must always have been some reaction, infinitesimally faint, stirring somehow through the vast, homogeneous inertia" (*P*, 432).

This long study, which Lawrence refers to in his letters as a philosophical discourse, is an elaborate network of cross-referenced dualities—male and female, love and law, unity and multiplicity, mind and body, the knowers and the known. He relies heavily upon these oppositions as a way of generating his thoughts and organizing his ideas. Although through most of the essay these dualities seem absolutely separate, there are certain moments when he stops to clarify their relationships. He tells us that the dualities are artificial, the vices of cognition. Even the most sacred of Lawrence's dualities is a mere convenience: "the division into male and female is arbitrary, for the purpose of thought." Differentiation is a necessary condition for analysis, for "motion and rest are the same when seen completely. . . . Since, if motion were infinite, there would be no standing-ground from which to regard it as motion" (*P*, 448).

Psychoanalysis and the Unconscious (1921) follows the same tendency to utilize dualistic paradigms, but it is far more

5. D. H. Lawrence, *Study of Thomas Hardy*, rpr. in Edward D. McDonald (ed.), *Phoenix: The Posthumous Papers 1936* (New York, 1978), 431. Subsequent page references to any works in this collection are hereinafter cited parenthetically as *P*.

systematic than the Hardy study. Perhaps because it is more systematic, it affords Lawrence fewer opportunities to detach his discussion from the polarities it establishes. Once he has buried himself in the task of analyzing the unconscious, he cannot stand back from his paradigm. One brief example shows what happens. Lawrence begins his argument against Sigmund Freud's description of the unconscious mind by formulating his own way of distinguishing between the conscious and the unconscious. Although his making this distinction is understandable, since his project is to redefine Freud's distinction, his divisions go well beyond the demands of responding to Freud. The initial distinction between the conscious and unconscious mind is transferred to the unconscious mind itself, which is then subject to further division and subdivision. The upper poles of the solar plexus, the first area of unconscious awareness Lawrence describes, are associated with the quest for others and are labeled "objective." The lower poles embody the self's turning inward toward itself and are associated with the subjective. As though these distinctions were not enough, Lawrence then distinguishes between the anterior and the posterior solar plexus poles, the former impelling us toward union and the latter toward separation. After Lawrence sets up his own distinction between cerebral (conscious) knowledge and vital (unconscious) knowledge, which induces wholesome connection, the unconscious mind itself is divided along analogous lines of subjectivity and objectivity.[6] It is as though Lawrence were caught up in the same thinking he is arguing against.

My saying that Lawrence lapses into dualism while he is advocating monism implies that Lawrence misrepresents himself at those moments when he is most intent upon making himself understood. Aside from defending Lawrence on the simple but reasonable grounds that he was an artist first and a philosopher second, we can explain his tendency to insist in his prose upon dualistic conceptions of knowledge by giving some attention to William James's seminal essay, "Does 'Consciousness' Exist?" As a philosophical essay, even James's discussion has

6. D. H. Lawrence, "The Birth of Consciousness," "The Child and His Mother," and "The Lover and the Beloved," *Psychoanalysis and the Unconscious* (New York, 1977). In the same volume with *Fantasia of the Unconscious*.

certain limitations, but these are too specialized to have any immediate bearing on what I am describing in connection with Lawrence.[7] The essay does tell us something important about what can happen as a result of thinking about rather than simply experiencing consciousness.

Although James does not suggest here that consciousness does not exist, he argues that our notion of consciousness as an entity—as a thing opposed to which there are objects of consciousness—is an illusion produced by reflecting back on our acts of consciousness in order to talk about them. The age-old problem in Democritus of accounting for the seemingly dual locations of the objects of knowledge is, according to James, an invented problem. When I see a chair, it seems to exist both in my knowledge of it and in the world independent of my knowledge. But for James, it seems to exist in two places not when I see it but when I think about having seen it: "The puzzle . . . is at bottom just the puzzle of how one identical point can be on two lines. It can, if it be situated at their intersection; and similarly, if the 'pure experience' of [a] room were a place of intersection of two processes, which connected it with different groups of associates respectively, it could be counted twice over, as belonging to either group, and spoken of loosely as existing in two places, although it would remain all the time a numerically single thing."[8] Precisely in this difference between the duality imposed through self-reflection and the homogeneity implied in "pure experience" can we begin to see the distinction in Lawrence between his discursive moods, which, more often than not, introduce a dualism that his creative moods militate against when they generate fiction that occasionally models direct presentation. Exactly in those aspects of his fiction where dualism is momentarily overcome does Lawrence modify the norms of realistic representation in the novel. Even in his novels, however, the dualism is to some extent maintained.

In a letter to Ernest Collings, Lawrence metaphorically describes how the mind relates to the external world: "I conceive

7. A. J. Ayer, *Philosophy in the Twentieth Century* (New York, 1982), 77–79.

8. William James, "Does 'Consciousness" Exist?" *Journal of Philosophy, Psychology, and Scientific Methods*, I (1904), 481.

a man's body as a kind of flame, like a candle flame, forever upright and yet flowing: and the intellect is just the light that is
shed on the things around—which is really mind—but with
the mystery of the flame forever flowing, coming God knows
how from out of practically nowhere, being *itself*, whatever
there is around it, that it lights up" (*CL*, I, 180). Making the
mind the wake of the body's motions, this perspective resembles Conrad's epiphenomenalism. Like objects surrounding
the flame, the mind is the body's boundary, and the intellect is
the middle term between the two. The dynamic flame (the conscious body) lives; the static objects surrounding the flame (the
mind) are the vanishing point of the body's life. In this description the mind is divided from the body (by the intellect), so
that we have a reversal of the terms in the Cartesian mind-body
dualism. In Descartes the body partakes of the realm of extended objects and the mind of the realm of the unextended. In
Lawrence's description here, this is reversed. This picture of the
mind as material correlates with those frequent instances, in
both the fiction and the discursive essays, where Lawrence suggests that the mind partakes in materiality and mechanism precisely because it generates ideas. "Ideal and material are identical."[9] This belief probably betrays Lawrence's immersion in
materialist philosophy, whose epistemology underwrites empirical psychology. We know from Jessie Chambers and from
some of Lawrence's critical biographers that he had read a fair
sampling of Locke, Bishop George Berkeley, T. H. Huxley, Ernst
Haeckel, and Charles Darwin.[10] From his published reviews we
also know that he was alive to the major trends in empirical
psychology.

During the late nineteenth and early twentieth centuries especially, psychology tried to model itself on the natural sciences' methodology. In this effort it had to utilize a concept of
mind that would render the mind amenable to empirical investigation; the mind had to be given to the senses. A seminal

9. Lawrence, *Psychoanalysis and the Unconscious*, 211.
10. Jessie Chambers, *D. H. Lawrence: A Personal Record* (2nd ed.; New
York, 1965), 94–123; Graham Hough, *The Dark Sun: A Study of D. H. Law-
rence* (London, 1956), 22–23; Delavenay, *The Man and His Work*, 47–48;
Daniel J. Schneider, *D. H. Lawrence: The Artist as Psychologist* (Lawrence,
Kansas, 1984), 10–21.

document in this effort is Franz Brentano's *Psychology from an Empirical Standpoint* (1874), translated in 1911 as *The Classification of Mental Phenomena*. Brentano does not oppose empiricism to its more usual rival in philosophy, rationalism, but rather to the spiritualism in which psychology was steeped before it emerged as a science. He takes as his methodological base the principle that in order for consciousness to be said to take place at all, it must implicate an object, or intention, of consciousness. This is the familiar starting point for phenomenological inquiries into consciousness. Brentano's argument for the necessarily "intentional" structure of consciousness is his way of defending psychology's empirical basis. Just as natural science investigates observable objects, so is psychology concerned with the mind as an observable object. If minds were not observable things among other observable things, he suggests, then psychology would partake in the spiritualism that he is trying to rid it of.[11]

Lawrence's characteristic identification of mind with matter, though it may betray his familiarity with certain materialist trends in contemporaneous thought, does not finally indicate his assent to them. He actually uses the identification of mind with matter as leverage for arguing *against* this concept of mind. In his view, empirical psychology turns the mind away from the blood and toward the lifeless condition of matter simply by employing its methodology for knowing other minds. Since he accepts the mind as a material entity only to use that concept against those who hold it, he seems to waver between the mind as matter and the mind as blood (or instinct). Thus, as Baruch Hochman observes, Lawrence moves back and forth as though to search for a compromise position between viewing the mind as abstracted from the world of objects and viewing it as object-bounded.[12] As a result, we are left with two models of knowledge: conscious knowledge, which is self-interested, and blood-knowledge, which is instinctive. Lawrence's shifts from one to the other are not restricted to his essays, where they

11. Franz Brentano, *Psychology from the Empirical Standpoint,* trans. Antos C. Rancurello, D. B. Terrell, and Linda McAlister (1874; rpr. New York, 1973), 100.

12. Baruch Hochman, *Another Ego: The Changing View of Self and Society in the Work of D. H. Lawrence* (Columbia, S.C., 1970), 124n.

often introduce contradiction, but also appear in the fiction as concessions to the norms of realistic representation.

In both *The Rainbow* and *Women in Love* knowledge is Janus-faced. In *The Rainbow* Ursula Brangwen in her experiences at the university dramatically conveys Lawrence's message about knowledge's tendency to divide man against himself. Ursula goes naïvely to the university after her initial experiences as a teacher, only to find that the university contracts the circumference of what it is possible to know. It is like the blinding light of an arc lamp [13]—blinding because it gives the impression that everything outside its purview, the darkness, is unworthy of the least consideration. The university as she discovers it is limited to the investigation of facts, to that which is commensurate with the analytical mind, and is concerned with nothing else. Its light serves the students as a candle does moths.

It does not take long for Ursula to see that the Gothic arches of the campus buildings disguise the university's affiliation with industrialism's mechanistic powers. In contrast is the role the university once had in its connection with religious truth, when scholasticism and religion were allies in the project of conducting man back to God: "Her soul flew straight back to the medieval times, when the monks of God held the learning of men and imparted it within the shadow of religion" (*R*, 430). At this point it seems to Ursula that the reunion of knowledge with Christian scholasticism would remedy the university's debilitating position as the arm of industrialism. However, since it eventually presents Ursula's later disaffection with Christianity, *The Rainbow* shows how unfeasible this remedy finally is. As an extension of the cathedral, which entraps Ursula's father in an embryonic condition, the university itself imposes a division between the mind and the vital reality outside of it: "within the great, whispering sea-shell, that whispered all the while with reminiscence of all the centuries, time faded away, and the echo of knowledge filled the timeless silence" (*R*, 431). In this shell-like world, knowledge is thrown back upon itself; the university impedes connection.

13. D. H. Lawrence, *The Rainbow* (New York, 1961), 12. Subsequent page references to this novel (hereinafter cited parenthetically as *R*) are to this Viking Compass edition.

So far, we have considered only one way in which knowledge's debilitating potential appears in Lawrence's fiction. The dangerous aspect of knowledge appears in *Women in Love*, in the character Hermione, who perfectly delineates herself: "To me," she says, "the pleasure of knowing is *so* great, so *wonderful*—nothing has meant so much to me in all life, as certain knowledge—no, I am sure—nothing."[14] It is exactly because Hermione directs her knowledge toward the goal of establishing certainty that she is such an enormous threat to Birkin. The description of Breadalby, her estate, suggests the effect her passion for certain knowledge has on herself and on everyone she meets; it isolates the mind from the reality surrounding it. At Breadalby, as in the cathedral and the university in *The Rainbow*, "there seemed a magic circle drawn about the place, shutting out the present, enclosing the delightful, precious past, trees and deer and silence, like a dream" (*WL*, 76).

Yet in the "Class-Room" chapter, where she and Birkin visit Ursula while Ursula is conducting a botany lesson, Hermione argues against knowledge, complaining that education alienates children from the world. Her lying about her true feelings, though at this point in the novel we do not yet know she is lying, perfectly dramatizes the nature of her threat to Birkin. It becomes apparent that she is converting Birkin's intuition of the pernicious character of knowledge into an intellectual proposition. By so doing, she sends Birkin's thoughts back upon himself and becomes his echo chamber, which incurs Birkin's rage and launches him into an intellectual debate. She thus converts his feelings into intellectual propositions, parodies of his own stance, and further alienates his thoughts from his feelings. The result is the very habit of intellectual polemicizing that he must get out of in order to enter into a harmonious relationship with Ursula.

By contrast, Tom Brangwen's intuitive knowledge of Lydia is effectively conveyed in *The Rainbow* by the immediacy of his recognition that she is the woman he will marry. Here Lawrence dramatizes the way knowledge can be used to escort the individual into a confluent relationship with the life forces that

14. D. H. Lawrence, *Women in Love* (New York, 1960), 78. Subsequent page references to this novel (hereinafter cited parenthetically as *WL*) are to this Viking Compass edition.

work within and around him. The moment he sees her he
knows: "'That's her,' he said involuntarily" (R, 24). Allied to
instinct, knowledge promotes his wholesome relationship with
her. It is her very foreignness that entices Tom, but he has no
urgent concern for certain knowledge concerning Lydia's past,
for example. He leaves the details sketchy. Their ability to
allow for the element of mystery beyond their certain knowledge of each other lends to Tom and Lydia's marriage an astonishing resilience. This is dramatically proven in their third
year of marriage, when he begins to feel caught and bound. Tom
forces Lydia to remind him of her needs, that she cannot be
treated "like cattle—or nothing" (R, 89). Following upon a bril-
liantly rendered sexual contact, they are "transfigured," because "at last they had thrown open the doors, each to the
other." They become each other's threshold to the mystery that
characterizes genuine living. The recent past of their two years
of marriage becomes as insignificant at this point as Lydia's
first marriage was when they initially met. They can undergo
this transfiguration only because they have the power to leave
behind their certain knowledge of the past, the kind of knowledge that arrests the unfolding of unthought possibilities. Tom
does not "know her any better, any more precisely, now that he
knew her altogether." Knowing her altogether means becoming
one with her, spiritually and sexually. By contrast, knowledge
which hopes for certainty inhibits the unfolding of further possibilities: "What was memory after all, but the recording of a
number of possibilities which had never been fulfilled? What
was Paul Lensky [her first husband] to her, but an unfulfilled
possibility to which he, Brangwen, was the reality and the
fulfilment? What did it matter, that Anna Lensky was born of
Lydia and Paul? God was her father and her mother. He had
passed through the married pair without fully making Himself
known to them" (R, 91).

Lawrence's portrayal of the pernicious face of knowledge is
his way of setting up a point of contrast to his monistic picture
of knowledge, which is thereby dramatized (insofar as it lends
itself to dramatization) in the context of realistic fiction. The
dualism of subject and object becomes the *duality* of mental
and blood-knowledge. Whereas in his discursive essays his falling back upon dualistic models can disrupt his project because

it generates contradictions that undermine his arguments, in his fiction he is right at home. There when he falls back upon a dualistic picture of the mind's relation to the world, he works successfully within the conventions of realistic fiction. It is exactly when he advances his monistic ideas about knowledge through his fiction that he pushes the representational possibilities of the novel beyond their accustomed boundaries and stakes out for himself his place in the modern transformation of the novel.

Knowledge and Representation: *The Rainbow* and *Women in Love*

In Lawrence's view genuine knowledge is possible only when nothing intervenes between subject and object. Following the retrospective consideration of consciousness, the self feels its separation from the object of knowledge: "With his consciousness [man] can perceive and know that which is not himself. The further he goes, the more extended his consciousness, the more he realizes the things that are not himself. Everything he perceives, everything he knows, everything he feels, is something extraneous to him, is not himself, and his perception of it is like a cellwall, or more, a real space separating him. I see a flower, because it is not me" (*P*, 431–32). The important thing in Lawrence's description is the "real space" separating the subject from the object. The felt distance implies no mediating term between the knower and the known; all we have is a real space which affords freedom to both. It is important to recognize that when Lawrence says, "I see a flower, because it is not me," he is not saying that he sees the real space between the flower and himself at the moment of consciousness, for then he would be conscious of the space and not the flower. He would not be knowing. The space between himself and the flower exists in the retrospective consideration of his initial consciousness of the flower.

Lawrence's positing of a real space militates against representational theories of knowledge that dualistic theories use to explain how the space between knower and known can be crossed. In representational theories such as Locke's, sense data bridge the gap between knower and known. Although Lawrence never argued against any theory that he recognized as representational, he would likely find the proposition of representational knowledge ludicrous. For at the moment of consciousness we have no intuitive awareness of the mind's *representation of* the world to our minds; the world seems to be given directly. Lawrence would probably say that the positing of mediating terms for knowledge only further exemplifies the intellect's capacity to render hopelessly complex the things we simply do. His fiction bears this out.

To Lawrence no representation of a thing can measure up to the thing itself, and the best representation relies on partial identity. Truly to know is directly to know, so Lawrence would agree with Edwin Holt, who in defense of epistemological monism asks, "What symbol or other device, human or divine, could represent a colour or a sound except just that colour or that sound? Obviously none. Nor can the representative theory [of knowledge] fall back on the notion of 'similarity,' for the concept of similarity is precisely synonymous with that of representation. Similarity is partial identity: and similars are completely identical in those respects in which they are similar." [15]

In *The Rainbow* the problem of representation and reality has a decisive role in the futures of its principal characters, as demonstrated in Will Brangwen's passion for the cathedral. In the cathedral's representations of holiness—the stained windows, the statues, and the church building itself—Will finds transcendent rather than immanent meaning, which he maintains only through his tendency to separate these representations of holiness from the objects of the banal world outside. That is, the church becomes for Will a world set apart from the real (quotidian) world; he erects a kind of partition between them in order to preserve the transcendent meaning he finds in the church. If the meaning were genuinely transcendent, then he would not have to protect it from external threat in this way. That he does so betrays his uncertainty about the endurance of transcendent meaning that it will be Anna's impulse to attack: "And he did not care about his trespasses, neither about the trespasses of his neighbour, when he was in church. Leave that

15. Edwin B. Holt, *The Concept of Consciousness* (1914; rpr. New York, 1973), 148.

care for weekdays. When he was in church, he took no more notice of his daily life. . . . In church, he wanted a dark, nameless emotion, the emotion of all the great mysteries of passion" (*R*, 154–55).

Even in the context of Lawrence's values, Will's desire for a dark, nameless emotion seems an entirely reasonable pursuit; Tom seeks just this nameless emotion in his relationship with Lydia. Taken in the context of his other drives, however, Will's quest is unreasonable, unwholesome, and finally impossible. By erecting a partition between the world of quotidian experience and the realm of the Holy Spirit, he constructs within his consciousness an artificial dividing line that he expects to mediate his knowledge of eternity. Since it is situated between the sacred and the profane worlds, the division must be maintained for the sacred to be comprehensible *as* otherworldly.

This partition Will erects between divine and profane is reproduced microcosmically within himself. Here we begin to see how Anna stands in contrast to him, for "whereas he seemed simply to ignore the fact of his own self, almost to refute it," in Anna "soul and . . . self were one and the same" (*R*, 155). Will internalizes the division by detaching his soul, associated with the sacred, from his self, associated with the profane, a disjunction that is one of *The Rainbow*'s most urgent messages.

Although Will is divided and Anna is whole, she is by no means a paragon of holiness. Nonetheless, she more directly contacts the sacred than does Will, for all his absorption in the accoutrements of the church. She begins to hate Will for this absorption and challenges his whole conception of the sacred by attacking the church iconography. When she refuses to see any but the most literal meanings of the church icons, she is not simply displaying a thick-headedness. When she sees the lamb as "only a silly lamb in the glass" (*R*, 156), she calls attention at once to real lambs, which the icon does not represent, and to the representational character of the icon—to the fact that it shows a lamb "in the glass," where real lambs obviously do not live. She exposes the distance between real lambs and the lamb in the glass in order finally to lay bare the even further distance between real lambs and the Lamb of God. In Anna's cold estimation, as long as the lamb's meaning transcends the lamb's actuality, it is "more than it appeared" (*R*, 156), so that the lamb has some covert message to embody. Much to Will's dismay, she tells him, "I like lambs too much to treat them as if they had to mean something" (R, 158). Just as her soul and her self are one, the lamb's meaning must not outrun its actuality.

In their discussion of Christ's miracle at Cana we are afforded another look at the difference between their perspectives—a difference that renders their marriage a mere imitation of the true marriage that Anna's parents, Tom and Lydia, modeled. At Cana, Christ attends a wedding where he changes water into wine, a miracle ordinarily interpreted as Christ's transformation of the couple's profane bond into the sacred bond symbolizing Christ's saving mediation between God and man. Unlike Anna's parents, she and Will can never be so transfigured, and their debate shows why. Will is trapped in the purely representational sacred world he has set apart for himself. Anna is trapped in the profane world, where she searches in vain for Christianity's transfigurations of the profane into the sacred. She cannot find this transfiguration in Christianity because she sees it divorced from the historical world; she demands to know whether Christ actually—in a particular historical moment—converted the water into wine.

She pushes Will to the wall by demanding that he prove to her that the miracle actually took place. The harder she tries to verify the historical moment of the miracle, the less actual it becomes, to both herself and Will. Once they both decide that the miracle could not have actually taken place, Anna directs her vision to the profane world, where her lapse into a continual condition of pregnancy signals her surrogate way of giving birth to herself as a transformed soul. Will, for his part, directs his vision to the sacred. If the miracle at Cana has no historical truth, then he will simply erect another partition and abstract the idea from the miracle that represents it:

> Very well, it was not true, the water had not turned into wine. But for all that he would live in his soul as if the water *had* turned into wine. For truth of fact, it had not. But for his soul, it had.
>
> "Whether it turned into wine or whether it didn't," he said, "it doesn't bother me. I take it for what it is."
>
> "And what is it?" she asked, quickly, hopefully.
>
> "It's the Bible," he said.
>
> That answer enraged her, and she despised him. She did not

actively question the Bible herself. But he drove her to contempt. (*R*, 169)

They can never be genuinely married. The further she drives him into the refuge of his soul, his as-if world, the more she pushes herself into questioning openly the historical grounds of what she is not yet emotionally prepared to question. Not unlike Conrad's Razumov in Geneva, where his isolation in a world that sustains a make-believe identity puts him in control of his quest for self-knowledge, Will isolates himself from Anna by taking refuge in an as-if world that sustains his self-image.

By forcing Will to recognize that the church is not an orderly world immune from the condition of the quotidian world, Anna tries to crack the partition mediating between sacred and profane, which presents as much a problem for her as it does for him. She forces him to see the church as a world within the world, not as a world above our world; and as a "world within a world, a sort of side show" (*R*, 202), the church becomes a fiction. When he recognizes momentarily that the church is not coterminous with the higher world it is supposed to represent, he loses his connection with eternity because he can love it only "as a symbol": "[H]e realised that the doorway was no doorway. It was too narrow, it was false. Outside the cathedral were many flying spirits that could never be sifted through the jewelled gloom. He had lost his absolute" (*R*, 203).

In light of this conflict, we can understand what is at stake for Ursula, whose experience is a compendium of her parents' desires and confusions about inferential knowledge of the absolute. At one point in her childhood, Ursula is more like her father than her mother, for she wants religion to remain abstract: "To her, Jesus was beautifully remote, shining in the distance, like a white moon at sunset, a crescent moon beckoning as it follows the sun, out of our ken" (*R*, 273–74). The phrase "out of our ken" strikes a familiar chord. She is as justified as her father was in insisting that religious mystery exceed her capacity for certain knowledge, but insofar as sustaining the mystery depends upon withdrawing from the world, her goal is unreasonable. Only later will she achieve what the rainbow promises, an unmediated contact with the eternal in *this* world.

As of yet, she requires a barrier between her soul and the world in order to follow her instincts outside the purview of knowledge. She lives with two identities—a dualism that renders the intersection of eternity with the contingencies of the moment impossible: "She lived a dual life, one where the facts of daily life encompassed everything, being legion, and the other wherein the facts of daily life were superseded by the eternal truth. So utterly did she desire the Sons of God should come to the daughters of men; and she believed more in her desire and its fulfilment than in the obvious facts of life" (R, 275). Through a systematic testing of Christian precepts, Ursula discovers that what Christian morality demands—gestures like turning the other cheek—has no place in this world at all: "Sin was absolute and everlasting: wickedness and badness were temporary and relative" (R, 272). She is her father's daughter.

We are not as far from our consideration of the role of representation in knowledge as it might seem. Skrebensky is to Ursula what the cathedral was to her father: the mediating term that she hopes will make eternity manifest to her consciousness in the moment. As Will tried to use the cathedral to render the eternal through its representative icons, so Ursula uses her sexual experience with Skrebensky to constitute her experience of the eternal; but because he is wholly gripped by his ideals of social servitude, Skrebensky is an inadequate conduit of eternity and therefore only partitions her off from it. He encourages her to maintain her internal disjunction between self—a contingent identity shaped by quotidian experience—and soul, the inviolate, presocial core of the individual that is independent of its surroundings.

In order to maintain her sacred soul, Ursula thinks she must cut it off from the external world, so she wedges her self between her soul and the world, where it then mediates between the two. The danger is this: if her self constitutes her image of the world, then the world will be nothing more than her ego-ideal and, as such, will be an inadequate representation of the world. Furthermore, by identifying the self with the world, she will widen the gap between the soul and the world, rendering genuine soul-intimacy, of the kind she will find only with Birkin, an absolute impossibility.

Ursula tries to marry her *self* to Skrebensky, who to her is a self and not a soul. She cannot truly marry him, however, because "to make public their connection would be to put it in range with all the things which nullified him, and from which he was for the moment entirely dissociated. If he married he would have to assume his social self" (R, 453). Theirs would be, like Will and Anna's, only a representation of marriage: "The living fact was that he and she were a delicious make-believe" (R, 454). In order to overcome the mediation impairing her contact with the world, Ursula must reject Skrebensky. As soon as she does, he marries someone else, "to screen himself from the darkness," for now Ursula is "the darkness, the challenge, the horror" (R, 482). Unlike Skrebensky, who shields himself from the realm of darkness where direct connection alone is possible, Ursula enters it and so to him is as if one with it. She thereby finds the courage to destroy the protective curtain between her soul and the world, and her reward is a vision that banishes the dividing line between time and eternity. Her vision of society is founded upon the individual and does not, as Skrebensky's view does, impose an abstraction upon individuals in order to see them as parts of a societal whole, as social selves. Therefore the society she sees is as firmly rooted in the blood as the heavenly arch of the rainbow is fixed upon the earth.

Because the social promise she envisions at the end grows logically out of her victory over the mediating, socially constructed self, it is understandable, in spite of what some commentators have suggested, that her vision should hold a social as well as a personal promise: "She saw in the rainbow the earth's new architecture, the old, brittle corruption of houses and factories swept away, the world built up in a living fabric of Truth, fitting to the over-arching heaven" (R, 495).[16] Since she no longer relies upon an inadequately mediating self, she can

16. Critics holding that the social promise in Ursula's vision is unwarranted include F. R. Leavis, *D. H. Lawrence: Novelist* (New York, 1956), 111; Hough, *The Dark Sun*, 71–72; Roger Sale, "The Narrative Technique of 'The Rainbow,'" *Modern Fiction Studies*, V (1959–60), 37; Julian Moynahan, *The Deed of Life: The Novels and Tales of D. H. Lawrence* (Princeton, 1963), 55; Keith Sagar, *The Art of D. H. Lawrence* (Cambridge, England, 1966), 71–72; and Stephen J. Miko, *Toward "Women in Love": The Emergence of a Lawrentian Aesthetic* (New Haven, 1971), 183. Alternate readings according with mine include those of Marvin Mudrick, "The Originality of *The Rainbow*," in Harry T. Moore (ed.), *D. H. Lawrence: A Critical Survey* (Toronto, 1969), 77–78; and Frank Kermode, *Lawrence* (N.p., 1973), 50.

recognize the liberating space between her soul and the world: "There was a space between her and the shell. It was burst, there was a rift in it. Soon she would have her root fixed in a new Day" (R, 492).

Representational knowledge separated Will from the relative world where Anna lived, Anna from the eternal sphere where Will lived, and Will and Anna from each other. As long as the representation of the world is superimposed upon it and not coterminous with it, direct knowledge is impossible and human fulfillment is delayed. For Ursula, however, the direct contact between her soul and the world eliminates all mediating terms. The abstraction that is the social self disappears, the shell falls away, and she knows directly and is fulfilled.

So far we have established Lawrence's preference for direct over representational knowledge, and we have seen how in *The Rainbow* he dramatizes the struggle to reach unmediated contact with reality. We now turn our attention to Lawrence's own struggle to make his fiction meet the representational demands that his ideal for direct knowledge requires—representational demands that are finally impossible. If his fiction is to represent anything at all, it cannot ultimately banish its mediating position between reader and meaning; but it can, as all realistic fiction tries to do, approach the ideal by suppressing the frame it unavoidably places on reality. Conrad pointed to the frame in *Heart of Darkness* by stationing a narrator between the reader and the reality the narrator spoke of. Because the truth itself is an absence that knowledge cannot grasp except by distorting it, by filling it with light and order, mediation served to delay the confrontation with absence that would render narrative impossible. Lawrence, by contrast, values that incomprehensible realm because it is an asylum from the death-blow of pernicious knowledge's certitude. Lawrence moves, then, in the opposite direction by suppressing rather than pointing to the mediating status of his fiction. Just as the supreme knowledge directly contacts its objects and obviates the self-reference that is the starting point in dualistic epistemology, so then does the supreme fiction directly contact the reality it represents without calling attention to its mediating role.

This suppressing of the frame is perfectly traditional in the realistic English novel, but the challenge to representational norms of realistic fiction comes in the nature of the reality Lawrence is trying to represent. Here the essential and the accidental, the symbolic and the banal, the subjective and the objective cannot be wholly set apart. The fiction is real not because, as in conventional realism, the world it imitates is a seemingly objectively verifiable one that stands the test of doubt, but rather because we accept it completely on its own terms—the only way to read Lawrence profitably. The reality Lawrence represents asks us to believe and imagine; conventional realism asks us to question and doubt.

It is a commonplace that the major thrust of Lawrence's originality lies in his importing into the novel experiences which have traditionally been left out. By incorporating these, he forces upon himself sometimes impossible demands for representation. The topic of marriage is a case in point. For Lawrence, as for Conrad and Woolf, marriage no longer served as the final resolution of personal conflict, as it had traditionally done in British fiction of the eighteenth and nineteenth centuries and as Ursula naïvely suggests at the beginning of *Women in Love*. As Robert Kiely explains it, "The conception of marriage as a 'final resting place,' suggests not only that plot is preparation but that it is preparation for a time in which the old, more interesting self ceases to exist."[17] The realistic novelist perhaps wisely avoided exploring marriage, not just because it was too private to be depicted but because it lacked conflict and would thus challenge the momentum of plot. We need hardly look further than the sequel to Richardson's *Pamela* for evidence of how including the ultimate personal fulfillment can serve to arrest the narrative's dramatic interest.

Although Lawrence posits marriage as the potential resolution of personal conflict, he directly inspects it in his fiction rather than using it as the end to which his narrative is the means. Intensely concerned with the state of marriage itself, he sustains dramatic conflict in his depictions of it by introducing a tension between marriage as a legal or social arrangement and marriage as a spiritual and even mystical level of experience.

17. Kiely, *Beyond Egotism*, 86.

Even the latter he considers to be an ongoing experience, not the goal of marriage. The legally married couples in *The Rainbow* and *Women in Love* may or may not be truly married; theirs may be only a representation of marriage. In *The Rainbow*, Tom and Lydia are truly married, but Will and Anna are not. Just because they are truly married, though, Tom and Lydia do not reach a *final* resting place in marriage, but rather experience a perpetual oscillation between stasis and movement, fulfillment and conflict, which is the best that can be hoped for in Lawrence's realistic fiction.

In representing their resting places Lawrence meets his greatest challenge, as in this description of Tom and Lydia: "Blind and destroyed, he pressed forward, nearer, nearer, to receive the consummation of himself, he received within the darkness which should swallow him and yield him up to himself. If he could come really within the blazing kernel of darkness, if really he could be destroyed, burnt away till he lit with her in one consummation, that were supreme" (*R*, 90–91). His consummation is in the subjunctive mood because, just as Conrad's does in "passing out" when it is time to reveal the heart of darkness, Lawrence's narration acknowledges its representational limits by shying away from the real consummation. It refuses to shed light on this darkness, but neither does it call immediate attention to its limits: where narration leaves off, we are asked to assume, the consummation begins. Lawrence suggests the consummation here in two ways—through dislocation and a blurring of perspectives. It suddenly becomes impossible to say where the characters are, and the narrator seems to speak from within them, no longer as an outside observer of the scene. While he speaks from within both characters at once, they seem to enter a whole new sphere of consciousness: "It was the entry into another circle of existence, it was the baptism to another life, it was the complete confirmation. Their feet trod strange ground of knowledge, their footsteps were lit-up with discovery. Wherever they walked, it was well, the world re-echoed round them in discovery. They went gladly and forgetful. Everything was lost, and everything was found. The new world was discovered, it remained only to be explored" (*R*, 91). At this moment Lawrence renders a state of being; the process of becoming has ended. Since their marriage is made both in heaven and on earth, Tom and Lydia must vacil-late between the higher and lower conditions, but at least in these moments they rest in their consummation.

Since this moment is so important in his fiction, Lawrence must figure out a way to make it a part of the whole narrative while yet making it seem to step out of the narrative sequence in order to distinguish it as ultimate. Such a consummate mo-ment cannot be understood as merely the end of a sequence of causes and effects, because what the couple does not do is more important than what it actively does, thus making it problem-atic to position the moment within a narrative sequence of causally related events. Because nothing the couples do seems to have any consequences for the outcome, it is hard to tell what makes one couple successful and another unsuccessful. Marguerite Beede Howe suggests that the outcome is rhetori-cally swerved in favor of some couples and against others.[18] If the outcome is simply narratively swerved, then Lawrence has failed, by his own standards: he would have us watching the words rather than the world they pretend to present.

In *The Rainbow* Lawrence places his renderings of ultimate fulfillment within the narrative sequence without establishing causal links by presenting a plurality of resting places for Tom and Lydia rather than one consummate experience that would render further narrative unnecessary. Stretching his narrative over a period of three generations, he can sustain narrative mo-mentum by including a range of successes and failures, since successes by themselves arrest the narrative and Lawrence uses failures to move the plot forward, just as he sustains dramatic action by holding successful marriages in a state of flux. The narrative can suggest the static condition of fulfillment only by surrounding it with a whirlwind of conflict. Similarly, Conrad had to use the light in order to reveal the dark, to engage the reader in a network of value-laden schemes in order finally to reveal their factitiousness. In Conrad that darkness is the end of human experience; in Lawrence it is the beginning. In Conrad the imagination, a participant in the factitious world, ceases to generate images when the narrative fails; in Lawrence the reader's imagination must take over where narrative leaves

18. Howe, *The Art of the Self in D. H. Lawrence,* 69.

off, for imagination, as called upon in the subjunctive mood, is the only possible way the reader has of filling in the narrative lacunae. Conrad's imperative is doubt; Lawrence's is belief. By following the imperatives of Lawrence's narration, we participate in his model of direct knowledge because direct knowledge eliminates the mediating term and therefore the possibility of doubt.

The Rainbow plots a series of consummate moments in a story with a broad historical scope and in that way preserves momentum by moving us forward in time, but *Women in Love* takes place over a matter of months. Here Lawrence relies on counterpoint rather than historical sweep to plot the consummate moments; we move back and forth between the story of Gerald and Gudrun and the story of Birkin and Ursula. By foreshortening the plot's temporal scope, though, Lawrence presented himself with another problem: to sustain the counterpoint, the consummate moments of Birkin and Ursula have to be as contracted as Gerald and Gudrun's relationship is protracted to show the prolonging effect of Gudrun's knowledge upon Gerald. She knows him not as a way of contacting mystery and otherness, but in order to fix him, to be certain in her relationship with him. The longer it takes for her to know him, the better off they both are and the longer they can continue together. When he is in her arms, she asks herself, "How much more of him was there to know?" (*WL*, 324). Even Gerald senses, at some unspecified level of awareness, that her knowledge of him will result in his death, so that when he senses that Gudrun is holding herself back from him, he is glad: "And even he was glad to be checked, rebuked, held back. For to desire is better than to possess, the finality of the end was dreaded as deeply as it was desired" (*WL*, 325). When the desire for the end equals and then surpasses the dread of it, the result is death.

This is true, however, only for those for whom the consummation is the death rather than the flower of experience; it is not true for Birkin and Ursula. For them the movement toward consummation is lesser than the consummation itself. Since their quest is to overcome the movement toward consummation, to meet and mingle in immediate contact, their becoming is more difficult to represent. Even in its state of being, their consummation escapes Lawrence's attempt at representation as much as it militates against clear, certain knowledge for Birkin and Ursula themselves. Because their consummation is contracted into single moments and because Lawrence tries to render it so specifically in the "Excurse" chapter, he cannot overcome the problem of representing it. Even his most sympathetic readers cringe at this depiction, which attempts to take representation beyond its reasonable limits. Among Lawrence's best critics, Stephen J. Miko most exactly describes the problem with the scene.[19] Precisely the scene's specificity mars it: "It was a perfect passing away for both of them, and at the same time the most intolerable accession into being, the marvellous fullness of immediate gratification, overwhelming, outflooding from the source of the deepest life-source, the darkest, deepest, strangest life-source of the human body, at the back of the loins. . . . And now, behold, from the smitten rock of the man's body, from the strange marvellous flanks and thighs, deeper, further in mystery than the phallic source, came the floods of ineffable darkness and ineffable riches" (WL, 306). If it is hard to read this passage with a straight face, perhaps it is because the specific location of Birkin's "ineffable darkness" makes the scene far more pictorial than the scene involving Tom and Lydia. There the dislocation and blurring of perspectives implicitly demanded that the reader imagine the scene, to see it as though for himself yet from the narrator's perspective within both characters' consciousnesses. Here the more one tries to picture this scene, guided by the narrator's graphic description, specifically the association of the life-source with the back of Birkin's loins, the more absurd it seems.

This depiction fails for another reason, having to do with the relationship between the narrator, the characters, and the reader that usually obtains in Lawrence's successful rendering of such scenes. Not the least of Lawrence's achievements was bringing the sex act into realistic narrative without rendering it as pornography, which he avoided by making the reader drop his position as an outside observer of the act. In real life, a third party's observation of the sex act is unwholesome; exactly because there is no chance of participation, being the observer ap-

19. Miko, Toward "Women in Love," 273–74; Hough, The Dark Sun, 81–82.

peals to the aberrant personality. When rendered in words with such specificity that the reader, alongside the narrator, feels his status as an observer, the sex act becomes pornographic. The "Excurse" scene makes the reader feel like an outsider, if not through its specificity in describing the act itself, then in its specificity in explaining the sources of ineffable darkness, which should remain ineffable. When the narrator claims direct and exclusive knowledge of such things, he sets himself apart, making the reader feel a distance from both the narrator and the scene he is witnessing.

When one considers the enormous strides Lawrence made by incorporating into the novel subjects and states of mind that realistic fiction has characteristically resisted, a failure like the "Excurse" scene should be easy to overlook. We can learn as much from his failures as we can from his successes, and we learn here that the direct rendering of characters' moments of unity—at once psychic and sexual—is beyond the purview of any narration. If such a final unity does exist, narrative can only represent it by suggesting it. Lawrence best disguises his narrative limitations by calling upon the reader's imagination, but when the narrator stands apart and tries to persuade, then he invites only doubt and calls attention to the limitations inherent in his narrative medium.

Lawrence's ideal of fiction as direct presentation also informs his use of the symbol. His symbols do not ordinarily lend themselves to a distinction between the symbol itself and the meaning it conveys; instead, the symbol becomes coterminous with its meaning. As a result, his fiction often effects a synthesis of the particular and the universal—a synthesis that modifies the character of realistic representation. In dualistic epistemology the mind verifies the objects of its knowledge after withdrawing from them in a moment of introspection, after which the distinction between the inner and the outer is ascertained. For Lawrence, however, the self cannot know itself in introspection and can make no final distinction between the internal and the external: they are one. Analogously, just as the mind cannot be partitioned off from what it knows, the vehicle of the symbol cannot finally be distinguished from its tenor. The symbol is no longer a middle term standing between the mind and a reality that seems to be outside the linguistic field of

the narrative. Instead, it is the mind and the world gathered together, coterminous with both. The symbol becomes a subject-
object; it is itself the very relationship of the mind to externality.

Tzvetan Todorov calls this family of symbolic theories, in
which he includes Friedrich Schelling's work, "syntheticism."
In his *System of Transcendental Idealism* Schelling calls the
symbol's synthesis "subjekt-objectivirung"—the subjectifica-
tion of objectivity, so complete that no distinction can be made
between the symbol and its meaning. The effect of such symbols is to defy precise explication, which holds true for some of
Lawrence's more demanding symbolic scenes in *Women in
Love.* The symbolic texture of this novel is at every point similar to Frank Kermode's definition of the Romantic image, which
he says is "without simple intellectual content, bearing the
same relationship to thought as the dancer bears to the dance.
As in the dance, there is no disunity of being; 'the body is the
soul.' . . . For this Dancer is one of Yeats's great reconciling images, containing life in death, death in life, movement in still-
ness, action and contemplation, body and soul; in fact all that
passionate integrity that was split when Descartes, as Yeats puts
it, discovered that he could think better in his bed than out of
it." It is without "simple intellectual content" because it does
not lend itself easily to explication; the moment one explains
it, one feels one has missed something. According to Kermode
this Romantic view of the symbol, preserved in French symbolism, appears once again in the best of early modern British
and American poetry.[20]

When these symbolist tendencies emerge in the midst of
a realistic narrative, they modify the reality that novels usually present, and Conrad, Lawrence, and Woolf all share these
symbolist leanings.[21] Conrad uses the silver's ambiguity in
Nostromo to make his point about the spiritual and the material: the silver is both a material thing and a spiritual interest
and functions as an ambience. So does Woolf use the lighthouse
as at once the object and the symbol of the characters' desires in

20. Tzvetan Todorov, *Theories of the Symbol,* trans. Catherine Porter
(Ithaca, N.Y., 1982), 184–89; James Engell, *The Creative Imagination: Enlightenment to Romanticism* (Cambridge, Mass., 1981), Chap. on Schelling;
Frank Kermode, *Romantic Image* (London, 1957), 48.
21. Daniel J. Schneider, *Symbolism: The Manichean Vision* (Lincoln, 1975).

To the Lighthouse. One can never make a certain determination of how far the symbol guides our interpretation of the story and how far it is part of the story we are interpreting. It does not simply mediate our knowledge of the story; it constitutes the story itself.

Eliseo Vivas calls such symbols in Lawrence "constitutive." As in Todorov's outline of syntheticism and Kermode's definition of the Romantic image, Vivas' constitutive symbol is a creative synthesis of meaning with the matter of experience.[22] This synthesis models the direct knowledge that is the ideal behind Lawrence's view of fiction, because it eliminates mediating terms between subject and object. Given what we have already learned about Lawrence's thoughts about representation—that the adequate representation of a thing is the thing itself—we can see why he should be philosophically predisposed toward accepting this model, since by merging the representation with the represented he reduces to zero the power of mediation. The symbol cannot damage the integrity of what it represents if it is continuous with its meaning and with the mind to which it is presented.

In contrast to the constitutive symbol Vivas posits the "quasi-symbol," in which "something stands for something else that can be grasped independently of the sign vehicle." Lawrence relies on quasi-symbols as well as constitutive symbols. As an example of a quasi-symbol Vivas describes the scene in *Women in Love* where Gerald subdues his white Arab mare while a train passes by. The scene lends itself to clear explication; not only can its meaning be unproblematically formulated, but the "Carpeting" and "Industrial Magnate" chapters discursively render the meaning.[23]

To Vivas' example we could add many, but just one more will help establish the contrast with constitutive symbols. In "The Industrial Magnate" the machine is the wholly adequate symbol of Gerald's lapse into abstraction and into the mechanism that, for Lawrence, abstraction necessitates. This does not mean that Lawrence tried and failed to find a constitutive

22. Eliseo Vivas, *D. H. Lawrence: The Failure and the Triumph of Art* (Evanston, 1960), Appendix, 273–91.
23. *Ibid.,* 275, 241–42.

symbol for Gerald; rather, Gerald is adequately symbolized by the machine because of his failure as a human being, not because of Lawrence's failure as a novelist. Although he thinks visual description inadequately characterizes, Lawrence nonetheless must render Gerald in strikingly visual terms, because Gerald conducts his life and sees the world as an "object-bounded" person. In fact, as Vivas well shows, in respect to his capacities as a friend and lover, Gerald is consistently embodied in constitutive rather than quasi-symbols.[24]

In contrast to quasi-symbols, constitutive symbols are difficult or impossible to explain discursively. Among the scenes showing Lawrence's use of the constitutive type are Anna's laughing out loud at Will in church, her dancing during her pregnancy with Ursula, and Ursula's vision of the horses that seems both a subjectively and objectively real experience, all in *The Rainbow*, and Gudrun's dancing before the cattle and her subsequently slapping Gerald, and the "Moony" chapter, both in *Women in Love*. A scene like Birkin's famous stone-throwing in "Moony" is never explained discursively in the rest of the novel the way Gerald's behavior with the mare is, nor is it ever fully explained in the commentary on the novel. There are about as many different interpretations of Birkin's throwing stones into the moon-reflecting water as there are critics who have made the attempt.

My point is not to offer yet another interpretation of any of these scenes but to register their peculiarity and their relevance to Lawrence's ideal for fictional representation. When we read a constitutively symbolic scene like "Moony" or the "Water-Party" scene between Gudrun and Gerald and try to confer a meaning upon the events, we feel that we have missed something; some meaning has wholly escaped us. If, on the other hand, we simply experience the scene in the act of reading it and make no conscious attempt to articulate it, then we sense a contact with its meaning. That is, when we try to explain discursively one of Lawrence's constitutive symbols, we automatically fall into the habit of dividing the symbol into separate terms, the representation and the represented. We impose a dualistic representational model of knowledge that the con-

24. *Ibid.*, 243.

stitutive symbol defies. The adequate response to a constitutive symbol is an ever-fluctuating, nonverbal, reciprocal relationship with it.[25]

Not only do constitutive symbols elude our attempt to specify their meanings, but they can also defy the norms of narrative sequence. Here we come back to the larger problem of representation in fiction. A constitutive scene, such as Gudrun's dancing before the cattle and her slapping Gerald, defies any attempt to specify its position within the narrative sequence of causally linked events. On one level of comprehension we can specify the position of this scene within the narrative easily enough. Gudrun slaps Gerald after he interrupts her dancing and before they leave the island to rejoin the Criches' party. Furthermore, the scene occurs well before Gudrun is fully acquainted with Gerald and before she could possibly know that she will have a part in his death. If we interpret her slapping Gerald as a consequence of the immediately preceding event, then we assume that she slaps him for interrupting her dancing. As soon as we begin deducing causal reasons from the sequence of events, however, we begin to sense the inadequacy of the explanation. When she accuses him of believing that she is afraid of his cattle and of him, when she is said to feel "an unconquerable desire for deep violence against him," and when he tells her, "You have struck the first blow," to which she as enigmatically responds, "And I shall strike the last" (WL, 162), we have the distinct sense that the full meaning of this scene is beyond the range of its specific chronological place among other causally linked events. This scene actually *constitutes* the whole relationship between Gerald and Gudrun; it surmounts the whole story of their desire and hatred, from their initial encounter at the wedding to Gerald's icy death in the Tyrolean Alps. Thus, its meaning has a place both within the individual moments of the narrative and outside the narrative, from the perspective of a reader who has seen the whole story. The meaning within the narrative's individual moments, voiced in the limited perspectives of the characters, is subjective. The

25. Dorothy Van Ghent, "[*Sons and Lovers*]," in E. W. Tedlock, Jr. (ed.), *D. H. Lawrence and "Sons and Lovers": Sources and Criticism* (New York, 1965), 181; Angelo P. Bertocci, "Symbolism in *Women in Love*," in Moore (ed.), *A Critical Survey*, 83–102.

objective meaning is afforded to the omniscient narrator or to the reader who knows the whole story. Both meanings overlap when the objective, usually reserved for the omniscient narrator, is given over to the characters themselves. Something like this happens in Woolf's *Mrs. Dalloway,* where Clarissa achieves the omniscient narrator's perspective and can therefore comprehend her own life by entering the life of a man she has never met. Similarly, in this scene Gerald and Gudrun unconsciously know that he will be the victim and she the victimizer. If they always knew this, then their continuing with each other would render their characters implausible. They are plausible only if they believe they have something to gain from their relationship, as they think through most of the novel.

It would be not only artificial but also at odds with Lawrence's intentions if in this or any other scene Gudrun and Gerald were deemed to have full conscious knowledge of the consequences of their relationship. As it is, their knowledge remains at a deep, unspecified level of awareness, a level inaccessible to them because of the pernicious nature of that knowledge. If all along they knew the course of their relationship, they would be essentially static models, but Lawrence resists abstraction at every turn. He apparently wants to exhibit their limitations as human beings rather than as paradigms, because through most of the novel they make free choices that are not tied to their knowledge of their future. Gerald and Gudrun are culpable because they strive for certain knowledge of each other instead of accepting each other's mysteries. If their behavior were determined by their knowledge of their future together, then they would not be responsible for their failure and Lawrence would not be able to make the point he wants to make, which requires that they be genuinely human first and then, as a result of misdirecting their knowledge, stumble into their deathly condition of stasis in abstraction.

The same holds for Ursula and Birkin. If their success were guaranteed and they knew it was, they would have no real responsibility for it. In *The Rainbow* and *Women in Love,* as in all of Lawrence's best works, including *The Plumed Serpent,* there is constant tension between the universal and the particular. Lawrence is concerned not to let his fiction succumb to the abstract. (It is another question whether he finally succeeds in avoiding the abstract or whether doing so is really a criterion for good fiction.) For him the abstract is static and dead; the particular active, indeterminate, and alive. If he allowed his fiction to call direct attention to his abstraction, then he would undermine his own intentions.

The Rainbow and *Women in Love* set up an ultimately impossible but approachable ideal: to banish fiction's mediating role in conveying the truths of the world it represents, while at the same time making that truth seem to exist independently of its fictional portrayal, perhaps in the reader's buried impulses. To do this forces the reader to participate in the construction of the fiction without his knowing it, as when the narrator turns toward the reader and implicitly asks him to construct the scene imaginatively. The narrator must do this; otherwise he would shed light on the darkness and disperse it when the point is to become immersed in it.

The Stable Ego: Psychological Realism in *Sons and Lovers*

We have been discussing the more general issues of representation pertaining to Lawrence's epistemological ideal for pure knowledge. Now we turn to a more specific instance of representation: characterization, the aspect of his fiction where Lawrence revealed his greatest innovations. In his best characterizations he convinces us that the criteria we assume are necessary for determining that we know another self are worse than inadequate. His new criteria, however, are not easily specified, partly because a major thrust in his characterization is his implicit request that we be comfortable in what seems like ignorance. At times, if our knowledge of his characters or their knowledge of each other loses all predictive power, if we cannot tell which actions are voluntary, and if we feel we somehow cannot *see* the character we study, we are asked to believe that our intimacy with that character has taken an unfamiliar form—a form that demands a new and better relationship with the other self and that invites an awareness of unfamiliar parts of ourselves.

A few of our ordinary expectations in knowing conventionally realistic characters can clarify matters. First of all, we expect our knowledge to be mediated; we know characters by outward signs. In conventional realism no less than in Lawrence, the narrator mediates our knowledge of characters. The omniscient narrator works by assuming the privilege of direct (unmediated) knowledge of characters, entering their minds and voicing otherwise unvoiced thoughts. This practice, which Dorrit Cohn distinguishes as psycho-narration, is especially prevalent in Lawrence because the knowledge he thinks most worth having is too far beneath conscious attention to be reported in any other way.[26] Although this method also appears in conventional realism, it moves into the foreground in Lawrence, becoming not just an instance of literary license but an important issue in the story: his characters' knowledge of each other is as direct as an omniscient narrator's. In conventional realism, knowledge of other selves is also mediated by "object-binding" characteristics—appearance, clothing, social background. The surroundings help to define the character and help the character define himself in introspection. These object-binding characteristics make us feel we know *about* the characters, and we assume that these observable traits are usually reliable; we cannot, after all, enter another's mind and think his thoughts unless we are omniscient narrators. In our usual sense of how others can be known in fiction, the more vivid these object-binding traits are, the easier it is to be sure there is a real person on the other side.

These mediating traits also individuate characters, another main standard for psychological realism. When each character has his own psychological history with specifiable causes and effects, we are taken in and we can set some limit on what it is conceivable for the character to do next, reinforcing another main expectation for psychological realism: consistency. Of course when a character becomes wholly predictable, we can no longer believe in him—we call him a cardboard character— but this usually happens when there is no attempt at detailing a psychological profile. A psychologically realistic character sometimes behaves in an unpredictable manner, but we can usually account for his behavior, even if only in retrospect, fitting his choices into the range of the conceivable, whose

26. Cohn, *Transparent Minds*, 100.

boundaries his psychological history defines. Within these borders lies the character's consistency.

Lawrence never wholly abandons any of these criteria for psychological realism—mediation, individuation, or consistency—but he subordinates them for the sake of other concerns, bringing a new logic to the inspection of characters. Some have argued that only he can read this logic, which comes near to saying that Lawrence's characters could live nowhere but in his novels. If we said only that Lawrence's novels were written by Lawrence, we would not be getting much further, and I hope we can.

The first time Lawrence effectively employs his new way of making selves knowable to the reader and to each other is in *The Rainbow*. He rejects what in a well-known letter to Edward Garnett he calls "the old stable *ego*" in search of "another *ego*, according to whose action the individual is unrecognisable" (*CL*, I, 282). That other ego is perceived directly, which is why Lawrence's most usual metaphor for that knowledge is tactual. Aldous Huxley formulates this true knowledge of other selves as "nocturnal and tactual—a touching in the night."[27] That designation is appropriate because Lawrence almost always associates visual perception with mentation and distance. For him it is mediated knowledge and can be rendered in mental images that arrest the object and cut it off from its life. Touch, though, is direct. Obviously tactual experience is not a possibility in narrative presentation; it is a metaphor reinforced by characters' contact with each other.

When the narrative registers this model of direct, tactual knowledge, however, it discredits specific assumptions behind psychological realism, which we can get at by examining Lawrence's dissent from Freudian psychology. For our purposes I link Lawrence's dissent from Freud to his dissent from conventional literary assumptions about psychological realism. This rough and dangerous link ignores two important points: Freudian psychology is at least as innovative as Lawrence's novels, and Lawrence's innovations have certain similarities to Freud's. What follows distorts Freud because the main issues

27. Aldous Huxley (ed.), Introduction to *The Letters of D. H. Lawrence* (2nd ed.; London, 1932), xiv.

in Lawrence's innovations in character presentation are what Lawrence *thought* Freud was saying, which is not always the same as what Freud said, and, even more important, what Lawrence objected to in Freud's methodology. That methodology is empiricist, in Lawrence's reading, and shares important assumptions with literary psychological realism. Here again, the assumption that Freud's methodology is empiricist requires the sort of qualification that would exceed the scope of this study. Suffice it to say that Freud's systematization of human behavior partook in psychology's widespread tendency, in the first half of this century, toward pseudoscience, even though more careful study of Freudian methodology reveals that, as Sigmund Koch says, "The widely shared idea that psychoanalysis is a 'science' which can cumulate and progress by a logic of verification similar to that of physics or even biology is absurd."[28] Freud's is, after all, a depth psychology; so is Lawrence's, but Lawrence could never get past the suspicion that Freud's scientific inspection of the unconscious mind dispersed its considerable powers.

Lawrence knew that psychoanalysis intended to bring the unconscious mind to conscious attention, but in his view, to do this was to violate the unconscious and to impede its connection with the vital will, which moves in and through the individual. For him the unconscious mind is the only part worth having, for its spontaneity and purity. Psychoanalysis would only idealize it, that is, in Lawrence's terminology, freeze it in a mental construct. A good instance of their difference is incest-craving. Freud sees it as a powerful complex operating on the level of the unconscious mind. As far as Lawrence is concerned, when the conscious mind turns inward to the unconscious mind, the resulting self-regard imports into the latter the incest-craving that the conscious mind only thinks it finds there. The incest-craving is then accepted as normal: "Once . . . you accept the incest-craving as part of the normal sexuality of men, you must remove all repression of incest itself. . . . Psychoanalysis will never openly state this conclusion that every analyst must, willy-nilly, consciously or unconsciously, bring his

28. Sigmund Koch, "Psychology as Science," in S. C. Brown (ed.), *Philosophy of Psychology* (New York, 1974), 31.

patient." We momentarily put aside the suspicion that Lawrence misrepresents Freud. The important part is the taboo of bringing the unconscious mind to conscious attention, which in part explains Lawrence's heavy reliance on indirect discourse, or psycho-narration, a practice that in Lawrence is often dismissed as a sleight of hand. For Lawrence, bringing the unconscious mind to the self's own conscious attention denigrates it: the unconscious becomes a source of horror in the process, as in Gerald Crich's inward journeys as well as in Lawrence's image of Freud's view of the unconscious mind—"Nothing but a huge slimy serpent of sex, and heaps of excrement, and a myriad repulsive little horrors spawned between sex and excrement."[29]

If the conscious mind is prohibited from journeying inward, what then is the alternative in terms of either psychological or literary presentation? A brief inspection of Trigant Burrow's *The Social Basis of Consciousness* (1927) provides a likely systematic answer in terms of psychology. Written by a lapsed Freudian psychologist, it challenges Freud's methodology. Lawrence read and reviewed this book with great admiration the year it appeared, perhaps because its formulations resembled the theory of knowing other selves that Lawrence's earlier narrative innovations embody.

The inspiration for Burrow's study is worth considering for a moment, since it defines his methodology. Originally a practitioner of Freudian psychoanalysis, Burrow began to question one of empirical psychology's fundamental assumptions, namely, the analyst's ability to detach himself from his patient and thereby objectively to observe the workings of his mind. This question arose when a student of his whom he was analyzing said he could make full use of the doctor's analyses and conclusions about himself only if he were allowed to psychoanalyze the doctor. This suggestion challenged the usual barrier between doctor and patient, for the authority of the doctor to analyze his patient objectively would then be conferred upon him not only by himself and his colleagues but by the observed patient. Wanting to break the barrier between the observing and the observed minds, Burrow concluded that the detachment of

29. Lawrence, *Psychoanalysis and the Unconscious*, 206, 203.

observer from observed is a fantasy that perpetuates the unconscious motives of the doctor/observer. The doctor's project of opening the unconscious areas of his patient's mind, if the distinction between observer and observed is upheld, amounts to an elaborate distraction from the patterns of unconscious drives hidden beneath the shared consciousness of doctor and patient.

Burrow posits a collective consciousness that ignores the boundaries between selves. The unconscious half of this collective consciousness is not to be confused with C. G. Jung's collective unconscious, because in Burrow the unconscious mind is by definition individuated. "Collective unconscious" would be a contradiction in terms because the unconscious mind derives from the delusory attempt to regard the mind as private, cut off from collective consciousness. As Burrow puts it, "The separative or the personal *is* unconsciousness. Discontinuity and unconsciousness are coterminous." Lawrence never adopted Burrow's terminology; I don't know that he ever called private consciousness the manifestation of unconsciousness. On the contrary, collective consciousness in Lawrence implies a redeeming lapse of consciousness. Terminology notwithstanding, the logical implications shed light on Lawrence's model of knowing other selves and on the innovative patterns of character presentation that that model occasions. If there is no boundary between the observer and the observed mind, then there is no fundamental difference between knowing another mind and knowing oneself: "The analysis of a patient is the analysis of oneself," Burrow insists. "It cannot be otherwise."[30] He does not mean what any psychologist would say, that we learn about ourselves through analogies to what we see in others; he says we directly know other minds in the experience of directly knowing our own. If there is no way to distinguish the observing from the observed mind, psychology cannot continue as an empirical enterprise. The assumption behind empirical investigation of any kind is that there is something "out there" that our senses report to us. Its goal requires detachment

30. Trigant Burrow, *The Social Basis of Consciousness* (New York, 1927), 126, 26–27.

so that the field of observation does not include the observer. Burrow's methodology, in reaction against Freud's, turns its back on these basic empiricist assumptions, and intuition reigns.

It is easy to see why Lawrence should be attracted to Burrow's thesis when Burrow says, "we are none of us thinking clearly because we are none of us feeling clearly," thus establishing the hegemony of feelings over thoughts. The concept of feeling clearly is problematic, but Burrow advances his thesis on the grounds that cognition fails to present us with a genuine contact with reality. However much he differs from Conrad and Woolf, Lawrence shares with them and with Burrow a sense of cognition's inadequacy when the mind is thought of as the private arena of its experiences. Burrow registers this sense of distrust by asserting that knowledge unguided by feeling is always knowledge *concerning*; it never augments the subject's contact with the essence of knowledge's objects: "If I consider any object . . . all that my knowledge will ever yield me is restricted to the attributes that pertain to the substance in hand." That is, knowledge never penetrates the attributes to reach the essence. Now, if it cannot reach the essence, then either there is something wrong with knowledge or the universe maintains a metaphysical dualism between minds and essences. Burrow explains this much the way Lawrence does, by suggesting that we posit a metaphysical and unreachable essence in the first place because our minds are too dissociated from our feelings to effect the connection that feelings alone can augment: "the alleged essence is merely that organic condition of matter with which our conscious processes are not organically continuous. There are, however, organic conditions or processes with which our consciousness is continuous—namely, the organic processes occurring within our own bodies and registering themselves within us as feeling."[31]

This description opens the possibility of feeling oneself into the objects of knowledge in the effort to achieve direct knowledge, and it accords with Lawrence's own narrative methods, defining his implicit request of his readers. He asks us to find the "carbon" in ourselves in order to find it in his characters: "The ordinary novel would trace the history of the diamond—

31. *Ibid.*, 125, 19, 20.

but I say, 'Diamond, what! This is carbon'" (*CL*, I, 282). It resembles what psychologist Sigmund Koch calls "meaningful thinking" when he argues that psychology should move away from pseudoscientific imperatives:

> There is an intimate, an organic determination of the form and substance of thought by the properties of the object, the terms of the problem. In meaningful thinking, the mind "caresses," flows joyously into, over, around the relational matrix defined by the problem, the object. Polanyi talks about the "indwelling" of the understanding in the objects of inquiry. There is a merging of person and object, problem, task: one is *inside* the problem or object; better, one *is* the problem; better still, "one" is not—only the problem or object, its terms and relations, exist, and *these* are real in the fullest, most vivid, electric, irrefragable way.[32]

Attempting this merging is the condition of reading Lawrence's fiction. If *Sons and Lovers* sets up psychological problems that it becomes unable to solve, it is because neither we nor, I'm afraid, the narrative feels its way into the problem.

Lawrence only gradually learned to make his narratives embody his emergent models of knowing other selves. Because *Sons and Lovers* stumbles in the attempt, it provides an unusual opportunity to follow Lawrence through the threshold from the familiar knowledge of the self to the new knowledge that gives birth to the new self, another ego. Especially in Part One, the novel is conventionally realistic; its depiction of character erects a set of expectations for mediation, individuation, and especially consistency. We detect this in William's characterization, which betrays the novel's interest in portraying a self that is knowable from the outside-in, whose actions follow a discernible path. More so than Paul, William follows the Oedipal paradigm exactly along psychologically realistic lines. Lawrence carefully plots the series of events that will define William's growth and decay because of his mother's hold on him. The consistency of character here is painstaking. We first see William's attachment when he is too terrified by his mother's absence to enjoy the fair he has begged her to let him attend. There is no mistaking that Mrs. Morel is the cause, inasmuch as William is born "just when her own bitterness of disillusion

32. Koch, "Psychology as Science," 10.

was hardest to bear."[33] Later when he brings his girl Lily home for a visit, he complains to his mother that the girl is shallow. If Mrs. Morel tries to stand up for her, it seems only in order to restrain herself from agreeing; presumably they both want him to have a shallow girl in order to preserve the mother-son bond. Lily is clearly too different from Mrs. Morel to provide any competition. She is a sexual object, and William rather tactlessly announces to his family that she's never finished a book. The characterization makes it clear and plausible that William does not care for the girl unless she is physically present. She is a body; his mother is the mind. As the narrator puts things, "She could understand nothing but love-making and chatter. He was accustomed to having all his thoughts sifted through his mother's mind; so, when he wanted companionship, and was asked in reply to be the billing and twittering lover, he hated his betrothed" (*SL*, 131).

The psychologically realistic profile of William delineates the mind-body dualism. It carefully works out through skillfully plotted causal sequences the Oedipal paradigm Lawrence relied on when he described this novel to Edward Garnett as he was revising it:

> It follows this idea: a woman of character and refinement goes into the lower class, and has no satisfaction in her own life. She has had a passion for her husband, so the children are born of passion, and have heaps of vitality. But as her sons grow up she selects them as lovers—first the eldest, then the second. These sons are *urged* into life by their reciprocal love of their mother—urged on and on. But when they come to manhood, they can't love, because their mother is the strongest power in their lives, and holds them. . . . As soon as the young men come into contact with women, there's a split. William gives his sex to a fribble, and his mother holds his soul. But the split kills him, because he doesn't know where he is. . . . The [next] son decides to leave his soul in his mother's hands, and, like his older brother go for passion. . . . Then the split begins to tell again. But, almost unconsciously, the mother realises what is the matter, and begins to die. The son

33. D. H. Lawrence, *Sons and Lovers* (New York, 1962), 14. Subsequent page references to this novel (hereinafter cited parenthetically as *SL*) are to this Modern Library edition.

casts off his mistress, attends to his mother dying. He is left in the end naked of everything, with the drift towards death. (CL, I, 160–61)

Paul's psychological profile, however, is not quite as neat. Lawrence says Paul drifts toward death, but when we analyze the conclusion of this novel, we suspect that the narrative hedges on this point, which is why equally astute readers can interpret the ending in opposite ways. This hedging about the Oedipal pattern when it comes to Paul probably stems from Lawrence's gradual shift in emphasis from the stable ego to another ego—a shift perhaps caused by Paul's being Lawrence's fictional counterpart and by Lawrence's seeing him from the inside as well as the outside. Whatever the cause, the result is a characterization that exceeds the Oedipal pattern's psychologically realistic parameters. Mark Schorer has argued that this Oedipal pattern was superimposed upon the novel, and certain evidence supports this reading. As Frederick J. Hoffman pointed out some time ago, Lawrence's acquaintance with Freud was indirect even when he was revising Sons and Lovers, so that it was at best "superficially affected by Lawrence's introduction to psychoanalysis" through Frieda. Subsequent attempts like Daniel A. Weiss's to discern the Freudian pattern at the heart of the novel therefore seem strained, especially when we come to analyze Paul's character in Part Two.[34]

Especially damaging to a clear understanding of the narrative innovations Lawrence reaches toward in Sons and Lovers is the implication that the Freudian pattern competes against other psychologically realistic patterns here. One line of argument says that the details of Miriam's background confuse the issue: if the Oedipal pattern suggests that Paul's inability to love another woman derives from his mother's hold on him, as the novel makes obvious at times, then Miriam's inability to satisfy Paul because of her own inhibitions disrupts the Oedipal pattern, putting the blame on Miriam rather than on

34. Mark Schorer, "Technique as Discovery," in Tedlock (ed.), "Sons and Lovers": Sources and Criticism, 164–69; Frederick J. Hoffman, Freudianism and the Literary Mind (2nd ed.; Baton Rouge, 1957), 154; Daniel A. Weiss, Oedipus in Nottingham: D. H. Lawrence (Seattle, 1962), 32–68.

Mrs. Morel. "Thus," as Mark Spilka writes, "the chief 'split' between Paul and Miriam comes from the abstract nature of their love, and not from the mother's hold upon the young man's soul" and, Daniel J. Schneider argues, "the only adequate test of Paul's Oedipal problem would have been to confront him with a woman who, unlike Miriam and Clara, was well suited to him, thus showing that he could not love even the right woman."[35] This does not amount to a flaw, aesthetic or otherwise; it merely leaves us with two complementary patterns: Paul's psychological bond with his mother aborts future sexual relationships *and* Paul's dissatisfaction with Miriam derives from her psychological history, which the novel insightfully delineates. If there is a problem here, it may derive from the attempt to read Lawrence's psychological profile into the novel. Such an attempt asks us to compare Miriam with Jessie Chambers, her historical counterpart, and to come to the novel with conventional realism's demands, to see whether Lawrence isn't making her more spiritual than she was as a way of disguising his bond with his mother. The truth we are left with, however, is that Miriam is as spiritual as the novel makes her.

This is not to say that if we accept the novel on its own terms it offers no contradictions. Even if we allow that the Oedipal pattern need not be the center of our attention, that its importance can shift throughout the novel, becoming very important in assessing William's life and only intermittently important in assessing Paul's, a certain narrative confusion remains. The blurring of the Oedipal pattern that I just described is not the source but the symptom of the novel's philosophical confusion—a confusion that appears in the pattern of imagery encompassing darkness, sexuality, and death. In this confusion Lawrence is grappling with an emergent epistemology that changes the rules by which other selves are knowable. Louis Fraiberg's assessment comes closest to mine when he says, "The search for life and its meaning perversely becomes for Paul the inadvertent but welcome union with death, the obliteration of self. This is both a logical and fictional contradiction,

35. Mark Spilka, *The Love Ethic of D. H. Lawrence* (Bloomington, 1955), 66; Schneider, *The Artist as Psychologist,* 140.

and it prevents the book from achieving full aesthetic integration."[36] I do not believe that logical contradictions necessarily
prevent aesthetic integration. Any successful art influenced by
Christian theology uses logical contradictions to its advantage.
Fictional contradictions do emerge in Sons and Lovers, though,
and their hedging at the end stems from unfortunate shifts in
imagery.

Especially in Part One, the imagery of darkness takes on traditional Judaeo-Christian associations, representing fear, evil,
and mystery. When it images mystery, mystery is evil. Early on,
Mrs. Morel is associated with spirit and light, Mr. Morel with
darkness and mystery. Their courtship and marriage consist
largely in her attempts to bring him to light. We see him walking home from work with the other men "down the trough of
darkness formed by the path under the hedges" (SL, 6), and as a
miner he is associated with the earth's cavernous darkness. In
Paul's mind, though, the darkness represents threat. After the
family moves from the Bottoms, there is a menacing sense of
space and darkness associated with the household turmoil:
"Having such a great space in front of the house gave the children a feeling of night, of vastness, and of terror. This terror
came in from the shrieking of the [ash] tree [that Mr. Morel
loves] and the anguish of the home discord" (SL, 59). Although
on one occasion when Paul returns from work this ash tree becomes a friend to him, when the parlor is arranged for William's
wake it represents death's horrifying mystery: "Paul went to
the bay window and looked out. The ash-tree stood monstrous
and black in front of the wide darkness. It was a faintly luminous night. Paul went back to his mother" (SL, 138). She is his
light, his means of understanding, and she takes root in him.

Past this point the associations shift in important ways that
change our understanding of Paul, in spite of the novel's invita-
tion that we interpret his character through the terms established in William's characterization. At the end of Part One
William is called a prophet (SL, 141), but we can use William as
a paradigm only occasionally because the novel strains against

36. Louis Fraiberg, "The Unattainable Self," in Tedlock (ed.), "Sons and
Lovers": Sources and Criticism, 226.

repetition. Trying not to circle back on itself, it looks for new ways of seeing Paul and registers this search in the shift in the imagery pattern.

During his early courtship of Miriam, Paul thrives in her atmosphere of chivalry and spirituality, with his "passion for understanding" through which "her soul lay close to his" (*SL*, 173). But he soon tires of this and wants to enter a sexual relationship. To do this he feels he must challenge her religious beliefs, which are allied to light and order. Later on, in a letter he tells her, "In all our relations no body enters. I do not talk to you through the senses—rather through the spirit" (*SL*, 251). As his sex drive increases, "a new self or a new centre of consciousness" comes alive (*SL*, 252). At about this point the pattern of association linking sexuality to darkness and death emerges; only now, the pattern becomes the touchstone of full living and of the purest form of knowing other selves:

> "I like the darkness," he said. "I wish it were thicker—good, thick darkness."
> He seemed to be almost unaware of her as a person: she was only to him then a woman. She was afraid.
> . . . She relinquished herself to him, but it was a sacrifice in which she felt something of horror. This thick-voiced, oblivious man was a stranger to her. (*SL*, 286)

He is somewhat of a stranger to us, too. As this other self emerges, the criteria for knowledge and certainty shift: to know the new self is to submerge the old self and sometimes even obliterate it by moving it toward its own extinction in death. Hence, "This strange, gentle reaching-out to death was new to him" (*SL*, 287).

Paul's association with death is a logical contradiction, but not one that presents any aesthetic problems in itself: finding oneself by losing oneself is an established pattern in Western literature. When the pattern shifts unaccountably, then we have a fictional contradiction and an aesthetic flaw. Even this stage, however, where the darkness that threatened him and that was associated with his father becomes the image of his salvation, may not be problematic if we consider that Paul has, after all, grown up. As he reinterprets his experience, so must the narrative reinterpret the images that convey it.

In his subsequent affair with Clara, especially in the rendering of its dissolution and the simultaneous death of Paul's mother, the imagery pattern quickly shifts back unaccountably. At the beginning of Paul's affair with Clara, the darkness embodies his salvation and even hers to some extent. In one sexual encounter, they "know the tremendous living flood which carried them always, gave them rest within themselves. If so great a magnificent power could overwhelm them, identify them altogether with itself, so that they knew they were only grains in the tremendous heave that lifted every grass blade its little height, and every tree, and living thing, then why fret about themselves? . . . Nothing could nullify [their mutual verification], nothing could take it away; it was almost their belief in life" (*SL*, 354). With the exception of that last "almost," where the narrative hedges, this passage renders the sort of heightened experience that appears in the later novels. We are asked here to believe that this is not enough for Clara, even though "something great was there, she knew" (*SL*, 354). At the same time, certain objections Clara raises come across as all too reasonable. Unlike Miriam, she can enter this state of heightened consciousness with Paul, yet she wants her relationship to encompass Paul's social self as well. Unlike Miriam, who wanted Paul's spirit and social self at the cost of having a mutual sexual relationship, Clara wants the whole man. In her attempts at meeting in the social sphere of work, she wants to "smash the trivial coating of business which covered him with hardness, get at the man again" (*SL*, 351).

Since Clara knows yet rejects "so great a magnificent power," and since she nonetheless searches out the vital self buried under the social dressings, she comes across in the first instance as unreasonable for rejecting the relationship and in the second as reasonable for expanding its parameters. This novel will not let Clara win. The simultaneous end of the affair and the gradual death of Paul's mother, with its attendant imagery patterns, hardly make matters clearer.

At this stage we are to believe that Paul's affair with Clara is now not enough for him; the "tremendous living flood" which "nothing could nullify" becomes nullification itself. The imagery pattern comes to associate his relationship to his mother with darkness, sexuality, and death—all three holding little promise for redemption. At one point Paul dejectedly watches one of his dying mother's hairs as it "floated and was gone in the blackness of the chimney" (SL, 376). During this period, as his sexual interest in Clara wanes, his behavior with his mother becomes more explicitly sexual: "He kissed her again, and stroked the hair from her temples, gently, tenderly, as if she were a lover" (SL, 376). His father hardly ever visits her, and after she dies, he can scarcely look at her body. Paul, however, can; he triumphs over his father, virtually escorting his mother to her death by conspiring with his sister to administer the overdose of morphine. Paul's connection with the darkness now horrifies Clara: "Clara wanted to run. She looked round. There was the black, re-echoing shore, the dark sky down on her. She got up terrified. She wanted to be where there was light, where there were other people. She wanted to be away from him" (SL, 388). Now the darkness that held them draws them apart.

The end of the novel shows Paul drifting in this darkness that has become the cessation of life, not the image of incipient rebirth, yet at the same time the narrative hesitates to commit itself to this scenario. It has backed itself into a corner by shifting the imagery pattern from what it was during the heights of Paul's sexual experience with Clara to what it is at the end of his mother's life. The overwhelming evidence seems to be that Paul's future holds little hope: "There seemed no reason why [anything] should occupy the space, instead of leaving it empty," and "The realest thing was the thick darkness at night. . . . He wanted everything to stand still, so that he could be with [his mother] again" (SL, 410). The narrative no longer recognizes this darkness as the image of redemptive bliss. In the fourth poem in Lawrence's Ship of Death sequence, absence takes a similarly powerful hold:

> And everything is gone, the body is gone
> completely under, gone entirely gone.
> The upper darkness is heavy as the lower,
> between them the little ship
> is gone
>
> It is the end, it is oblivion.[37]

37. D. H. Lawrence, Selected Poems (New York, 1959), 142.

In that poem the darkness is not the end, but rather the occasion for the dawn, for new birth. *Sons and Lovers* offers a far more tentative outcome than does the *Ship of Death* sequence, yet its scenario, like the poem's, defies ordinary logic and psychological realism. If Paul's survival were unequivocal, he would be a Kurtz resurrected, but the novel makes this an extremely tenuous possibility, as if unsure of how Paul's new self could be imaged.

When he steps into this heart of darkness, Paul is the solitary inhabitant of a universe turned upside down: "Little stars shone high up; little stars spread far away in the flood-waters, a firmament below" (*SL*, 420). The narrative maximizes his solitude and disorientation as if to discover what would be left of Paul if everything were torn away. It nearly doubts itself— "Who could say his mother had lived and did not live?" (*SL*, 420)—as if to erase the psychological history that had given shape to Paul's old self. All that is left, though, is an oscillation that skirts along a series of connectives, qualifying the scene nearly into oblivion: "but yet," "and yet" (twice), and finally "but now." The first qualifying affirmation registers Paul's awareness of his body: "But yet there was his body, his chest, that leaned against the stile, his hands on the wooden bar. They seemed something." In the light of his relationship with Clara, this realization seems unpromising. The narrative's assessment of Paul's condition boils down to this: he is and he is not. "On every side the immense dark silence seemed pressing him, so tiny a spark, into extinction, and yet almost nothing, he could not be extinct"; he is, with everything else, even the stars, "at the core a nothingness, and yet not nothing" (*SL*, 420).

The narrative spins out in a series of oscillations that betray the incipient birth of a discontinuous self whose portrayal defies the sort of logic we are accustomed to finding in psychologically realistic portrayals. This discontinuous self—that other ego—is born from the conflict in *Sons and Lovers* between psychological realism and spiritual autobiography. Psychological realism makes the darkness Paul associates with sex an image of Paul's shame (*SL*, 345); spiritual autobiography makes it the occasion of supernal knowledge. This is not the first time this sort of conflict has appeared in the English novel. We run into something very similar in the complaints readers perhaps unfairly bring to Daniel Defoe's fiction, where expectations for emergent realism compete with the prerogatives of spiritual autobiography. Moll Flanders has no more trouble than St. Augustine in erasing her psychological history at the moment of her spiritual rebirth, nor does Richardson's Mr. B. Similarly, *Sons and Lovers* exhibits the logic of spiritual autobiography that G. A. Starr describes this way: "Between two successive episodes . . . a direct, causal connection may be altogether lacking; nevertheless they will be significantly related by virtue of having a common point of reference."[38] Unlike the later fiction, *Sons and Lovers* does not maintain a consistent attitude toward its reference point. Sometimes a drift toward death is a movement toward a more rewarding future; sometimes it admits of no future. *Sons and Lovers* wants it both ways.

The Other Ego: The Transindividual Self in *The Rainbow* and *Women in Love*

In *The Rainbow* Lawrence finds his bearings when he adjusts his narrative technique to accommodate his epistemological ideal for knowing other selves. In *Sons and Lovers* his emergent claims turn the paradoxes built into his ideal into fictional contradictions and, to some extent, aesthetic failure. His impulse to follow a single character through a causally linked set of psychological events moves that character to the margins of existence, where being and not being open up to each other and where we do not know what kind of self could survive such a crisis. After several drafts of *The Rainbow* Lawrence told Edward Garnett, "I don't think the psychology is wrong: it is only that I have a different attitude to my characters, and that necessitates a different attitude in you, which you are not prepared to give." Thus, we cannot "look for the development of the novel to follow the lines of certain characters: the characters fall into the form of some other rhythmic form." Where in *Sons and Lovers* Paul's psychological history needed to emerge from plausible causes that went back before his birth, in *The Rainbow* they follow a new pattern and do not try, and there-

38. G. A. Starr, *Defoe and Spiritual Autobiography* (Princeton, 1965), 43.

fore do not fail, to follow any other pattern. In this same letter Lawrence explains that he has discarded the "old stable ego" in search of another:

> You mustn't look in my novel for the old stable *ego*—of the character. There is another *ego*, according to whose action the individual is unrecognisable, and passes through, as it were, allotropic states which it needs a deeper sense than any we've been used to exercise, to discover are [*sic*] states of the same single radically unchanged element. (Like as diamond and coal are the same pure single element of carbon. The ordinary novel would trace the history of the diamond—but I say, "Diamond, what! This is carbon.") . . . Again I say, don't look for the development of the novel to follow the lines of certain characters. (*CL*, I, 282)

Lawrence's suggestion helps us come to terms with the difficulty of deciding who is, after all, the main character of *The Rainbow*. Although some commentators have little trouble deciding that Ursula is the main character, it has never been clear to me why she should be so designated. Through the first half of the novel she does not even appear, since she is not yet born. This differs from Sterne's project in *Tristram Shandy*, where the hero is unborn through a major portion of the novel, because Sterne's point is to reduce to absurdity the attempt to show every minute event that bears on the future development of character. Lawrence's outline of the preceding two generations of Brangwens, however, has no necessary—or better, no causal—bearing on Ursula's character. To suppose she is the main character would be to demand that the history preceding her have a contingent effect on what it is possible for her to become and achieve. If that were the point, the novel's first half would be a miserable failure. That is not its point: the connection between the earlier Brangwens and Ursula is not a linear, causal sequence in which Ursula's life has its separate place, defined by her personal characteristics and psychological history. Her mind is not a private arena. Beneath the "stable ego"— the individuated self—is the "other ego" that cannot be recognized by individual actions because this ego—a transindividual selfhood—passes beyond the boundaries between individuals. Thus, at the very deepest level of her experience Ursula is a continuous event in the Brangwens' collective identity. The same blood passes through them all.

This conception of *The Rainbow* perhaps explains why our experience of it does not meet our expectations for a family history.[39] While we are always aware in the back of our minds of the novel's historical sweep, there is nonetheless a timeless quality about each moment within that history. A sometimes unsettling interpenetration of the moment and the historical breadth often compensates for any loss of the ordinary dramatic conflict that more traditional presentations of family history employ. At any given moment in the narrative the reader is encouraged to feel that this moment is all, yet we keep moving on to another moment in the history. This technique bears on characterization and the way we know the people in the drama; it explains why we seem to have moved our interest so easily from one character to the next (considering the novel retrospectively) when in specific moments of our reading experience our attention was so wholly devoted to a single character. There is, for example, the rather offhand way the narration reports Lydia's death several years and several pages after she has been the focus of our attention: "[Ursula's] grandmother had been dead two years now" (*R*, 367). We are too involved in Ursula's struggles to care, and so, apparently, is the narrator. (Woolf uses the same technique when she literally brackets Mrs. Ramsay's death in a single sentence in *To the Lighthouse*.)

The sequence in which characters in *The Rainbow*'s family history come to the foreground is logical rather than causal; their relationships are not contingent. The personality of Anna is no more determined by the character of Tom and Lydia's marriage than Ursula's is by the character of Will and Anna's. Nor is the order random. If we step back from the individual characters, we discover a trajectory in the collective Brangwen identity: Tom and Lydia, though their lives are certainly not without conflict, present the exposition, the period of relative tranquility preceding the conflict that Anna and Will introduce; that is followed by Ursula, whose life is a compendium of conflict, climax, and resolution. Each character is a window on a larger identity. We recall that in Conrad the self is a sham because it is ultimately ungrounded and has no stability. In Lawrence the self is a sham exactly because there is a more

39. Kiely, *Beyond Egotism*, 104.

rudimentary self that is mingled with other selves in a collective unity.

Despite the wholeness in which separate characters are ultimately grounded in *The Rainbow*, Lawrence maintains character differentiation. As Julian Moynahan puts it, "If the essence of a character is carbon, then the essence of all characters is carbon."[40] If Lawrence's concern were exclusively with the carbon and never with its manifestations in diamond or other individuating states, then his fiction would not sustain any dramatic conflict. Not until we get to the later Woolf or to Samuel Beckett do we have the full thrust of interchangeable characters. That there is a family history at all in *The Rainbow* shows that Lawrence holds to a remnant of the linear plot and to ordinary character presentation. By placing his characters in specifiable positions within a family tree, he sets a limit upon his challenges to ordinary characterization. It is just that now the circle around the self is widened, drawn around the whole family.

In *Women in Love* the time scheme is contracted, and Lawrence therefore confronts slightly different representational challenges. He substitutes individual psychological development with counterpoint and uses traditional characterization in order to set up a contrast between object-bounded and boundless characters. Precisely those characters who are easiest to visualize are portrayed with more conventional novelistic methods. Gerald and Gudrun, in comparison with Ursula and Birkin, are not only easier to visualize but are also alienated from their deepest selves and therefore further away from fulfillment.[41] A passage from Lawrence's essay "[The Individual Consciousness v. the Social Consciousness]" helps explain the conceptual link between two seemingly unrelated issues: the debilitating effect of self-regard and the amenability of self-regarding characters to visual and object-bounded characterization: "The moment any individual creature becomes aware of its own individual isolation, it becomes instantaneously aware of that which is outside itself, and forms its limitations. That is, the psyche splits in two, into subjective and objective reality.

40. Moynahan, *The Deed of Life*, 41–42.
41. Miko, *Toward "Women in Love,"* 218.

The moment this happens, the primal Integral *I*, which is for the most part a living *continuum* of all the rest of living things, collapses, and we get the I which is staring out of the window at the reality which is not itself" (*P*, 761). By providing *certain* knowledge of and to Gudrun and Gerald, the novel establishes their object-boundedness and collapses their "primal Integral *I*." We can immediately picture Gerald's and Gudrun's physical features—his strong physical presence, her meticulous adornment.

Birkin and Ursula, however, are much harder to picture, and our difficulty in visualizing them is an important part of what they themselves are trying to achieve. In their early discussions Birkin explains to her that he wants to contact her not through visual experience (which Lawrence associates with mental knowledge) but rather through immediate (unmediated) contact, in which the moment of awareness excludes self-reflection. In her disarming response to his proposition, we still can see them as psychologically realistic characters. Birkin tells her,

> "I don't *want* to see you. I've seen plenty of women, I'm sick and weary of seeing them. I want a woman I don't see."
>
> "I'm sorry I can't oblige you by being invisible," she laughed.
>
> "Yes," he said, "you are invisible to me, if you don't force me to be visually aware of you. But I don't want to see you or hear you."
>
> "What did you ask me to tea for, then?" she mocked. (*WL*, 138–39)

When Birkin tells her, "I want to find you, where you don't know your own existence, the you that your common self denies utterly" (*WL*, 139), he is hardly clearer to her. It is difficult to imagine how such a relationship would fit into the plot of a realistic novel.

The central questions prompted by Ursula and Birkin's encounter are these: how would it be possible for them to know they had achieved such a relationship if one condition of the achievement is the impossibility of introspection? Furthermore, if the participants cannot know it, how can the reader? These questions are intimately connected with the problems of character differentiation and of immediate knowledge of other minds. What apparently Birkin and Ursula aim to achieve, and what Lawrence represents through them, is a mystic unity in which body and mind, and self and other, are one, hence Lawrence's portrayal of Birkin and Ursula's "mystically-physically satisfying" union in the "Flitting" chapter (*WL*, 306) as the melding of the two characters together. This portrayal requires a rather abrupt narrative shift. First, we have the sequence of causally related events—Ursula's announcement that she will marry Birkin, her father's anger over the abruptness of her announcement, her removal from her parents' home, and then her meeting with Birkin at his home. When Birkin takes Urusla in his arms, the narrative texture changes. As in *The Rainbow*, the narrator only briefly suggests their consummation. Then he begins to address the reader, whom he eventually posits as his lover:

> In the new, superfine bliss, a peace superseding knowledge, there was no I and you, there was only the third, unrealised wonder, the wonder of existing not as oneself, but in a consummation of my being and of her being in a new one, a new, paradisal unity regained from the duality. How can I say "I love you" when I have ceased to be, and you have ceased to be: we are both caught up and transcended into a new oneness where everything is silent, because there is nothing to answer, all is perfect and at one. Speech travels between the separate parts. But in the perfect One there is perfect silence of bliss. (*WL*, 361–62)

While the narrator addresses the reader, the description of Birkin and Ursula falls into the very "perfect silence of bliss" that characterizes their mingling. Seen from the outside, Ursula and Birkin would be two individuals together, but seen from the inside, from where the narrator's voice seems to emanate, they are one. The narrator gives a voice to the transindividual self, the primal I that renders the walls between individuals permeable, and speaks in and through Birkin and Ursula, who have at this moment dropped their stable egos. Where there is communion, there is no need for communication.

Lawrence does not sustain this tone, nor do Birkin and Ursula sustain this intensity of union. Through most of the novel they are two persons. However much Lawrence insisted upon portraying the "carbon" of the character, he was wary of the abstraction into which his characters might fall if they were sustained in that manner; he saw the novel as his opportunity to express the particular and the concrete, not the universal or the absolute. Precisely for this opportunity he admired the genre: "The novel is a great discovery: far greater than Galileo's telescope or somebody else's wireless. The novel is the highest form of human expression so far attained. Why? Because it is so incapable of the absolute. In a novel, everything is relative to everything else, if that novel is art at all. There may be didactic bits, but they aren't the novel."[42] In Lawrence the novel's insistence upon quotidian experience deconstructs abstract propositions—even his own.

The impossibility of making such unity present is betrayed in the novel's subtheme—Birkin's attraction for Gerald. The discarded outline of *Women in Love* tells us something about the novel as we have it in its final form. In its original conception the novel's plot achieved its principal momentum through Birkin's homosexual feelings for Gerald. The story depended on a sustained mind-body dualism; the homosexual plot advanced a purely physical relationship with Gerald that was a foil to the purely spiritual or intellectual relationship with Hermione: "It was the men's physique which held the passion and the mystery to him. The women he seemed to be kin to, he looked for the soul in them. The soul of a woman and the physique of a man, these were the two things he watched for, in the street."[43] Since in the novel as we have it Birkin searches for the unseeable dimension of Ursula and since he says elsewhere that sex is "such a limitation" (*WL*, 191), we could be led, in light of this sketch's dichotomy, to believe that the object of Birkin's quest is a wholly spiritual mingling with Ursula. That would not be the whole truth, however, either about the novel or about this sketch. Birkin's regard for Ursula actually repairs the mind-body schism; he does not pursue just half of her. In the preliminary sketch, though, Ursula has not entered the story. Hermione, not Urusla, is the rival of Gerald's claim on Birkin's attention.

In its present form *Women in Love* subdues the homosexual plot, possibly to accommodate Ursula in Birkin's view of love. Even though the homosexual plot is subdued in order to spotlight the nearly perfect relationship Ursula's introduction into

42. D. H. Lawrence, "The Novel," *Reflections on the Death of a Porcupine,* in Warren Roberts and Harry T. Moore (eds.), *Phoenix II: Uncollected, Unpublished, and Other Prose Works by D. H. Lawrence* (New York, 1978), 416.

43. D. H. Lawrence, "Prologue to 'Women in Love,'" in Roberts and Moore (eds.), *Phoenix II,* 104.

the novel makes possible, it nonetheless impairs the ideality (if ideality is even what was intended) of Ursula and Birkin's unity. Birkin's need to enter a relationship with Gerald competes with his relationship with Ursula.[44] At the end of the novel he tells Ursula that he needs a relationship with a man because he can find in it something that his relationship with a woman cannot provide. Ursula calls this "an obstinacy, a theory, a perversity" (*WL*, 473). The novel leaves us with an unresolved tension, which Lawrence allowed in order to suggest an ongoing conflict and to expose the limits of Birkin and Ursula's relationship. If we insist upon reading Ursula and Birkin as paragons of the Lawrencian ideal—a frequent misreading of the novel—then we will wholly overlook the real struggles that Lawrence means us to see—the struggles of Birkin and Ursula to overcome human limitations. Part of the limitation comes from their beginning as two separate persons. The conclusion of the novel, in suggesting Birkin's need for Gerald, betrays its representational limits. This is not an aesthetic flaw; it is the exposure of a logical impossibility. Just as direct presentation is beyond the capacity of any narration, so also is the presentation of the transindividual self. In order for it to be rendered knowable, that self must have boundaries somewhere. As it is, the narration can only imply its presence; it cannot illuminate that patch of darkness without pushing it away.

Birkin's need for Gerald betrays his separateness from Ursula because where Birkin and Ursula begin their relationship as sexual opposites, man and woman, and move toward a state of unity in which they are at once themselves and each other, Birkin and Gerald begin in physical unity, in the sense of sharing sexual identity. Since this physical unity Birkin desires is already a given of their identity, reveling in it is no more than an act of debilitating self-regard; it is only an imitation of the unity he can momentarily sustain with Ursula. Obviously, in Lawrence's view the latter is to be preferred because mystical-physical unity, which opposes self-regard, makes the boundaries between selves permeable. By contrast, Woolf goes a step further: for her, sexual identity is never a barrier, as it is for

44. Kiely, *Beyond Egotism*, 157–64; Vivas, *The Failure and Triumph of Art*, 267–68.

Lawrence, in the early stages of sexual relationships or in relationships between persons of the same sex. In Lawrence homosexuality is the pursuit of a sham-identity, and so Gerald and Birkin's relationship requires that Lawrence fall back on object-bounded characterizations.

Object-binding characterization, in Lawrence's view, not only prevents the narrator from seeing his characters but also prevents characters from knowing each other and thereby finding themselves. The same logic governs his portrayal of volition. There is a close connection between his view of character and his characters' problematic grapplings with the transindividual forces that work both through and around them. Lawrence establishes that connection in his essay on Benjamin Franklin, whom he sets up as the archetypal deliberate man. There he says: "We are only the actors, we are never wholly the authors of our own deeds or works. IT is the author, the unknown inside us or outside us. The best we can do is to try to hold ourselves in unison with the deeps which are inside us. And the worst we can do is to try to have things our way, when we run counter to IT, and in the long run get our knuckles rapped for our assumption."[45] His portrayal of volition has philosophical sources in his reading of Schopenhauer, for whom a cosmic, transindividual will generates man's highest aspirations. It also contributes to his experimental interest in literary realism, marking an important break from a basic psychological belief in the individuated will—a break which Bruce Johnson has discerned in Conrad.[46]

Ordinarily, realistic fiction maintains a division between the *res cogitans* and the *res extensa* by localizing volitional forces, so that it is reasonably certain what actions are intended, who intends them, and what actions are accidental. There is nothing new about Lawrence's placing volitional forces outside of his characters, who sometimes then seem to be carried along. Even within the generic context of the novel, which Georg Lukács describes as "the epic of a world that has been abandoned by God,"[47] naturalism, before and after Lawrence,

45. Lawrence, *Studies in Classic American Literature*, 20.
46. Johnson, *Conrad's Models of Mind*, 65–66.
47. Georg Lukács, *The Theory of the Novel: A Historico-Philosophical Essay on Great Epic Literature*, trans. Anna Bostock (Cambridge, Mass., 1971), 88.

portrays the individual's almost total inability to challenge the claims of the wholly external volitional forces around him. The world of Thomas Hardy's novels, for example, places the responsibility for all decisive events in the hands of either pure accident or a vaguely godlike but malicious presence. In both cases, the character has no controls over his future: Jude is carried along by a series of unlikely accidents, Tess Durbeyfield by the hauntings of "the President of the Immortals." To render volitional powers wholly outside the character, as Hardy and Conrad do, is still to specify them marginally, to say they are "out there," not "in here." Lawrence goes yet further by rendering that location ambiguous. "We are never wholly the authors" and "the unknown inside us or outside us"—these phrases from the essay on Franklin disperse such forces. In his fiction Lawrence similarly evades the localization of volitional forces, one more way in which he breaks down the boundaries between the subjective and the objective.

The work probably most explicitly concerned with the problem of volition is *Women in Love.* In this novel we find that just as those characters least worthy of penetrating the deeper mysteries of living are also most object-bounded in their characterization and are most frequently portrayed through quasi-symbols, so those characters who find it easiest to localize volitional forces inside or outside themselves are most excluded from the deed of genuine living. Gerald's whole life is a relentless struggle to take full control over his own actions, to render himself the supreme power over his workers, friends, and lovers. The often discussed incident in which he holds the Arab mare under his control with a "mechanical relentlessness" in front of a passing train most succinctly indicates his desire to bring all other wills under his control (*WL*, 104). His justification is what he calls the natural order of the world. As he explains it to Ursula, "It is more natural for a man to take a horse and use it as he likes, than for him to go down on his knees to it, begging it to do as he wishes, and to fulfil its own marvelous nature" (*WL*, 130). Gerald's absolute certainty that man's will is unequivocally distinguishable from animal will is the basis for his claim about the natural order.

The machine is Gerald's way of maintaining his control over man and beast alike. Between the mind and the world of objects that he hopes to subjugate Gerald positions the machine, which he worships for its inhuman capacity to mediate his control over the world: "He, the man, could interpose a perfect, changeless, godlike medium between himself and the Matter he had to subjugate. There were two opposites, his will and the resistant Matter of the earth" (*WL*, 220). In Gerald's dualistic view of the world, all human history dramatizes the imposition of man's will upon the world of matter and lower animals: "was not mankind mystically contradistinguished against inanimate Matter?" (*WL*, 221).

The distinction between self and world that Gerald maintains, and that is mediated only through the imposition of the machine as a surrogate for direct contact, is exactly what brings Gerald to destruction. Although he can distinguish himself from the world, he cannot, in certain moments, distinguish himself from the machine. The longer he sees himself as—to borrow Gilbert Ryle's famous phrase—a ghost in the machine, the harder it is for him to recognize his control over anything. As a mere ghost, he appears to himself in some moments to lack all presence; he becomes a nonentity: "And he went to the mirror. . . . He looked at his own face. There it was, shapely and healthy and the same as ever, yet somehow, it was not real, it was a mask. He dared not touch it, for fear it should prove to be only a composition mask. . . . He could see the darkness in [his eyes], as if they were only bubbles of darkness. He was afraid that one day he would break down and be a purely meaningless babble lapping round a darkness" (*WL*, 224–25). Gerald's heart of darkness is his buried living soul, which it would be his salvation to recognize. At this instant he strikes Kurtz's pose before Conrad's darkness, but in Lawrence, as Birkin and Ursula show, that darkness is his only hope. Through the very device by which he sought to impose his will upon the world— the machine—he becomes the ghost of his living soul, and as long as the soul that keeps him living is a horror, death is his only peace.

Birkin's and Ursula's ideas about volition, illustrated by their interpretations of Gerald's accidentally shooting his brother, explain their contrastingly greater potential for achieving a wholesome relationship. When he learns from Mrs. Crich that as a child Gerald had shot his brother, Birkin asks whether any action is really accidental. "Is every man's life subject to pure accident, is it only the race, the genus, the species, that has a universal reference? Or is this not true, is there no such thing as pure accident? Has *everything* that happens a universal significance? . . . He did not believe that there was any such thing as accident. It all hung together, in the deepest sense" (*WL*, 20). In concluding that there is no such thing as an accident, Birkin is far from solving the problem of agency. If there are no accidents, there are still the actors and the acted upon. Solving the riddle of agency by saying there are no accidents is like solving the riddle of the mind's relationship with the world by saying the world is all made up of idea. We are still left with the knowers and the known. Nor does Birkin's later discussion of victims and victimizers do much better in clearly distinguishing between the two: " 'No man,' said Birkin, 'cuts another man's throat unless he wants to cut it, and unless the other man wants it cutting. This is a complete truth. It takes two people to make a murder: a murderer and a murderee. And a murderee is a man who is murderable. And a man who is murderable is a man who in a profound if hidden lust desires to be murdered' " (*WL*, 27). As a way of sorting out the guilty from the innocent, this "complete truth" is complete nonsense. The idea here, though, is not to sort out responsibility, but to confuse it. If the self is going to achieve a full harmony with the life forces that run through and around it, we cannot reasonably expect to find a specification of agency, because it cannot be delimited.

Ursula shares Birkin's view, but she expresses it in a more presentable fashion. Although we have no certain way of knowing if Gerald regards his having killed his brother as an accident, we could safely guess that he does, for the least of Gerald's difficulties is sorting out his intentions from the forces that work outside him. Gudrun also interprets the incident as purely an accident. She defines murder by locating the intention to commit murder. Where Ursula, sharing Birkin's perspective, finds it difficult to sort out accidents from intentions, Gudrun does not:

> "Murder, that is thinkable, because there's a will behind it. But a thing like that to *happen* to one—"
> "Perhaps there *was* an unconscious will behind it," said Ursula. "This playing at killing has some primitive *desire* for killing in it, don't you think?"

"Desire!" said Gudrun, coldly, stiffening a little. "I can't see
that they were even playing at killing. I suppose one boy said to
the other, 'You look down the barrel while I pull the trigger, and
see what happens.' It seems to me the purest form of accident."

"No," said Ursula. "I couldn't pull the trigger of the emptiest
gun in the world, not if someone were looking down the barrel.
One instinctively doesn't do it—one can't." (*WL*, 42)

Gudrun can imagine a situation in which one boy pulled the
trigger of the gun he thought was empty because she herself
stakes her life—and finally Gerald's—upon her knowledge.
Ursula can stake nothing upon her knowledge, because in hers
there is no certainty.

The difficulty in knowing the difference between a person's
intended and unintended actions aggravates the problem of
knowing other minds. Knowing whether he is an intentional
killer makes a big difference in our estimation of Gerald. We
have no certain clues in the novel as to which explanation is
true, only the question and some speculation. This question is
especially important because our inability to answer it modifies our expectations for the novel's psychological realism. In
Sons and Lovers, the competition between spiritual autobiography's and psychological realism's standards for knowing and
revealing character yielded an unsettling tendency to change
the rules capriciously for the sake of an as-yet unspecified
metaphysic. In *The Rainbow* and *Women in Love*, that metaphysic emerges, lending aesthetic unity to the fiction by marrying Lawrence's spiritual and psychological interests.

Art and Imagination: *Women in Love* and "None of That"

Earlier I said that to read Lawrence sensitively we enter a con-
tract whose terms require that we accept his richly imaginative
vision so fully that it seems to be an undeniable reality; to do
otherwise is to hold oneself back. Perhaps the reason that Lawrence's fiction is so notoriously demanding is that it requires
that we give ourselves over to it completely—we must at least
momentarily embrace his vision as reality, because he did not
think his vision imaginative at all. Lawrence scarcely ever
speaks about his imagination (and I have so far not spoken
about it) because he has a puritanical contempt for that faculty.

For him it is only the most extreme solipsism; it models all the forms of self-reflexive knowledge we have considered.

Conrad shares Lawrence's distrust for the imagination, yet he embraces it because he sees no alternative: knowledge collapses into it, and all that is left is the chaotic void that threatens human existence—the heart of darkness. For Lawrence, however, there is an alternative to ordinary knowledge: direct knowledge, which is vital, instinctive, and incorrigible. Since imagination is only pernicious knowledge in its most dangerous form, it must be left behind; it is the mirror held up to the stable ego. In connection with Lawrence's view of imagination, we head into one of the most paradox-ridden issues in Lawrence: his assessment of art. Artist though he was, there always lingers behind in his efforts the glimpse of a puritan distrust for art. This paradox comes through most clearly in his portrayal of Gudrun and Loerke, artists in *Women in Love,* and in "None of That."

In Gudrun and Loerke, Lawrence contemplates the worst scenario for the artist's power. In the peculiar "Rabbit" chapter, where Gudrun watches Gerald subdue his sister Winifred's wildly kicking rabbit, Gudrun's reactions show how she uses Gerald to mediate her control over others the way Gerald uses the machine to mediate his. The machine is a greater threat to Gerald than Gerald is to Gudrun; at least Gerald can die and Gudrun be free of him, whereas the machine relentlessly continues in its mechanization. Gudrun stands at a further remove from the machine than Gerald does, and so the threat is less immediate to her, but she relishes power from a kind of mental distance. An artist to the core, she has a detached, aesthetic appreciation of her surroundings.

In her observations of Gerald's crucial actions—his domination over the mare and his restraining the angry rabbit (*WL,* 104–106, 233–34)—Gudrun observes the scene with a kind of relish prolonged by her feeling of detachment. She is both horrified and fascinated in both scenes: as long as she feels her immediate presence before a real occurrence, she is horrified; but as long as she is detached, she views it with pleasure, as though it were the subject for one of her works of art. Gudrun's capacity for aesthetically detaching herself from her surroundings is her indirect way of exerting her will.

The willful localization of volitional forces in the subject is conceptually linked with Gudrun's view of art, which appears at the end of the novel, where in her discussion of art with Loerke and Ursula she takes Loerke's side. When he shows the sisters his statue of the horse mounted by an adolescent girl, Ursula complains about the horse's stiffness, which suggests that his art has lost contact with the fluidity of life. Loerke defends his art this way: "'Wissen Sie,' he said, with an insulting patience and condescension in his voice, 'that the horse is a certain *form*, part of a whole form. It is part of a work of art, a piece of form. It is not a picture of a friendly horse to which you give a lump of sugar, do you see—it is part of a work of art, it has no relation to anything outside that work of art'" (*WL*, 420). Taking his side, Gudrun insists that her art is also a world apart: "My art stands in another world, I am in this world," she says (*WL*, 421). Ursula diagnoses their problem as a sickness and suggests that, far from reflecting another world, Loerke's art projects his true neurosis: "'As for your world of art and your world of reality,' she replied, 'you have to separate the two, because you can't bear to know what you are. . . . The world of art is only the truth about the real world, that's all—but you are too far gone to see it'" (*WL*, 422). "Art and Life were to them the Reality and the Unreality" (*WL*, 439) because art is their reality while life is only make-believe. Ursula's view of art corresponds to the premium Lawrence puts on narration as a form of direct presentation, because it models art's direct contact with life. In the opposing view Gudrun and Loerke express, the individual artist grants himself the Godlike power to re-create reality. Lawrence's puritan heritage is nowhere clearer than in his opposition to such a view, but even beyond his puritan distrust for artifice, Lawrence's objection stems from his insistence that no genuine and rewarding human effort can be so self-contained and self-justifying. An artist can no more be the source of his own world than the mind can be the object of its own knowledge or the self can be the source of its own existence. Instead, the power to create, for Lawrence as for Ursula here, moves *through* the artist. It is transindividual and dynamic, and the art it creates yields a truth that exceeds the powers of any one individual.

At the heart of this perspective is the view of imagination

Lawrence entertains in "None of That," which originally appeared in *The Woman Who Rode Away and Other Stories*
(1928). As few of Lawrence's works do, this story explicitly examines the imagination. It is not one of his best short stories;
at times it is far more schematic than dramatic. Aside from its
explicitly handling the topic of imagination, it is anomalous
in its narrative technique, which is intimately related to its
message.

"None of That" frames a narrative within a narrative. Our
immediate narrator is unnamed, and he reports a conversation
with Luis Colmenares, whom he runs into in Venice. In the conversation Colmenares tells the story of their common friend,
Cuesta, a Mexican bullfighter who has the power to see into
the innermost depths of an individual to that part of the self
that is beyond the personality and that is the deepest part of
everyone—the transindividual self:

> "It is strange that I have never seen eyes anywhere else like
> his. Did I tell you, they were yellow, and not like human eyes at
> all? They didn't look at you. I don't think they ever looked at any-
> body. He only looked at the little bit inside your body where you
> keep your courage. I don't think he could see people, any more
> than an animal can: I mean see them personally, as I see you and
> you see me. He was an animal, a marvellous animal. I have often
> thought, if human beings had not developed minds and speech,
> they would have become marvellous animals like Cuesta, with
> those marvellous eyes."[48]

He can see directly into others, and his power is therefore pure;
his is not, like Gerald Crich's, the power of the individual will
but of the transindividual self, whose strength is as incorrigible,
as we saw in *Women in Love*, as fate. His power is greater than
that of anyone else in the story, including the storyteller: to
those who do not share his power to penetrate, he retains a depth
that is always one step beyond their cognitive powers. When
he stands naked, "it seemed he would have many, many more
nakednesses before you really came to *him*" (*CSS*, III, 704).

The main subject of the story, however, is Ethel, the rich

48. D. H. Lawrence, *The Complete Short Stories* (3 vols.; New York, 1977),
III, 702–703. Subsequent page references to "None of That" are to this Penguin
edition (hereinafter cited parenthetically as *CSS*).

American woman to whom Colmenares introduces Cuesta in Mexico. She is Cuesta's antithesis; she meets his incorrigible physical power with her indomitable mental power—the power to translate the core of being into an imaginative vision. She has been married twice, and in her relationships with other men she has been able to keep a safe distance by translating them into her own imaginative terms: "It was like her lust for brocade and old chairs and a perfect aesthetic setting" (CSS, III, 706). In this respect she is like Gudrun, who exercises her will by creating self-contained aesthetic objects whose autonomy images her own solipsistic mental life. Like Ursula's before the end of The Rainbow, her knowledge of other persons is indirect, mediated by an abstraction her socially induced self-image shapes: "She could never go out without a man to stand between her and all the others" (CSS, III, 706). She uses men as Ursula used Skrebensky, to embody a social ideal by which alone she could contact others. When she first goes to Mexico, Ethel meets several romantic opportunities that she rejects; she discovers that the men do not really want her except as a mistress. "None of that" is her characteristic response, and she says it as though she were "hitting a mirror with a hammer" (CSS, III, 707), because part of her—her unrecognized identity—wants to break through her imagination, which does nothing but reflect her ego.

Her initial response to Cuesta proves that a part of her requires him. Because her urges are perverted by her imagination, her quest to know him is an attempt to control both their bodies with her imagination. When she first responds to Cuesta while watching him kill the bulls, the reversal in her psychological life is registered by the phrase "Ya es bastante! Basta!" (CSS, III, 713). "None of that" becomes "that's enough," because at this moment he has reached the part of her that her imagination cannot control: "'And she was trying to catch his look on her imagination, not on her naked inside body. And they both found it difficult. When he tried to look at her, she set her imagination in front of him, like a mirror they put in front of a wild dog'" (CSS, III, 174). Her knowledge of him is mediated, and Cuesta knows it.

During the early stages of their relationship, a translator mediates their conversations, much as Colmenares must mediate our knowledge of Cuesta because Cuesta's true character cannot be verbalized. He can express himself not through language but only by his immediate presence; otherwise, what he truly is would be distorted. This is the story of a conversation in which one man tells another the tale of a bullfighter and his lover, and this framed narrative reproduces the same sense that Cuesta's naked body produces—the feeling that there is a nakedness beyond the nakedness that is seen. The ultimate nakedness cannot be made present in the story, just as Cuesta's dark core cannot be presented, only sensed; no words can presume to shed light on it. Thus when Colmenares tells the narrator *about* Cuesta's final nakedness, he must fall back on an agreement with our narrator/listener: "Do you understand me at all? Or does it seem to you foolish?" The narrator/listener keeps the story moving and in a sense jumps the gap in Colmenares' description by registering his interest: " 'It interests me,' I said" (*CSS*, III, 704). He agrees to believe Colmenares at least long enough for him to go on with his story; otherwise, he could not maintain his interest. This agreement between the narrator/listener and the storyteller models the agreement between the reader and Lawrence, which demands that the reader give himself completely to the fiction.

Cuesta, sensing Ethel's desire to control him with her imagination, protects himself by erecting mediating barriers between himself and her. The translator is one such barrier; Cuesta himself "never once *spoke* to her—always spoke to his interpreter, in his flat, coarse Spanish." She can exercise her power, then, only when a translator is there. The only weak spot in Cuesta's armor is the topic of money, and he knows Ethel is rich: "He actually *had* no mental imagination. Talk was just noise to him. The only spark she roused was when she talked of money" (*CSS*, III, 716). After he arranges to meet her alone and there stages a gang rape, Ethel poisons herself and leaves him her fortune, as though to exercise one last hold on him.

Ethel had said that any woman can render herself immune to violations of her body, as long as the damage is not organic, by exercising her imagination. Thus when she speaks about a famous case of raped nuns, she says, "it was all nonsense that a woman was broken because she had been raped. She could rise above it. The imagination could rise above *anything*" (*CSS*, III, 711). Obviously hers could not after the rape in Cuesta's bedroom, for she had forewarned, "If my body is stronger than my imagination, I shall kill myself" (*CSS*, III, 718).

A narrative that lies beyond even the framed narrative would report the scene in the bedroom, but that is absent. We can have only indirect speculative knowledge about it, for Colmenares heard it from one of the men who raped her, and he was shot afterward. That absent narrative would tell us who won the battle. As it is, we have no way of knowing. Since Ethel killed herself, it seems obvious that she lost, but then we are left with the question of why Cuesta had her gang raped instead of raping her himself. If he was sexually incapacitated by her imaginative grip on him, a hold that uses money as its leverage, then he was defeated when she left her money to him. If his plan from the beginning, however, was to have her gang raped in order to protect himself from the imaginative power that he only sensed in her but to which he had not yet fallen victim, then Ethel was defeated. We cannot know the answer, because the answer is the unnarrated core of the story, a core like Cuesta's final nakedness that can never be verbalized.

The contest between Ethel and Cuesta is like the contest between the two halves of Lawrence's paradoxical character, the half that disdains the imagination and the half that is irrepressibly driven toward literary creativity. It is just as difficult to tell which half of Lawrence dominates as it finally is to tell whether Ethel or Cuesta wins out at the end. As Ethel willfully directs her imagination in order to capture Cuesta's vital power, so Lawrence directs his toward capturing the instinctive part of human experience that always runs a step ahead of the intellectual and literary drive to grasp and communicate it. If she loses, she is like the part of Lawrence that is in the grip of an imagination that can only pursue the world he wants to present but can never reach it.

These possibilities echo the two principal ways that literary history has viewed Lawrence so far: he is thought either to have discovered a direct line to the truth or to have been gripped by a diabolical imagination. Between these tiresome views there has been scarcely any middle ground, but Lawrence's place in literary history will not finally depend on whether he is a true or a

false prophet. It helps thus to remember Northrop Frye's observation about the criteria for evaluating literary utopias: the
question is not whether they are likely to exist, but whether
they are imaginatively conceivable.[49] Lawrence's achievement is
partly in the way he renders his vision imaginatively conceivable, for in his renderings lie the experimental contributions to
the novel engendered because he faced the representational
challenges that his epistemological ideals demanded.

49. Northrop Frye, "Varieties of Literary Utopias," *The Stubborn Structure*
(Ithaca, N.Y., 1970), 111–34.

3

VIRGINIA WOOLF

> Suppose the looking glass smashes, the image disappears, and the romantic figure with the green of forest depths all about it is there no longer, but only that shell of a person which is seen by other people—what an airless, shallow, bald, prominent world it becomes! A world not to be lived in.
>
> —Woolf
> "The Mark on the Wall"

Epitome and Inventory

In her thoughts about her craft, Virginia Woolf betrays two seemingly contradictory interests. One is in turning the novel's back on quotidian experience; the other is in capturing in the novel a reality more intimate and urgent than conventional modes of presentation have been able to render. Both of these interests are at the heart of her experiments in fiction and her contribution to the form of the novel. It was primarily the concern to take the novel beyond its mimetic features that first captured the attention of her critics, for she attacked head-on the conventions of social realism that had been in the mainstream of the English novel for the last two hundred years. The popular novelists of her day—John Galsworthy, Arnold Bennett, and H. G. Wells—were regarded as skillful craftsmen precisely because they were capable of drawing lifelike characters who lived in lifelike settings. In both her literary criticism and her experimental fiction, Woolf challenged her reading public's assumptions about what constituted realism. Her achievement was not simply to muffle realism; she reconstituted it.

More recent criticism especially has recognized Woolf's fundamental concern with the balance between the rival claims of reality and the imagination. Undoubtedly arising out of this climate in Woolf criticism, there has been a closer examination of her sources in philosophical realism. G. E. Moore's realistic epistemology, and not just his ethical philosophy, seems a more likely source than the idealistic models of consciousness advanced by John McTaggart and Henri Bergson. The relative merits of these two lines of influence have been examined carefully, but unfortunately according to a model of philosophy's relationship to literature that makes the appearance of one line of influence the basis for denying the viability of the other. According to that model, if *To the Lighthouse* betrays the author's philosophical realism and thus the influence of G. E. Moore, then the influence of the idealist Cambridge philosopher McTaggart in that same work, or perhaps in any other, is a moot point at best.

By employing the term *metatheory*, I hope to adjust this model. It is unquestionably important that we ascertain the degree of her exposure to the different influences in the Bloomsbury circle. We are left, however, with the embarrassing fact that Woolf's novels set forth a mixture of contradictory epistemological views, and yet this mixture is central to her place in literary history. The epistemological monism and philosophical idealism of McTaggart and the realism of G. E. Moore are both relevant to Woolf's fiction and to its place in the history of the novel, which accommodates philosophical contradictions. However sharply she differs from them in other respects, in combining the claims of epistemological dualism and monism Woolf takes her place with Conrad and Lawrence in changing the direction of the English novel.

Moore's philosophy is probably more thoroughly ingrained in Woolf's thinking than is anyone else's, and consequently she is fundamentally realistic in her thoughts about and portrayals of the mind's relationship with externality. Nonetheless, there are moments in her fiction when the realistically conceived boundaries between subjects and objects and between one mind and another collapse. Furthermore, these counterrealistic moments exceed even the idealistic claims of McTaggart. They are also at the core of Woolf's experimental contribution to the English novel.

Woolf herself had ambivalent feelings toward the claims of realism. She often had to confront the accusation that in her disinclination to animate living characters in realistic social settings, she was actually betraying a fundamental weakness in her skills. Her private reactions to such accusations were different from her public ones. In the private voice she reserved for her diary, she would characteristically acquiesce. There her insecurities would surface. After *Jacob's Room* appeared in 1922, Arnold Bennett wrote that she was incapable of creating a lifelike character.[1] In her diary she responded, "I daresay its [*sic*] true, however, that I haven't that 'reality' gift. I insubstantise, wilfully to some extent, distrusting reality—its cheapness. But to get further. Have I the power of conveying the true reality? Or do I write essays about myself?"[2]

Her essays tell a different story about her interest in and possession of the gift of conveying reality. In her public voice, instead of acquiescing she claims that if the novel is to have a future as an artistic genre, it must learn to rid itself of its blind commitment to representing quotidian experience. It can do this, she suggests, by taking on the responsibilities formerly accorded only to poetry. In her estimation, the novel would then become to the twentieth century what poetry had been to the nineteenth. In "Phases of Fiction" (1929) she says, "The novel, it is agreed, can follow life; it can amass details. But can it also select? Can it symbolize? Can it give us an epitome as well as inventory? It was some such function as this that poetry discharged in the past."[3] In asking the novel to epitomize, Woolf invites into the genre a form of abstraction that can potentially arrest the narrative momentum ordinarily associated with realistic fiction—the push and pull, the chains of causes and effects that the representation of daily life necessitates. Lawrence also introduces epitome into his realistic narratives: when he portrays "mystical-physical" consummations or uses what we have identified as constitutive scenes, he epitomizes in single moments the meaning of the whole narrative. These moments seem to stand above or outside the narrative, yet they are pre-

1. Arnold Bennett, "Is the Novel Decaying?" *Cassell's Weekly*, XXVIII (March, 1923), cited in Anne Olivier Bell (ed.), *The Diary of Virginia Woolf* (5 vols.; London, 1977–84), II, 248n.

2. Bell (ed.), *The Diary of Virginia Woolf*, II, 248. Subsequent page references appear after the title *Diary*, hereinafter cited parenthetically.

3. Virginia Woolf, *Collected Essays* (3 vols.; London, 1966), II, 102. Subsequent page references to this collection are hereinafter cited parenthetically as *CE*.

sented as parts of the whole causally linked sequence of events. Reliance on epitome introduces the representational challenges Woolf describes in "The Art of Fiction" (1927), where she sardonically recognizes that "the story might wobble; the plot might crumble; ruin might seize upon the characters. The novel, in short, might become a work of art" (CE, II, 55). In an age when narrative had almost wholly disappeared from serious poetry, she invited poetry into the novel and thus reacquainted us with a challenging use of language. She asked language at once to epitomize and to inventory, to transform the accidental into the essential, to make a miracle out of a moth. The English novel already had its poets: Emily Brontë had made her mark; and Woolf was not transporting from the French novel anything that hadn't already found its way into English fiction by way of Conrad. The lyrical intensity of Woolf's voice, however, is different in degree if not in its essential character.[4]

Woolf was also introducing into the novel an emphasis that rendered the characters' environment subordinate to their mental lives. Its effect is to detach the character from the particulars of his surroundings and to make his mentation valuable in itself and the primary justification for rendering his environment, thus modifying the psychological realism embedded in the tradition of the novel. Ordinarily, psychological complexity, except in rare examples, emphasizes not only private deliberation but also the decisive actions that arise out of deliberation; but Woolf's psychological details are often conveyed for their own sakes. They are supreme and incorrigible values—like Moore's "good." To display them as unquestionable values, Woolf often detaches her characters from the social and moral schemes against which we are accustomed to measuring characters. This detachment has a singular effect on her readers: we ourselves seem to be transferred from an intersubjectively verifiable realm to one in which experience cannot be firmly judged on common moral or metaphysical grounds. What characters do they simply do, and what is simply is. As Woolf suggests, this incorrigible realm has closer affinities to the worlds of music and mathematics than it does to our daily experience be-

4. See Ralph Freedman, *The Lyrical Novel: Studies in Hermann Hesse, André Gide, and Virginia Woolf* (Princeton, 1963).

cause the relationship between its parts is not causal but formal and logical, internal to the work itself and not in accordance with an exterior model. Precisely in these terms does she describe the audience's reaction when it is confronted with a genuine work of art and not just an "inventory novel." In "Phases of Fiction" she says,

> [W]e get another pleasure which comes when the mind is freed from the perpetual demand of the novelist that we shall feel with his characters. By cutting off the responses which are called out in the actual life, the novelist frees us to take delight, as we do when ill or travelling, in things in themselves. . . . Then we see the mind at work; we are amused by its power to make patterns; by its power to bring out relations in things and disparities which are covered over when we are acting by habit or driven on by the ordinary impulses. It is a pleasure somewhat akin, perhaps, to the pleasure of mathematics or the pleasure of music. (*CE*, II, 82)

In this incorrigible realm, where experience of the world's laws is heightened and direct, are placed the characters and readers of the genuinely artistic novel. This is a quasi-ideal realm where knowledge is unmediated and the mind is directly related to the object of its knowledge. This realm characterizes what Woolf calls "the moment"—that instant when the self comprehends both itself and its surroundings so fully that no further readjustment of perspective seems either necessary or possible. In life these moments of reconciliation are fleeting; that is why they are called moments. In art they are arrested as a perpetual possibility of experience, and therefore they are always one step beyond actuality. This is true in Woolf's fiction, where we always have one foot in a realistic world, because the moment that lifts us out of our realistic perspectival limits is almost always possible, not actual. When the moment is presented as actual—when characters are suddenly granted a total view that resolves the particles of experience in a homogeneous perspective—even then it is, for the reader, only a possible experience.

That the moment is only a possible experience does not discredit its role in our experience of the novels. It is not just possible; it is possible in a profound sense that my attaching the word *perpetual* is meant to convey. Because the possibility is perpetual, it acquires a spatial and temporal perdurability that in ordinary experience only our ideas of space and matter share. It is worth noting J. S. Mill's analogous theory that our concept of matter is founded upon what he calls permanent possibilities of sensation. Just as in Woolf's fiction the transcending of knowledge's limits is always a latent possibility in the realistic world her fiction presents, so in Mill's view our idea of matter is acquired not from actual sense experience but from our notion of what it is possible to sense: "My present sensations," he says, "are generally of little importance, and are moreover fugitive: the possibilities, on the contrary, are permanent, which is the character that mainly distinguishes our idea of Substance or Matter from our notion of sensation."[5] The analogy is reversible: just as in Mill this substance right outside of sensation is the rudimentary stuff out of which all things are made, so in Woolf is the substance of the vision a momentary gathering of each into all. Woolf thus lends to the imagination a power as great as the one Mill lent to the rational mind in making it the seat of the most fundamental recognition—that matter exists, that the universe is made out of something. The imagination envisions possibilities that Woolf renders as permanent possibilities; in so doing, she assigns to the imagination the power to comprehend reality as it "truly is," beyond the mind's realistically defined perspectival limits, according to which the vision is never actual. Though she shares with Conrad and Lawrence profound doubts about the mind's power to know reality, she empowers the imagination, as Conrad did and as Lawrence would not consciously do, to repair the mind's cognitive limits.

More directly influencing Woolf's motivations for and technical innovations in portraying the moment in fiction were Roger Fry's aesthetic theories, especially those he outlined in his "Esssay on Aesthetics" (1909). Roger Fry was, of course, a close friend of Woolf's and a member of the Bloomsbury Group. Near the end of her life, she would write his biography. The epistemological implications of his aesthetic theories had at least as much effect on her as did the theories of Moore and

5. John Stuart Mill, *An Examination of Sir William Hamilton's Philosophy* (Toronto, 1979), 180. Vol. IX of *Collected Works of John Stuart Mill*, 21 vols.

McTaggart.[6] Especially in her insistence that the artistic novel help the reader leave behind the responses that are called forth in daily life, Woolf borrows heavily from Fry's theories of pictorial art. The detachment from quotidian experience that she urges is analogous to what Fry calls an "absence of responsive action." He illustrates his point by asking us to consider the difference between what we would observe as passengers at a train station and what we would observe if the same scene were presented to us in a cinematographic image while we were reposing privately. He suggests that when we are actually present, we are caught up in the scene; we would be concerned with luggage and seats, and we would not have the presence of mind to observe the same details about the people around us. Viewed from a reposeful perspective, however, the same scene would be transformed: "It then, at once, takes on the visionary quality, and we become true spectators, not selecting what we will see, but seeing everything equally, and thereby we come to notice a number of appearances and relations of appearances, which would have escaped our notice before, owing to that perpetual economising by selection of what impressions we will assimilate, which in life we perform by unconscious processes."[7] From a detached vantage point, we are able to minimize our habits of selection. In her application of Fry's concept of responsive action to the novelistic technique of characterization, Woolf steadily pushes us away from the habits of selection that we employ in our daily lives and that we bring to our experience of the novel—habits that have been only reinforced by the portrayal of conventional reality in nineteenth-century fiction and its early twentieth-century imitations.

Thus far I have emphasized Woolf's interest in cleansing the novel of its mimetic features. Sometimes thinking herself unable to represent reality and at other times emphasizing poetic models for prose fiction, epitome rather than mere inventory, she seems to move toward an ideal whose realization would

6. Leon Edel, *Bloomsbury: A House of Lions* (Philadelphia, 1979), 162; J. K. Johnstone, *The Bloomsbury Group* (London, 1954); John Hanley Roberts, "'Vision and Design' in Virginia Woolf," *PMLA*, LXI (1946), 835–47.

7. Roger Fry, *Vision and Design* (New York, 1937), 25–26.

perhaps be the utterances of a single lyrical voice. The lyrical impulse is an important part of her experimental interest, but it is not the whole. The thrust of her objection to the novel's inventory of reality is not primarily to the representation of reality itself, but rather to the conventional manner of apprehending that reality. In a sense, her concern is not simply to pass a veil before her reader's eyes, but also to lift the veil; she wants her reader to see reality as though for the first time.

This concern helps explain her objection to the modes of radical subjectivity she sees in the work of James Joyce and Dorothy Richardson. In the earliest planning stages of *Jacob's Room*, she resolved to avoid falling into what she called "the damned egotistical self"; she asks, "Is one pliant & rich enough to provide a wall for the book from oneself without its becoming, as in Joyce & Richardson, narrowing & restricting?" (*Diary*, II, 14). The narrow view refers specifically to the stream-of-consciousness technique used in the final chapter of *Ulysses*. Woolf herself avoided the same kind of stream-of-consciousness technique, which plunged the reader wholly into a particular subjectivity. Usually in her fiction there is an omniscient narrator who retains a wider perspective even while reporting the experiences of single characters.[8] Woolf followed *Ulysses* with interest when the *Little Review* published it serially. She admired it for its departures from the norms of Edwardian fiction, but she had more complaints than praise. She particularly objected to its tendency to shut the reader within a narrow perspective. In her essay "Modern Fiction" (1919), she asks: "Is it the method that inhibits the creative power? Is it due to the method that we feel neither jovial nor magnanimous, but centred in a self which, in spite of its tremor of susceptibility, never embraces or creates what is outside itself and beyond?" (*CE*, II, 108). It is doubtful that she read Joyce patiently. Even if we grant that *Ulysses* anchors us to a subjectivity in certain moments, we can hardly imagine a narrator with a more capacious mind than the one this novel presents to us. What is more important here than the accuracy of Woolf's observations

8. James Naremore, *The World Without a Self: Virginia Woolf and the Novel* (New Haven, 1973), 64–75.

is their indication of her ongoing and genuine interest in the genre's capacity to represent reality *as it is.*

To portray reality as it is means to go beyond particular subjective apprehensions of it, or at least to seem to do so. It is to posit a reality that exists independently of anyone's observation of it, and this Woolf does. For all her interest in portraying a character's perceptions, she is also concerned to portray the character himself—as he is and not merely as he is seen either by himself or by anyone else. In this she is like almost any eighteenth- or nineteenth-century novelist. Her essay "Mr. Bennett and Mrs. Brown" (1924) closely examines what she calls "character in itself" (*CE*, I, 321), by which she means that core of the self that eludes the grasp of conventional novelistic tools, especially those of the Edwardians—Wells, Bennett, and Galsworthy. Her essay uses a fictional incident in which two Edwardian novelists observe Mrs. Brown in a railway carriage, but neither Wells nor Bennett is able to capture the real Mrs. Brown before she gets off at the next stop. The incident is designed to illustrate that what we mean by character is a convention, and she goes on to say that the English reading public is so suggestible to these conventions that it would believe all women have tails and all men have humps if its novelists repeatedly told them so (*CE*, I, 332). Her point is that there are, on the one hand, our conventional manners of seeing and, on the other, the objective correlatives of our subjective apprehensions—the character or thing in itself—which the novelist must always adjust his tools to capture but which he never will. Life outruns art.

The nonrepresentational characteristics of Woolf's fiction, which make her art seem more in accordance with the claims of idealism than of realism, are her way of registering the inevitable sense of loss that accompanies the attempt to make art represent life. Her struggle in this endeavor might be considered a covert impulse to make life more like art, but in any case, she always recorded and recognized the distance between her imagination and reality. In her best fiction, she does two things at once: she registers, within her novels, the distance between her aesthetic vision, which resolves disjunctions, and the reality outside; at the same time, she uses her art to effect a synthesis that she did not believe existed anywhere but in art and in the imaginative visions that are the motive for art. These two purposes most plausibly explain her novels' tendency to embody at once dualistic and monistic models of the mind's relationship to externality. In Lawrence's novels, both monistic and dualistic models also appear, but there the imagination inhibits the subject-object synthesis, whereas in Woolf's fiction precisely the imagination produces that synthesis. For Lawrence, when the synthesis is effected, the novel tries to banish its status as a product of the imagination and, turning away from the imagination, which inhibits unmediated connection, opens out toward the reality beyond all mentation. For Woolf, on the other hand, when the synthesis is effected, the novel turns inward upon itself and away from the disjunctive reality outside. Like Fry, she struggled to make art produce a harmony in life that she could hear only in art, and like him she could realistically appraise the alienation of the mind from its surroundings. As Fry puts it, "Nature is heartlessly indifferent to the needs of the imaginative life; God causes His rain to fall upon the just and upon the unjust."[9]

More clearly than Conrad's or Lawrence's, Woolf's novels follow chronologically along a line of artistic development intimately connected to the epistemological metatheories her novels gradually develop. For that reason, we begin with *Jacob's Room* and end with *Between the Acts*, analyzing in each work the epistemological implications of the narrator's relationship with the characters as well as the characters' relationships with each other. From novel to novel Woolf shows an increasing dissatisfaction with the epistemological claims of philosophical realism, whose boundaries the realistic novel customarily observes, and so she gradually transgresses. But even in the culmination of her experimental interests, in *The Waves*, she betrays her recognition of the mind's boundaries that real life upholds and that only art can render permeable. By making this recognition felt in her novels, she takes her place within the realistic tradition of the genre, but the degree of her dissent sends irrevocable shock waves ahead of her.

9. Fry, *Vision and Design*, 39.

The Shadow of Doubt: The Protagonist as Cipher in *Jacob's Room*

Jacob's Room is centrally concerned with the problem of knowing other minds. In literary realism this problem appears in the relationships between characters who must contend with perspectival limitations that profoundly affect their lives. In philosophical realism this problem emerges mainly from the Cartesian assumption that introspection affords privileged knowledge, that I can know myself better than anyone knows me; after all, who is closer to my thoughts than I am? Philosophers in the twentieth century, however, have begun to dismiss this as an artificial problem. Among others, Ludwig Wittgenstein has argued that the problem of knowing other minds can be approached if we clarify our thinking about language so that we do not lend absolute priority to first-person statements and then deduce that, since we know our own minds best, third-person statements are intrinsically more problematic. Woolf's later fiction lessens the problem of knowing other minds for reasons that also discredit specific Cartesian assumptions.[10]

In literary realism the problem of knowing other minds inheres in the characters' relationships, not in the disembodied narrator's knowledge of characters. There direct apprehension of characters' thoughts gives us no pause because the conventional novel rarely brings such knowledge into question; a reader's questioning such knowledge would impose from the outside a demand for explanation that the novel has no obligation to meet. Omniscient narrators' direct knowledge of characters' minds is a given just as knowledge of other minds is a given in philosophical realism, which assumes that mediated knowledge is usually reliable.

10. My discussion of the problem of other minds is indebted to, among others, G. E. Moore, "The Nature of Reality of Objects of Perception," *Philosophical Studies*, 31–96; P. F. Strawson, *Individuals: An Essay in Descriptive Metaphysics* (London, 1959), 87–116; H. H. Price, "Our Evidence for the Existence of Other Minds," *Philosophy*, XIII (1938), 425–56; Stuart Hampshire, "The Analogy of Feeling," *Mind*, LXII (1952), 1–12; Norman Malcom, "Knowledge of Other Minds," *Knowledge and Certainty*, 130–40; Moritz Schlick, "Meaning and Verification," in Herbert Feigl and Wilfrid Sellars (eds.), *Readings in Philosophical Analysis* (New York, 1949), 146–70.

Jacob's Room considers knowing other minds an enormous problem, but if it explored the problem only through inter-character relationships, it would probably not contribute much to Woolf's experimental interests. It *is* experimental, though. It deflates conventional realism's assumptions that other minds are knowable, even to nonparticipating narrators, by sifting the story through the mind of a narrator who doubts both the reality of the world she looks out upon and the powers she must rely on to give it order. When Woolf makes doubt the starting point for an omniscient narrator's knowledge, she reduces to absurdity a basic assurance literary realism gave itself when it allowed omniscient narrators direct and indubitable knowledge against which characters' knowledge could be tested. The result is a relentless display of the narrating mind's failure to apprehend others' experiences. The work that is immediately suggested by association is Sterne's *Tristram Shandy*, since in that novel, too, a philosophically realistic model of knowledge is taken to its absurd limits. There, associationist psychology becomes the most extreme solipsism; in *Jacob's Room* the intersection of philosophical and literary realism, which ordinarily provides the narrator with an unproblematic view of his characters, renders the main figure an enigma.

Because of the things that make it unique among Woolf's novels, *Jacob's Room* is misjudged because the reader finds it difficult to make a distinction between the novel as a story of failure and the novel as itself a failure.[11] As long as we can see it as an ironic commentary upon its own methods, we can appreciate what it sets out to do. Admittedly, though, there are whole passages where the sheer tedium of the narrator's insistence upon her own failure to tell the story makes it difficult to make the distinction. Although *Jacob's Room* does not, therefore, sustain the same level of excellence as do her subsequent major novels, it nonetheless provides important insights into those later works. Furthermore, we are already familiar with narrators for whom characters are enigmatic: precisely these limitations, imposed in realistically conceived models of knowl-

---

11. See Josephine O'Brien Schaefer's evaluation of the novel's last chapter in *The Three-Fold Nature of Reality in the Novels of Virginia Woolf* (Folcroft, Penn., 1969), 80.

edge, prevented Marlow from comprehending Jim, or Birkin and Ursula from consistently understanding each other. Conrad and Lawrence both confronted a sense of cognition's failure, and until they could find their way through the space between knower and known, they were, as Woolf is in *Jacob's Room*, at a loss to provide the reader with as clear a sense of what these characters were really like as he might demand from conventional realistic novels. *Jacob's Room* is, as one critic puts it, a novel in search of a character.[12]

The narrator straightforwardly examines these problems in the opening of *Jacob's Room*'s third chapter. The dramatic situation here is remarkably similar to that posited in "Mr. Bennett and Mrs. Brown": Jacob enters a railway carriage and seats himself near a woman he has never met. In this scene we enter the mind of the woman, Mrs. Norman, where a contest to know who Jacob is takes place. The contending forces are her previous knowledge of young men who look like Jacob and her immediate confrontation with him in a defensive frame of mind. Both her prejudices and her defensiveness prevent her from knowing who Jacob really is.

Initially Mrs. Norman's defensiveness renders her too preoccupied with herself to do anything that would acquaint her with Jacob. In case he attacks her, she has a strategy: "She would throw the scent-bottle with her right hand, she decided, and tug the communication cord with her left."[13] She warns him that this is a no-smoking compartment, hoping to discourage him from seating himself at all, but Jacob neither smokes nor attacks her. At this point the narrator takes the opportunity, in a manner that becomes familiar throughout the novel, to indicate the larger, more general reasons for Mrs. Norman's errors in judging Jacob's character: "Nobody sees any one as he is, let alone an elderly lady sitting opposite a strange young man in a railway carriage. They see a whole—see all sorts of things—they see themselves. . . . Mrs. Norman now read three pages of

12. S. P. Rosenbaum, "The Philosophical Realism of Virginia Woolf," in Rosenbaum (ed.), *English Literature and British Philosophy* (Chicago, 1971), 326.

13. Virginia Woolf, *Jacob's Room* (New York, [1959]), 30 (in the same volume with *The Waves*). Subsequent page references to this novel (hereinafter cited parenthetically as *JR*) are to this edition.

one of Mr. Norris's novels. Should she say to the young man (and after all he was just the same age as her own boy): 'If you want to smoke, don't mind me'? No: he seemed absolutely indifferent to her presence . . . she did not wish to interrupt" (*JR*, 30–31; marks of ellipses in the original). Not only does her defensiveness prevent Mrs. Norman from knowing Jacob well enough to predict what he will do in even the next few minutes, but her assumptions about young men she has heard or read about make her anticipate danger: "it is a fact that men are dangerous" (*JR*, 30). Her habits of thought are no doubt acquired from the Norris novel she reads. In an instance of dramatic irony, thus, she deflates the absolutist privilege of omniscient narrators, for whom a fact can be a fact. Later, in "Phases of Fiction" Woolf would place W. E. Norris among those she facetiously called the "Truth-Tellers." With Norris in mind she says, "it is the mark of the second-rate writer that he cannot pause here or suggest there. All his powers are strained in keeping the scene before us, its brightness and its credibility. The surface is all; there is nothing beyond" (*CE*, II, 61).

In light of this observation we can see at least one more way in which the carriage scene comments on the conventions of realism, for here the narrator does nothing if not pause and suggest. Hardly anything else occurs, and the incident has no direct bearing on the rest of the story except to show us how Jacob got to Cambridge. For all it tells us about Jacob, it might have been skipped over entirely: it is a meditative passage like those Woolf calls for, but it tells us more about the narrator than it does about her character.

The scene's meditative quality, however, makes it a continuation of, rather than a corrective for, the weaknesses that Woolf complains about. The irony is that if the weakness of conventional realism is its tendency to build details upon fundamentally unknown characters, then this scene perpetuates the shortcomings of the fiction it tries to improve upon. If we had to decide which of the two characters we felt we knew better on the basis of this scene alone, we would probably choose Mrs. Norman. We have less access to Jacob's thoughts about this woman and about himself than we do to the thoughts of the woman who watches him. Mrs. Norman's personality is, at least, a set of actual characteristics, while Jacob has only a set of possible ones. In this, the carriage scene is not at all an isolated case; throughout *Jacob's Room* we have the haunting sense that we know more about the people around him than we do about Jacob himself.[14] The titular hero is a cipher; all the surrounding characters are not.

We also know more about Jacob's mother, Mrs. Flanders, than we do about Jacob. The second chapter opens with a series of random and unidentified voices that communicate a sense of pity for her. The speakers wonder, for example, why she does not remarry. One speaks of a Captain Barfoot who regularly calls on her on Wednesday nights but never brings his wife. These and other details add up to a characterization of Mrs. Flanders that even the narrator wants to be certain we catch. In summing her up, the narrator does more to build up Mrs. Flanders' character than she ever does to build up Jacob's: "Elizabeth Flanders, of whom this and much more than this had been said and would be said, was, of course, a widow in her prime. She was half-way between forty and fifty. Years and sorrow between them; the death of Seabrook, her husband; three boys; poverty; a house on the outskirts of Scarborough; her brother, poor Morty's downfall and possible demise—for where was he? what was he?" (*JR*, 15). Although we never feel that the picture of Mrs. Flanders we build out of these details is complete, we feel we know her; we feel it is possible to know her. But the details of Jacob's life—the life that would seem to be the central one—do not add up to a coherent whole. The reader is brought to share in the same exasperation that the narrator feels in attempting to make sense of Mrs. Norman's perceptions of Jacob: "One must do the best one can with her report. Anyhow, this was Jacob Flanders, aged nineteen. It is no use trying to sum people up. One must follow hints, not exactly what is said, nor yet entirely what is done" (*JR*, 31).

Our exasperation is most intense whenever the narrator's refusal to sum up Jacob is handled in isolation from either her own attempts to sum up surrounding characters or other characters' attempts to sum up Jacob, for then the refusal seems willful and irritating. At one point, for example, we are afforded

---

14. James Hafley, *The Glass Roof: Virginia Woolf as Novelist* (Berkeley, 1954), 52.

a glimpse of Jacob in another student's room at Cambridge as we sit with the narrator just outside the window. The effect is almost that of a dumb-show, for though we hear Jacob's laughter and sense his rebuking of another student in a heated discussion, all the details—details, such as the subject of the discussion, that would make the scene dramatically interesting—are conspicuously left out: "The laughter died out, and only gestures of arms, movements of bodies, could be seen shaping something in the room. Was it an argument? A bet on the road races? Was it nothing of the sort? What was shaped by the arms and bodies moving in the twilight room?" (*JR*, 44). Jacob's movements, like the narrator's thoughts, give shape only to an absence. The question at this point is why the narrator refuses to turn that absence into a presence.

Although it seems that we know more about surrounding characters than we do about Jacob, that is only because our ideas about what qualifies as knowledge of a character differ from Woolf's. The details concerning other characters add up to a satisfying whole, while those concerning Jacob do not, because Woolf is trying to indicate that we should not be satisfied with the sums of details that make other characters seem real. Precisely the inadequacy of the details of Jacob's life should make him the most intimately felt and therefore justify his centrality in the novel. Details make a character this or that; they are exclusionary. The essence underlying everything, however, is inclusive, turning "either/or" into "both-at-once." Ideally the novel's characters should expand the reader's sense of self; they should make the reader feel capable of embracing other identities as though they were his own. This is the import of Mrs. Swithin's compliment to Miss La Trobe on the effect of her play in *Between the Acts*: "What a small part I've had to play! But you've made me feel I could have played . . . Cleopatra!"[15] In Woolf's view, the essence of the character is so much more inclusive that it takes in the reader more directly. Identifying with an unspecified character like Jacob, thus, makes the reader feel greater intimacy with the enigmatic es-

15. Virginia Woolf, *Between the Acts* (New York, 1941), 153. Marks of ellipsis are in the original. Subsequent page references to this novel are hereinafter cited parenthetically as *BA*.

sence than he would with characters whose traits were specified and therefore exclusionary. As the narrator of *Jacob's Room*
puts it,

> Either we are men, or we are women. Either we are cold, or we are
> sentimental. Either we are young, or growing old. In any case life
> is but a procession of shadows, and God knows why it is that we
> embrace them so eagerly, and see them depart with such anguish,
> being shadows. And why, if this and much more than this is true,
> why are we yet surprised in the window corner by a sudden vision
> that the young man in the chair is of all things in the world most
> real, the most solid, the best known to us—why indeed? For the
> moment after we know nothing about him.
>   Such is the manner of our seeing. Such the conditions of love.
> (*JR*, 71–72)

Jacob seems to be the shadow at the center of this novel, yet
the essence of the self cannot be a shadow; it is what casts the
shadows. The truth behind this apparent contradiction is that
the portrayal of Jacob is lost in the shadow of the narrator—the
shadow of her doubt about the efficacy of her own knowledge.
We can see why she doubts herself if we posit a definition of
what Jacob's real essence is. In Conrad's terminology, the real
essence of Jacob is not a hidden kernel; it is, in Woolf's, the
semitransparent envelope that is life itself. Cipher that he is,
Jacob is whatever is added to him, that is, whatever he is conscious of. Thus, his essence is supremely capacious because
anything might be the object of his consciousness. In trying to
portray that consciousness, Woolf tries to embody what can
never be experienced by anyone but Jacob himself.

To portray consciousness is not simply to portray its content, yet that is exactly what the narrator tries to do, and it is
understandable that she should fall back on the details contained in Jacob's consciousness—most notably his room—as a
way of making his essence felt. In her attempt there is an important similarity to the problem of describing consciousness
that G. E. Moore discusses in his essay "The Refutation of Idealism" (1903). There he points out the conspicuous absence in
the history of philosophy of precise definitions of consciousness: "this omission is . . . due to the fact that though philosophers have recognised that *something* distinct is meant by consciousness, they have never yet had a clear conception of *what*

that something is." As Moore explains it, when we try to describe or even think about our consciousness of the color blue, we naturally give our attention to the color rather than to the act of awareness itself, for the consciousness through which we see blue is "as if it were diaphanous."[16]

It is in just such an image of translucence that the narrator describes the self in *Jacob's Room*: "We start transparent, and then the cloud thickens. All history backs our pane of glass. To escape is vain" (*JR*, 49). In terms befitting this concept of the self, to escape would be to lift one's consciousness clear of its potential objects or intentions. The narrator's portrayal of Jacob can be seen to follow precisely this path: she is caught in a struggle to draw a line between Jacob's consciousness and the world it experiences. By doing this, she avoids object-bound definitions of him, much as Lawrence wanted to do in order to portray the dynamic character of the "other ego," the irreducible self that cannot be defined within the limits of its surroundings. At the end of *Women in Love* Birkin wants to keep his surroundings as sketchy as possible, never to define himself or Ursula according to them, contrary to what Gerald Crich does. In portraying Birkin, Lawrence had to suggest the infinite potentialities and the unforeseeable unfoldings of his deepest self. Similarly, the narrator of *Jacob's Room* tries to keep Jacob's potentialities before us by not fixing him and by not defining him according to his surroundings. In situating the narrator so obviously outside Jacob, however, as Lawrence's narrators are never situated in their relationship to his characters, Woolf sets the narrator up for failure. All the narrator gets from her attempt to erect a barrier between Jacob and his world is the realization of the barrier between herself and him, a barrier that makes him inaccessible.

Not the least of the reasons that the narrator cannot turn the story into an embodiment of Jacob's consciousness is her inability to enter that consciousness. As long as she remains outside—she thinking her thoughts, he thinking his own—the novel will be as much about her as it is about him, perhaps even more about her. And as long as the novel is about the narrator, it is not about Jacob, who is then an object of her aware-

16. G. E. Moore, *Philosophical Studies*, 25.

ness and not a subject whose mind is directly presented. I am
not the first to observe that this novel's narrator is by far the
most self-conscious of all of Woolf's narrators.[17] She often refers
to herself by indicating not only her sex and age but also by defining the limits to her knowledge that sex and age impose.
Thus she casts a shadow across Jacob partly by taking on a
body. Insofar as we see her as Woolf's fictional construct, however, the narrator's limitations are not imposed just by her sex
and age—after all, Woolf could have made her anything—but
rather the limits are imposed by her own self-reflection.

When the narrator feels herself falling short in her rendering
of Jacob, she characteristically begins speaking about herself,
as though hoping to find something deep inside her consciousness that would intersect Jacob's. But whether or not her hopes
are reasonable, the effect of her introspection on the reader is
to cast doubt on her knowledge of Jacob, because her self-
reference never forms an adequate basis on which her knowledge of Jacob can be predicated. All it does, finally, is to drive
a wedge between herself and Jacob. In her moments of self-
consciousness, Jacob's consciousness gets lost in the shuffle,
becoming simply all that the narrator's consciousness is *not*.

The narrator's unpredictable alternations between telling
her story and talking about herself create interesting difficulties in point of view. For example, in the incident where
Jacob and his friend Durrant are described in their boat, the
question is whether the meaning of the incident is shaped by
Jacob's or the narrator's perspective. Though both perspectives
on Durrant amount to the same thing—both explaining why
Jacob is not at the moment admiring Durrant—they arise from
very different motives: "[Durrant's] calculations had worked
perfectly, and really the sight of him sitting there, with his
hand on the tiller, rosy gilled, with a sprout of beard, looking
sternly at the stars, then at a compass, spelling out quite correctly his page of the eternal lesson-book, would have moved a
woman. Jacob, of course, was not a woman. The sight of Timmy
Durrant was no sight for him, nothing to set against the sky

17. Hafley, *The Glass Roof*, 50–51; Barry Morgenstern, "The Self-
Conscious Narrator in *Jacob's Room*," *Modern Fiction Studies*, XVIII (1972),
351–61.

and worship; far from it. They had quarrelled" (*JR*, 47). There
are two reasons for Jacob's not admiring Durrant. One is the
narrator's, that Jacob is not a woman; the other is Jacob's, that
the two have just quarrelled. Though the two distinct reasons
add up to the same result, they arise from wholly different categories of motives. By including her own perspective on the incident, the narrator tries to make her own character the basis on
which to interpret Jacob's behavior. Her perspective's motives
are incommensurate with Jacob's, however, and therefore her
perspective is not an adequate basis for interpretation. This incommensurability reinforces the realistic sense that the narrator's story of Jacob is independent of her knowledge of it, that
conceivably all this would go on even if she were not there to
report it.

If this gap between the narrator and Jacob establishes the
story's realism, it at the same time establishes her at a distance
from the characters whom she wants to know more intimately
than the boundaries of realistically conceived knowledge will
allow. This distance is the reason the narrator does not consistently hold herself to the same spatiotemporal boundaries
throughout the novel. Although in the boat incident she remained somewhere outside Jacob and did not enter the spatiotemporal realm where he lives, in other places in the novel she
does seem to enter that realm. She does, for example, enter his
room when no one is there: "reaching his door one went in a
little out of breath; but he wasn't there" (*JR*, 38). In this scene
the narrator comes very close to taking on the identity of the
"one" who loses his breath at the top of the stairs, and therefore
seems to be present in Jacob's spatiotemporal domain. But since
she is in his room when he is not, she withholds herself from
interacting with him on the level where other characters inter-
act with him. In conventional realism, omniscient narrators dis-
obey physical laws all the time. We do not notice because they
rarely specify their spatiotemporal locations to begin with.

At another point, however, the "one" that the narrator posits and with whom she eventually identifies herself is no longer
a delimited self as the characters are. This "one" is a consciousness with an unrestricted potential for knowing and reporting
things unavailable to minds with realistic perspectival limits.
The moment of identification appears in the curious scene

where the narrator's perspective breaks into two distinguishable parts. When she sees Jacob on the street walking home, the narrator begins by seeing him from a perspective characterized by nothing more than the usual limits of her age and sex. When she enters Jacob's spatiotemporal domain, however, the limitations become so constricting that she leaps clear of them:

> Whether we know what was in his mind is another question. Granted ten years' seniority and a difference of sex, fear of him comes first; this is swallowed up by a desire to help—overwhelming sense, reason, and the time of night; anger would follow close on that—with Florinda, with destiny; and then up would bubble an irresponsible optimism. "Surely there's enough light in the street at this moment to drown all our cares in gold!" Ah, what's the use of saying it? Even while you speak and look over your shoulder towards Shaftesbury Avenue, destiny is chipping a dent in him. He has turned to go. As for following him back to his room, no—that we won't do.
>
> Yet that, of course, is precisely what one does. (*JR*, 94–95)

That "one" who does enter Jacob's room, and who thereby sets aside the limitations that she had just imposed upon herself, is the part of the narrator that refuses to be object-bounded. This nonbounded part can conceivably meet Jacob in the space that presumably only the imagination can allow her to enter.

On the other hand, the part of the narrator that refuses to take advantage of the privileges afforded to fictional narrators is constantly having to choose and to suffer the inevitable anxiety that being free to choose brings. To choose one place, one person, is to exclude all others and then be anxious lest that choice be wrong or inadequate. Knowledge imposes this anxiety when it falls within a self that is spatially and temporally bounded, as the narrator suffers herself to be whenever she refuses to imagine. But that other part of the narrator that is willing to give up her epistemological authority as a real, specifiable person with inferential knowledge of others dares to imagine. She is the one who enters Jacob's room when no one would be admitted. If daring to imagine means suffering others' doubts about one's epistemological authority, then the consolation is relief from the anxieties about choosing.

In Woolf, to know is to exclude unrealized possibilities, and to imagine is to make everything possible. This attitude is nowhere clearer than in the despair into which the narrator falls when describing the aisles and stalls at the opera house where Clara must bid good-bye to Jacob at the end of an intermission. The aisles, stalls, and seats suggest the dividing lines that separate individuals in life as we know it, rather than as we imagine it. Because they impose our absence from one another, they are like the "death in effigy" that Clara feels when Jacob must go back to his seat (*JR*, 68). As long as the narrator designates her own spatiotemporal boundaries, she must undergo the same agony; she must take a seat. In her description of the amphitheater, she sets aside, with an abrupt "but no," the capaciousness of mind into which only her imagination could deliver her:

> The moulds are filled nightly. There is no need to distinguish details. But the difficulty remains—one has to choose. For though I have no desire to be Queen of England—or only for a moment—I would willingly sit beside her; I would hear the Prime Minister's gossip; the countess whisper, and share her memories of halls and gardens; the massive fronts of the respectable conceal after all their secret code; or why so impermeable? And then, doffing one's own headpiece, how strange to assume for a moment some one's— any one's—to be a man of valour who has ruled the Empire; to refer while Brangaena sings to the fragments of Sophocles, or see in a flash, as the shepherd pipes his tune, bridges and aqueducts. But no—we must choose. Never was there a harsher necessity! or one which entails greater pain, more certain disaster; for wherever I seat myself, I die in exile: Whittaker in his lodging-house; Lady Charles at the Manor. (*JR*, 69)

Here the narrator is resigned to her exile. By announcing it, she upholds at once her status as an identifiable self as well as the limitations to knowledge that that status imposes.

This refusal to allow her imagination to interpose is something we do not see in Woolf's later novels. There she goes back to conventions of realism that allow the narrator to enter characters at will and interpolate their private experiences. She goes even further in her next two novels: she takes philosophical and literary realism's assumption that absolute knowledge of other minds is always a potential, brings it to the foreground, and then turns the potential into an accomplished feat when she brings characters to direct and indubitable knowledge of each other, thus collectivizing consciousness and thereby trans-

forming realistic narrative. In *Jacob's Room*, however, the narrator's self-scrutiny dominates as both a response to and the
cause of her inability to know Jacob: a response when it arises
out of her exasperated attempts to make Jacob's essence present, a cause when it requires her to think less about Jacob in
order to think more about herself.

Thus far we have overlooked Jacob's self-awareness, easy to
do because it is virtually nonexistent. As Jean O. Love observes,
"others contemplate him but he does not contemplate himself."[18] There is one passage, however, in which Jacob comes
closest to expressing a self-awareness. This one seems to be an
exception to the rule that Jacob is the only nonreflective character in the novel:

> Anyhow, whether undergraduate or shop boy, man or woman,
> it must come as a shock about the age of twenty—the world of the
> elderly—thrown up in such black outline upon what we are; upon
> the reality; the moors and Byron; the sea and the lighthouse; the
> sheep's jaw with the yellow teeth [which Jacob found on the beach
> when he was a child]; upon the obstinate irrepressible conviction
> which makes youth so intolerably disagreeable—"I am what I am,
> and intend to be it," for which Jacob will be no form in the world
> unless Jacob makes one for himself. The Plumbers will try to pre-
> vent him from making it. Wells and Shaw and the serious six-
> penny weeklies will sit on its head. (*JR*, 36)

Even here Jacob's self-consciousness is interpolated by the narrator. We are not to believe that he came out one day and actually said, "I am what I am, and intend to be it," as the narrator
puts it. Rather, this whole event is a decidedly indirect rendering of a particular stage in Jacob's cognitive development. As
the narrator says, it is the way any undergraduate or shop boy
would feel at the age of about twenty. This passage is an almost
clinical generalization of an introspective moment, not the moment itself. By positioning herself between the reader and Jacob
in his self-reflective moment, the narrator almost totally ob-
scures Jacob's self-consciousness. It is as if she were taking
upon herself the self-consciousness that she denies to Jacob.
This is *my* character, she seems to say, and in a sense it is.

18. Jean O. Love, *Worlds in Consciousness: Mythopoetic Thought in the
Novels of Virginia Woolf* (Berkeley, 1970), 39.

The narrator does the thinking while Jacob does the acting, so that they appear as two parts of a single identity that is made up of action and contemplation. If this conjunction is not obvious, it is because action and thought are as divorced in this novel as the character and the narrator are. The *res cogitans* and the *res extensa* are bifurcated, and it is one part of Woolf's subsequent experimental achievement to bring them back together. By diffusing subject and object, the narrators of the later novels work within monistic models of knowledge. The result is that both narrators and characters are decreasingly able to hold themselves apart from the objects of their knowledge well enough to register, in any moment of self-awareness, the space between the act and the intention of consciousness. The enigma of the irreducible self then becomes a record of consciousness that makes us feel we know the characters directly, not inferentially.

Language and Consciousness: *Mrs. Dalloway*

In *Mrs. Dalloway* Woolf first discovered the novelistic techniques by which she could not only criticize the traditional realistic novel but actually add something new to it. Her advance in this novel is both technical and thematic. Whereas in *Jacob's Room* she avoided entering the consciousness of Jacob because of her resolve to circumvent what she called the "damned egotistical self" (*Diary*, II, 14), in *Mrs. Dalloway* she plunges deep into the radically subjective experiences of her characters. She calls this her "tunnelling process," but she does not thereby succumb to the egotism that she had wanted to avoid. The more she tunnels, the more she realizes, as she indicates in her diary, that the tunnels meet: "The idea is that the caves shall connect, & each comes to daylight at the present moment" (*Diary*, II, 263). This tunneling process is the major breakthrough that *Mrs. Dalloway* constitutes.[19] Both the techniques that establish the connecting of subjectivities and the thematic concern with the relative virtues of privacy and collective experience work together to stage a rich, dramatic challenge to the

19. Edward A. Hungerford, "'My Tunnelling Process': The Method of 'Mrs. Dalloway,'" *Modern Fiction Studies*, III (1957), 164–67.

philosophical and literary realism that underlie not only the tradition of the novel but also certain aspects of this novel as well. *Mrs. Dalloway* is an especially complex novel because it entertains a view of the relationships between subject and object and between consciousness and language that it also denies.

Mrs. Dalloway is at once monistic and dualistic in its meta-theories of knowledge and imagination. Insofar as it is dualistic, it is as conventional in its presentation of consciousness as *Jacob's Room* is, and it works within the same limitations in rendering consciousness. Its epistemologically monistic implications, however, fuse subjectivities that realism characteristically holds apart. *Mrs. Dalloway* merges subjectivities in a special way—by abolishing the distinction between language and consciousness—yet it simultaneously maintains another level of meaning where language and experience, as well as subject and object, are held apart. These two levels I refer to as the collective and the private.

We begin to see how these levels work when we inspect the most simple of the narrator's verbal patterns. When the narrator sets Clarissa Dalloway's words off in quotation marks, we have a clear sense of the difference between her voice and the narrator's, not just because of the punctuation but because of the differences between the narrator's and Clarissa's idioms. Most of the time, however, Clarissa's experience is rendered through the narrator's interpolations of her thoughts. Then, what the narrator reports Clarissa as thinking is not what she is actually saying to herself; rather, the narrator attributes thoughts to Clarissa that she herself does not or could not express. The result is what Dorrit Cohn labels psycho-narration.[20] Conventional realism insists that we look beyond the inherent contradiction that these publicized thought experiences are private. They are Clarissa's and no one else's. Furthermore, they logically precede the language in which they are expressed, if we assume that the narrator's articulation of them does not itself create those experiences but reports only what she would think anyway and what we would otherwise not know about. In realistic fiction psycho-narration is perfectly conventional. As a measure of the independence of isolated subjectivities, this

20. Cohn, *Transparent Minds*, Chap. III; Kiely, *Beyond Egotism*, 123.

mode of narration is dualistic in its model of mind and entirely consistent with the assumptions behind empirical psychology. It also, though, advances a view of language and experience that the novel's collective level of meaning undercuts. The collective level turns private thoughts into shared experiences and banishes the distinction between what is thought and what it is possible to experience.

Wittgenstein formulated similar ideas in his *Philosophical Investigations* (1953), where he argues that there is no private language in the sense that we can establish for ourselves individually the relationship between our private experience and the words which refer to it. According to him language and experience become one, because experience is not logically prior to the language in which we express it; in fact, the words do not refer to our sensations the way the notion of a private language would encourage us to think they do. Wittgenstein says: "If one has to imagine someone else's pain on the model of one's own, this is none too easy a thing to do: for I have to imagine pain which I *do not feel* on the model of the pain which I *do feel*. That is, what I have to do is not simply to make a transition in imagination from one place of pain to another. As, from pain in the hand to pain in the arm. For I am not to imagine that I feel pain in some region of his body. (Which would also be possible.)"[21] A private language would not overcome this problem. When I arrive at the meaning of the word *pain*, unless I want to reach the solipsistic conclusion that I am the only one in the world who experiences pain, then I will have to say that the word *pain*, inextricably bound to my sensation of pain, is not bound by the private application of the word to the sensation, but rather is a part of the collective experience, embodied in language, in which my sensation partakes. Norman Malcom articulately explains Wittgenstein's position on this: "If I obtain my *conception* of pain from pain that I experience, then it will be part of my conception of pain that *I* am the only being that can experience it. For me it will be a *contradiction* to speak of *another's* pain. This strict solipsism is the necessary outcome of the notion of private language."[22] Wittgenstein ex-

21. Ludwig Wittgenstein, *Philosophical Investigations,* trans. G. E. M. Anscombe (New York, 1953), par. 302.

22. Malcom, *Knowledge and Certainty,* 106.

plains our associations of words to sensations in roughly this way: we do not apply the sensation, say, of pain to the word *pain* in a private moment of introspection, as is commonly assumed in Cartesian epistemology and in the sense-datum theories derived from it, for this assumes there is such a thing as a private rule of application, something Wittgenstein reduces to absurdity when he asks what would count as a correct application of the rules when he who judges is he who applies the rules. Instead, he suggests, we attach the words we learn to our primitive, nonverbal, innate expressions of pain. Following rules we learn from others, we translate a cry of pain into the word *pain*.[23]

As a result, language is not just evidence for another self's sentience, and it is more than assurance of another's sentience, since assurance implies varying degrees of evidence. Rather, it is the *criterion* for sentience. To ask for evidence for the existence of another mind, rather than settling for criteria, erroneously assumes a private arena whose introspections are its privileged knowledge. In Wittgenstein's view, Cartesian epistemology and its derivatives in sense-datum theory invent the problem of knowing other minds.

Although what I said about *Mrs. Dalloway*—that it asserts private experience through the use of private language rendered in psycho-narrations and thus relates experiences or sensations logically prior to their expression—seems to undercut the philosophical perspective of Wittgenstein, I use his idea that language is the criterion for our knowledge of others' experience in order to qualify *Mrs. Dalloway*'s conventional narrative practices. I do this for the simple reason that this novel itself qualifies these practices and assumptions, primarily through its reliance on psycho-narration. Of course, psycho-narration is perfectly ordinary in conventional realism; even there, it forces language to be the criterion for our knowledge of the thoughts it conveys: it would be absurd to doubt an omniscient narrator who reported that "Clarissa thought she was happy, but unconsciously she was in agony." We take the narrator's word, for this is conventional realism's way of assuring us that the space between private minds could be spanned if we could only draw closer together. Nevertheless, Woolf's manner of using psycho-

23. Wittgenstein, *Philosophical Investigations*, par. 244.

narration comes dangerously close to abolishing the mind as a private arena whose criteria for existence exceed its own or the narrator's language. I say it only comes close because *Mrs. Dalloway* is concerned with seeing how long it can work at erasing the line between private and collective experiences without making that line vanish altogether. That faint line keeps the novel within important realistic assumptions that the narrative technique keeps trying to undercut.

In Wittgenstein's view and Woolf's prose, language becomes the criterion for our knowledge of others' experience: when a man says he *thinks* he smells fish, there is no evidence that would discount him. Hence we believe him because he said so. Using psycho-narration as much as it does, *Mrs. Dalloway* emphasizes just this sort of statement that cannot be verified except through language: it is more concerned with what its characters think they experience than with what could be intersubjectively verified by comparing others' accounts. In the process, this novel collectivizes its characters' experiences by merging their verbal accounts of those experiences. J. Hillis Miller and Elizabeth Deeds Ermarth have shown that even conventionally realistic narrators collectivize their characters' consciousnesses, but conventional realism does not force this to our attention, preferring to keep us believing in the characters' independent existence. The collectivization of experience that *Mrs. Dalloway* intermittently foregrounds is sustained in *The Waves,* forcing on us an ambiguity that Miller describes this way: however difficult it is to mistake one character for another, it is quite easy to mistake all the characters for the narrator. At this collective level the narrator's words do not, strictly, refer to characters' thoughts but constitute them, becoming the criterion for their experiences. So it is not surprising that Miller should come to feel that in *Mrs. Dalloway,* at the deepest level of individual minds, the one-way relationship that allows a narrator to know a character, but not the character to know her, becomes reciprocal.[24]

In *Mrs. Dalloway* the collectivizing of experience is most explicit when the language the narrator uses employs the same

24. Schaefer, *The Three-Fold Nature of Reality,* 138; Miller, *Fiction and Repetition,* 181.

phrasing and imagery to interpolate more than one character's thoughts. One imagery pattern comes from William Shakespeare's *Cymbeline*: "Fear no more the heat o' the sun / Nor the furious winter's rages." Coming from the dirge sung for Imogen (IV, ii, 255–78), these lines suggest Clarissa's latent fear of death. She first sees these lines through a bookstore window,[25] and they later enter her psycho-narration on at least two more occasions (*D*, 44, 59). They also appear, even if somewhat transmuted, in Septimus' psycho-narration shortly before his suicide (*D*, 211, 226). The linked imagery patterns in the language that verbalizes their separate experiences effect a unity in their patterns of thought. That unity, along with other indications, gives the impression that these two characters who never met each other have direct access to each others' minds and that they are thinking in the narrator's collective consciousness.[26]

On a private level the novel still posits a world where minds are independent, private arenas. Here Clarissa and Septimus are two persons. Their experiences are prior to and independent of the narrator's verbalization; the narrator, in entering the private arenas of their minds, reports the thoughts they conceivably would have had even if there were no narrator to report them. This world perfectly accords with conventional literary realism and implies a realistic model of knowledge.

On the collective level, however, the novel posits a world where minds have as direct access to each other as the narrator has to them. Clarissa and Septimus are, as Woolf says in her preface to the Modern Library edition, one and the same character.[27] On this level, no experience precedes the narrator's verbal formulation because there is no private self behind which the narration can lag. Clarissa and Septimus' union is effected by the indistinguishability of the narrator's language and their own experiences—experiences that are finally gathered together in the narrator and that are constituted by the narrator's language. This collective level of meaning implicates a monistic model of knowledge and moves the novel to the edge of literary,

25. Virginia Woolf, *Mrs. Dalloway* (New York, 1925), 13. Subsequent page references to this novel are hereinafter cited parenthetically as *D*.

26. For the aesthetic theories behind the patterning I am discussing, see Roberts, "'Vision and Design' in Virginia Woolf," 835–47.

27. Virginia Woolf, Introduction to *Mrs. Dalloway* (New York, 1928), vi.

psychological, and philosophical realism. Both levels appear in the novel and are defined by the similarities and differences between Clarissa and Septimus. Measuring these similarities and differences can spotlight for us the paradoxical intersection of the private and the collective.

Septimus is cut off from all that surrounds him because he privately invents his union with his surroundings instead of earning it as Clarissa does. He tries to commune without communicating and hence slides further into isolation. "Communication is health," he says; "communication is happiness" (D, 141). But he is not really communicating: the only person he wants to speak with is his deceased friend Evans, a figment of his imagination. To Septimus there is no distinction between real and imagined persons because all are equally extensions of his own mind. They might as well be rocks. He lives in a psychological condition of radical isolation that approximates the solipsistic extremes of philosophical idealism; he is what the collective consciousness of the narrator would be if it were a self. Even in *Mrs. Dalloway* the collective consciousness that the narrator voices is not a self. Idealist philosopher McTaggart surprisingly anticipates this cul-de-sac when he troubles to point out that "a whole of which a self is part cannot be a self." As P. F. Strawson has argued, the imputation of a collective consciousness has the mysterious but indubitable power of instantly banishing the consciousness of the constituent parts.[28]

Seeming to think he is the only conscious self, Septimus' experience is irredeemably private, as is his language. He attaches words to sensations according to his own rules, so the people who try to contact him are at a complete loss. To them his experience is beyond language. Neither his wife, who has the most emotional sort of contact with him, nor his doctor, Bradshaw, who has a decidedly clinical interest in him, can break the private code that expresses his private experience and that further isolates him. For all her efforts Rezia cannot tell whether Septimus' insanity is in remission or not. Only moments before he jumps from the window, she is under the impression that he is cured (D, 219). Earlier, when Bradshaw asks

28. McTaggart, *The Nature of Existence*, II, 86; Strawson, *Individuals*, 114–15.

Septimus if he served with distinction in the war and he responds only by interrogatively repeating the word *war*, Bradshaw concludes that he is "attaching meanings to words of a symbolical kind" and that this is a "serious symptom, to be noted on the card" (*D*, 145).

The narrator, however, expresses in language what Septimus' experience is like and thereby recovers it. As a result, we can see why his experience of the world should be so impossible to communicate: he experiences the world as an undifferentiated mass, a chaos of images. The external world behaves only in accordance with Septimus' private moods; it is animated by his thoughts about it: "And the leaves being connected by millions of fibres with his own body, there on the seat, fanned it up and down; when the branch stretched he, too, made that statement. The sparrows fluttering, rising, and falling in jagged fountains were part of the pattern; the white and blue, barred with black branches. Sounds made harmonies with pre-meditation; the spaces between them were as significant as the sounds" (*D*, 32–33). The description has the qualities of a mystical experience in which the self is an indistinguishable part of a monistic whole. Sounds make harmonies with premeditation because no event is accidental; the whole universe is animated by a single will. There is as little difference between the sounds and the intervening silence as there is between Septimus and the trees he is observing. There is no hierarchy, for no event is more important than another, because all is one. We can so easily tell that Septimus' picture of reality is nothing more than a serious mental illness because on one level *Mrs. Dalloway* advances a realistic model of knowledge. We know he is insane because there is an implied independent and intersubjectively verifiable reality that serves as the backdrop to his psychotic experience and that makes it identifiable as psychotic.

If the whole novel were viewed through Septimus' eyes, there would never be any tension between subjects and objects or between one consciousness and another because in his experience the world has no existence independent of his consciousness. There would also be no death. From his ego-bound perspective, the world cannot go on after his death, so there would be no perspective outside of his own that would register his mortality. Thus, even when he jumps from the window, he does not interpret his actions as leading to his death, only as a way of escaping the doctor who will take him away. To Septimus, jumping is only a melodramatic gesture, not tragic as the doctor sees it because it will mean the failed ending of a case history. Through Septimus' eyes we have this perspective:

> There remained only the window, the large Bloomsbury-lodging house window, the tiresome, the troublesome, and rather melodramatic business of opening the window and throwing himself out. It was their idea of tragedy, not his or Rezia's (for she was with him). Holmes and Bradshaw like that sort of thing. (He sat on the sill.) But he would wait till the very last moment. He did not want to die. Life was good. The sun hot. Only human beings—what did *they* want? . . . Holmes was at the door. "I'll give it you!" he cried, and flung himself vigorously, violently down on Mrs. Filmer's area railings. (*D*, 226)

He says that this is not Rezia's idea of tragedy either, "for she was with him." Insofar as she is with him, she is part of his consciousness—the consciousness whose ending he cannot comprehend. The fact is that this *is* her tragedy because she will have to live on after his death. But Septimus will not allow her her own ideas; he will not allow her her independent existence.

Then, too, if this narration were wholly given from Septimus' point of view, we would not be able to read it, because he makes up the rules of his own language. That he does so is evident in that only he can understand his words, which the narrator demonstrates when she renders his thoughts in cryptic language. So Septimus' view of life, with its premium on unity and its abolition of death, is rendered in a language that barely asserts anything other than his perspective's radical separation from community and life: with no communication there is no community, and with no urge to grant the feelings and thoughts of others there is no life. Septimus is the walking paradox that turns the single identity behind Clarissa and himself into two persons and that splits this novel down the middle, creating a fissure that the novel itself scrambles to repair.

In several ways Septimus radically differs from Clarissa. Where Septimus denies others an existence independent of his own, at almost every turn Clarissa feels herself into others' lives. He has ceased to feel, but she can do hardly anything but feel. He lives in radical isolation, while she makes her preparations for the party she will give on the day he kills himself. Septimus and Clarissa are in most ways opposites—mirror images—but even mirror images have something in common with what they are reflections of. Their similarities, as well as their differences, make sense of the epistemological implications of their relationship to one another.

For all her differences from Septimus, Clarissa shares his sense of isolation. She even desires isolation. In fact, it is mainly Peter Walsh's wanting to share everything with her that has discouraged her from marrying him: "with Peter," she reflects, "everything had to be shared; everything gone into. And it was intolerable" (D, 9). She cannot bear the intimacy that gives her no space but in which Peter takes such pleasure. On one occasion he relishes the thought that "they had always this queer power of communicating without words" (D, 90), and later that "they went in and out of each other's minds without effort" (D, 94). Under such circumstances, where intimacy is forced upon her rather than achieved by her own conscious efforts, there is no reason to have romantic love, for in such conditions love has no barriers upon which to exert its powers. Clarissa, for these reasons, is more comfortable with her husband. They also can communicate without words, as when Richard, unable to bring himself to tell her he loves her, manages to make himself understood with subtle, nonverbal gestures (D, 179). There is nonetheless a space between them—a space in which Clarissa takes comfort: "And there is dignity in people; a solitude; even between husband and wife a gulf; and that one must respect, thought Clarissa, watching him open the door; for one would not part with it oneself, or take it, against his will, from one's husband, without losing one's independence, one's self-respect—something, after all, priceless" (D, 181).

Living in and cherishing a certain degree of isolation, Clarissa then is like Septimus in an important way, but there is a major difference in their forms of isolation. While Septimus can conceive of no reality outside his consciousness and therefore lives in a condition of unredeemed solipsism, Clarissa has a genuine belief in and concern for the world beyond her immediate awareness. Septimus is plunged into his isolation whether he wants to be or not; Clarissa, by contrast, has the luxury of choosing the degree of isolation that suits her. It is out of respect for her own independent existence, and out of respect for others', that Clarissa reserves a space for her privacy.

Unlike Septimus, Clarissa can make a deliberate distinction between her ideas about others and the others as they are in themselves. Her attitude toward Miss Kilman, her daughter's friend, is the most explicit indication of this. Clarissa's ideas about Miss Kilman arise out of egocentric concerns; she is jealous because, in befriending her daughter Elizabeth, Miss Kilman seems to have taken her away. Clarissa is afraid, too, that Miss Kilman's newfound and intense Christianity will make Elizabeth turn against her for living in luxury among the socially elite. Unlike Septimus, however, Clarissa can make a distinction between her own idea of Miss Kilman and Miss Kilman herself. The woman herself, most notably in her physical presence, is a pitiable German girl who had to suffer the persecution that was inevitable while she lived in England during the war. Clarissa recognizes in her physical presence Miss Kilman herself, the woman who has suffered and whose history is independent of Clarissa's ego-bound opinions: "how she lost her malignity, her size, became second by second merely Miss Kilman, in a mackintosh, whom Heaven knows Clarissa would have liked to help" (D, 190). As soon as the woman leaves, though, Clarissa's idea of Miss Kilman takes over and her egocentric feelings condition her attitude: "For now that the body of Miss Kilman was not before her, it overwhelmed her—the idea" (D, 191). Yet Clarissa can see the idea for what it is.

Septimus and Clarissa also share a feeling of being everywhere at once, as though spread out over all other consciousnesses. Septimus' consciousness seems to enter and to animate everything he observes. Clarissa, similarly, is so acutely aware that the walls separating one self from another can at times seem permeable that she only hesitantly specifies her identity or anyone else's: "She would not say of any one in the world now that they were this or were that" (D, 11). This insight leads her to ask whether the death of an individual self can make any difference, if consciousness in one self can spread out into adjacent selves. When she decides that death makes no difference, Clarissa comes very close to making the same observations about the continuance of consciousness after death that Septimus' refusal to acknowledge his mortality implied:

Did it matter then, she asked herself, walking towards Bond Street, did it matter that she must inevitably cease completely; all this must go on without her; did she resent it; or did it not become consoling to believe that death ended absolutely? but that somehow in the streets of London, on the ebb and flow of things, here, there, she survived, Peter survived, lived in each other, she being part, she was positive, of the trees at home; of the house there, ugly, rambling all to bits and pieces as it was; part of people she had never met; being laid out like a mist between the people she knew best, who lifted her on their branches as she had seen the trees lift the mist, but it spread ever so far, her life, herself. (D, 12)

One difference between hers and Septimus' view makes all the difference in the world; she can picture at once both her immortality and her mortality. She can conceive of her awareness as falling within a particular self and as spreading out into others. She has a kind of double vision that allows her, unlike Septimus, to operate on both private and collective levels of this novel. For it is she who will comprehend her relationship with Septimus, but Septimus himself will not understand. She will merge with him, but he not with her.

Clarissa's observations of the elderly lady in her room in the next building take on an epistemological significance that is built upon her relationship with Septimus. She watches this woman on two separate occasions, before her party and then during her party but after she has recognized the complicity of her life in Septimus'. What fascinates Clarissa while she watches the elderly lady is the woman's essential privacy: "Somehow one respected that—that old woman looking out of the window, quite unconscious that she was being watched. There was something solemn in it—but love and religion would destroy that, whatever it was, the privacy of the soul. The odious Kilman would destroy it. Yet it was a sight that made her want to cry" (D, 191–92). This lady's privacy, which Clarissa fears Miss Kilman would seek to destroy or overcome as though it were an intolerable problem, is precisely what turns Clarissa's observation of her into a solemn event. The occasion for solemnity is the paradox that in watching the old lady in her privacy Clarissa might abolish that privacy by virtue of her outside perspective, and yet she is not abolishing that privacy. The lady remains an unwatched woman as long as Clarissa puts aside her self-awareness, her knowledge of herself as a watcher. To remain unaware of self is to surmount her act of knowing and to know the lady as intimately as the lady knows herself—not indirectly, through a window, but directly, intuitively, unmistakably. Private experience, paradoxically, is shared and yet remains sanctified as private:

> Clarissa tried to follow her as she turned and disappeared, and could still just see her white cap moving at the back of the bedroom. She was still there moving about at the other end of the room. Why creeds and prayers and mackintoshes? when, thought Clarissa, that's the miracle, that's the mystery; that old lady, she meant, whom she could see going from chest of drawers to dressing-table. She could still see her. And the supreme mystery which Kilman might say she had solved, or Peter might say he had solved, but Clarissa didn't believe either of them had the ghost of an idea of solving, was simply this: here was one room; there another. Did religion solve that, or love? (D, 193)

Clarissa's way of entering another's private experience arises, as Septimus' does not, out of an intense impression that there are separate selves (separate rooms) to begin with. Her observations of the elderly lady are also built upon her relationship with Septimus, because the narrator exacts a correspondence between the old man who descends the stairway and looks straight at Septimus just before he commits suicide (D, 226) and the old woman who ascends the stairway and looks straight at Clarissa just after she has comprehended Septimus' meaning for her (D, 283). When Clarissa discovers that she shares Septimus' identity, she also discovers that the way up is the way down. Her discovery comes in a "moment"—the instant when all the seemingly irrelevant, incoherent, and random events and feelings in Clarissa's life suddenly coalesce. This moment is built up slowly and brings the novel to a stunning close.

When Lady Bradshaw first tells Clarissa and Richard about Septimus' death, Clarissa's initial response is a sudden feeling of violation: "in the middle of my party, here's death" (D, 279). One could hardly imagine a less sensitive response to the news. But then Clarissa has never met Septimus, and suicides occur every day in cities as big as London. What turns out to be more remarkable than her initial indifference is her final concern, her sense that Septimus' disaster is her own. Her initial feeling that there is something profoundly incongruous about mentioning death at her party indicates, in light of her subsequent understanding, that she is as yet not ready to understand that the gesture of gathering at a party and the act of dying both render the walls between consciousnesses permeable—in short, that death is also an attempt to communicate. Given that language is the criterion for our knowledge of others' experiences, we see that death becomes an experience when it becomes an attempt to communicate; death is no longer the end but merely a part of our experience. In death, as in language, the self communes with others instead of plunging into an irredeemable privacy.

When Clarissa goes off into an adjoining room, her intention is not to hide away in isolation to contemplate the death, but rather to seek out the prime minister, who she thought had gone into the other room. Thus, to stave off the aura of death and isolation, she tries to spread herself over her guests. She finds herself alone there, however, and the incongruity of her isolation in the midst of her gathering is like the incongruity of death at her party: "so strange it was to come alone in her finery" (D, 280). When she comprehends Septimus' death, the incongruity disappears. There is life in death, society in privacy.

Interestingly, the narrative takes no pains to tell us explicitly what details of Septimus' death Clarissa was told, and this is significant. Her knowledge of his death is as if passed directly from the narrator, whose collective consciousness she attains at the moment she comprehends Septimus' gesture. As a way of examining his experience, Clarissa rehearses what it would have been like: "Always her body went through it first, when she was told, suddenly, of an accident; her dress flamed, her body burnt" (D, 280). But even here her consciousness remains outside his, for she is more acutely aware of her difference from Septimus than she is of their points of similarity: "She had once thrown a shilling into the Serpentine, never anything more. But he had flung it away" (D, 280). Clarissa has not yet flung herself away. The image of the falling coin, which has entered into the narrator's accounts of Clarissa's private experience throughout the novel, becomes a basis for the contiguity of Clarissa's private experience and Septimus' suicide, which so far has not been a part of her experience. The falling coin becomes an image of Septimus' body: the image is hers, the body his. At this instant the private and collective levels of experience intersect. The narrator's language gathers Clarissa and Septimus into its collective fold, transcending private language and private experience. The whole embraces the part when life embraces death.

First we hear, "He had been killed—but how?" Then it is as if the narrator's voice tells Clarissa what she has not known: "He had thrown himself from a window. Up had flashed the ground; through him, blundering, bruising, went the rusty spikes. There he lay with a thud, thud in his brain, and then a suffocation of blackness. So she saw it" (D, 280). Precisely because she never met Septimus, did not actually see the details of his death, and had to learn about them in her meditation, her knowledge is privileged. In her ability to think the dead man's thoughts, she can now understand that death is not the cessation of consciousness: "Death was an attempt to communicate; people feeling the impossibility of reaching the centre which, mystically, evaded them; closeness drew apart; rapture faded, one was alone. There was an embrace in death" (D, 280–81).

Throughout the novel the image of the window is central as an emblem of the act of consciousness, for both Clarissa and Septimus pass through windows in one way or another. Clarissa makes a mental leap from the inside of the glass to the outside, by comprehending both Septimus' death and, without violating it, the elderly lady's isolation; thereby she retains her individuated identity while at the same time transcending its boundaries. Septimus, by contrast, literally jumps to the other side of the glass, ridding himself at once of both his selfhood and the consciousness through which he could conceivably have transcended his isolation. What Clarissa sees through the window he meets face to face. As an image of consciousness the window has two sides: it both separates selves and joins them.

So is the narrator's use of language double-edged, since it both sets the boundaries between selves, by assigning each his individual life, his private experience, and gathers distinct selves into itself by constituting their experience. It is in Clarissa's moment of clarity (clarity is what her name means), when her private experience is fleetingly transcended, that the novel sets forth an alternative model of knowledge and imagination. The language by which we know Clarissa's private thoughts is joined to the collective voice of the narrator, who is all characters at once. By even momentarily raising Clarissa's consciousness to this inclusive level of awareness, Woolf boldly challenges the norms of literary realism and posits a model of knowledge at odds with the philosophical realism that she for the most part accepts. She thus injects into her art an ideal concerning the nature of the mind left out of realistic accounts.[29]

Subject, Object, and the Nature of Reality: *To the Lighthouse*

In her major technical advance in *Mrs. Dalloway*, Woolf dropped the self-conscious narrator of *Jacob's Room*, finding an imaginative space that would break down the realistic perspectival limits. Not restricted to individual points of view, the narrator is able to move in and out of the characters freely and to gather them into a collective consciousness that the narrator's language constitutes. This technique advances a metatheory of knowledge and imagination that tears down the boundaries between subjectivities—the monistic epistemological model that is central to her contribution to the history of the novel. These technical innovations persist in *To the Lighthouse*, but the novel has additional aspects that make it a unique addition to Woolf's canon.

To the Lighthouse employs a plot and structure that together advance, first, the realistically conceived separation of the categories of subjectivity and objectivity and, then, the synthesis of those categories. The three parts of this novel roughly correspond to a tripartite model of consciousness: a subject, an object, and a reality constituted by the intersection of the two.[30] Part I, "The Window," stresses subjectivity, especially

29. Gabriel Franks reaches this conclusion in "Virginia Woolf and the Philosophy of G. E. Moore," *Personalist*, L (1969), 222–40.

30. Norman Friedman, "The Waters of Annihilation: Double Vision in *To the Lighthouse*," *ELH*, XXII (1955), 61–79.

through its sympathetic and distorted portrait of Mrs. Ramsay, which contrasts with the antagonistic portrait of Mr. Ramsay. "Time Passes," Part II, stresses the austerity of objectivity, the realm that continues to exist when no one is conscious of it. Despite its intense lyricism, and partly because of it, this section is the most impersonal section of the novel and advances a view of nature totally at odds with human desires. "The Lighthouse," Part III, strikes a balance between the rival claims of subjectivity and objectivity by holding them in an equipoise. When translated into Lily Briscoe's visionary painting, the rivals are fused in the monistic realm afforded through art, but not found in the midst of life itself except in those fleeting moments that are the motive for art.

As in *Mrs. Dalloway*, the image of the window, appearing as the title of Part I, appropriately suggests the act of consciousness and the subjectivity that the narrative emphasizes here. Even though "The Window" stresses the subjective dimension of experience, the characterization of Mr. Ramsay advances a way of seeing the world that only seems at odds with this emphasis. If we look at the three parts of the novel together, however, it becomes clear that his place in this section is as a foil, to set Mrs. Ramsay's perspective in relief.

Mr. Ramsay is a philosophical realist not only by profession but also in his dealings with his family: "What he said was true. It was always true. He was incapable of untruth; never tampered with a fact; never altered a disagreeable word to suit the pleasure or convenience of any moral being, least of all his own children."[31] In his insistence upon the facts rather than individuals' subjective and emotional investment in those facts, Mr. Ramsay has his importance in the novel's guiding plot intrigue—the journey to the lighthouse that his son James so much desires. For all we know in the first part of the novel, there is no strong reason to believe that the weather will impede the journey, so Mr. Ramsay's insistent warnings seem unwarranted: "There wasn't the slightest possible chance that they could go to the Lighthouse tomorrow, Mr. Ramsay snapped out irascibly." Although his predictions turn out to be right, his re-

31. Virginia Woolf, *To the Lighthouse* (New York, 1927), 10–11. Subsequent page references to this novel are hereinafter cited parenthetically as *L*.

actions at this point have an intensity disproportionate to the issue at hand, which encourages us to suspect an underlying emotional need that he will not acknowledge: "The extraordinary irrationality of her remark, the folly of women's minds enraged him. He had ridden through the valley of death, been shattered and shivered; and now, she flew in the face of facts, made his children hope what was utterly out of the question, in effect, told lies. He stamped his foot on the stone step. 'Damn you,' he said. But what had she said? Simply that it might be fine tomorrow. So it might" (L, 50). His emotional needs, which begin to come through here, are pertinent because they establish the relative merits of his philosophical position in the scheme of attitudes that the novel as a whole advances.

Mr. Ramsay wants to be recognized for his complicity in that realm outside his family's and, by extension, everyone's direct conscious awareness. As a philosophical realist he insists upon the existence of a reality that goes on independently of anyone's consciousness; he sees himself as the sole explorer of that new frontier. Consistent with this attitude is his insistence that the weather, which both Mrs. Ramsay and James would rather ignore, will impose unsuspected restrictions upon their subjective desires. His view of his professional role as a realistic thinker puts him in the same stoical light:

> It was his fate, his peculiarity, whether he wished it or not, to come out thus on a spit of land which the sea is slowly eating away, and there to stand, like a desolate sea-bird, alone. It was his power . . . to stand on his little ledge facing the dark of human ignorance. . . . [H]e kept even in that desolation a vigilance which spared no phantom and luxuriated in no vision, and it was this guise that he inspired in William Bankes . . . as a stake driven into the bed of a channel upon which the gulls perch and the waves beat inspires in merry boat-loads a feeling of gratitude for the duty it is taking upon itself of marking the channel out there in the floods alone. (L, 68–69)

As a stake that marks out unseen hazards, Mr. Ramsay here is a miniature lighthouse. In taking upon himself the role of the pure and unadulterating skeptic, he is reminiscent of Decoud in *Nostromo*. Like Decoud he thinks he can strip himself of illusion, that he can predicate his identity upon the cogitation in which he pridefully invests himself. That, according to the narrator, is a guise, a supreme illusion. Unlike Decoud, though, he suspects his own limitations before it is too late.

Here his sense of his own limitations is not nearly as strong as the narrator's sense of them, however, and the narrator's attitude toward him powerfully spells out Mr. Ramsay's ideas' significance. "The Window" is skewed toward the subjective apprehensions of reality, as is borne out by the narrator's rather barbed manner of describing Mr. Ramsay's thinking: he takes the usual formulation "If P then Q" and changes it to the ludicrous formulation "If Q then R." Thus, the narrator calls attention to the formulas themselves by which Mr. Ramsay tries to reach his proof of a reality outside of consciousness and, in calling attention to them, makes his realism a covert solipsism. The narrator's subsequent description of Mr. Ramsay as a fearless leader of men on an expedition, a leader who would not lie down and die (L, 55), renders him little more than a Don Quixote fighting windmills. He is a realist with the embarrassing problem of being unable to make contact with the real world.

Lily Briscoe's peculiar understanding of Mr. Ramsay's epistemological theories further intensifies the criticism of his character implicit throughout "The Window": "Whenever she 'thought of his work' she always saw clearly before her a large kitchen table. It was Andrew's doing. She asked him what his father's books were about. 'Subject and object and the nature of reality,' Andrew had said. And when she said Heavens, she had no notion what that meant. 'Think of a kitchen table then,' he told her, 'when you're not there'" (L, 38). The kitchen table when it is not seen represents the reality that exists independently of consciousness. This example is the classic refutation of idealism, and it is no doubt intended to help Lily comprehend the realistic epistemology Mr. Ramsay espouses. Her understanding is still vague, however, so she converts his realism into the terms of radical subjectivity; Lily understands the kitchen table as nothing more than an idea, however austere in its conception, and not as the independent fact it is supposed to represent. The image of the table finds its way into some humorous and almost surrealistic scenes. When she is taking a walk with Bankes, for example, Lily thinks about Mr. Ramsay's table: "It lodged now in the fork of a pear tree, for they had reached the orchard. And with a painful effort of concentration, she focused her mind, not upon the silver-bossed bark of the tree, or upon its fish-shaped leaves, but upon a phantom kitchen table" (L, 38).

The largely unsympathetic perspective that "The Window" affords on Mr. Ramsay is complemented by the contrastingly sympathetic portrayal of his wife. If it is Mr. Ramsay's place in this section to emphasize the distance between consciousness and its intentions, desire and fulfillment, imagination and reality, then it is precisely Mrs. Ramsay's place to abolish that distance. While he emphasizes what seems only a remote possibility that the weather will prevent the journey to the lighthouse, she is alive to James's emotional comprehension of that journey. For Mr. Ramsay the lighthouse is an austere fact, and the journey there thus involves the ability to confront and endure the elemental obstacles that fill the distance between it and their summer home. For Mrs. Ramsay the lighthouse stands at a mental distance that can be closed in on by changing one's attitude: "To pursue truth with such astonishing lack of consideration for other people's feelings, to rend the thin veils of civilisation so wantonly, so brutally, was to her so horrible an outrage of human decency that, without replying, dazed and blinded, she bent her head as if to let the pelt of jagged hail, the drench of dirty water, bespatter her unrebuked. There was nothing to be said" (L, 51). Her reading the fairy tale to James through most of "The Window" betrays her impulse to make believe that reality takes the shape of our desires. We are not to believe that Mrs. Ramsay lies to James or that she is incapable of distinguishing fact from fantasy, but we are given to believe that she emphasizes imagination as intensely as Mr. Ramsay emphasizes reality.[32] Her emphasis gives her access to a frame of mind in which she is capable of becoming one with objects of her consciousness, abolishing *all* distance: "Often she found herself sitting and looking, sitting and looking, with her work in her hands until she became the thing she looked at—that light, for example" (L, 97).

Mrs. Ramsay's gifts—her astonishing moments of heightened consciousness, her sincere concern for others' feelings, her humility—all invite our sympathy with her, but it is im-

32. Freedman, *The Lyrical Novel*, 229–32; Kiely, *Beyond Egotism*, 72.

portant to recognize the serious limitations in her perspective if we are to see the epistemological bias the whole novel advances. Only in light of these limitations can Lily's ability to surmount Mrs. Ramsay's subjectivity be comprehended. "Time Passes" gives us a perspective on her that we could not have in "The Window," for in Part II Mrs. Ramsay's designs meet the test of time and her subjectivity confronts reality. When at the end of "The Window" she throws her shawl over the boar's skull and tells her children the story of the mountains the shawl now reminds her of, she is filling the void that is death— her death. But in "Time Passes," things are reversed and the chasm she cannot fill is opened: she herself dies. The literal short-sightedness that seemed harmless enough in "The Window" comes to indicate her inability, revealed later in the novel, to foresee the consequences of her designs: Lily does not marry Bankes, as she had hoped; and the marriage of Paul to Minta, which she had been instrumental in arranging, turns sour.[33]

Subjectivity's hegemony is undercut by the passage of time, which emphasizes that Mrs. Ramsay's perspective is not privileged over other characters'. When the novel's three parts are taken together, the underlying austere objectivity of "Time Passes" is more apparent. The language here makes it difficult to view the second section as impersonal or objective, yet its lyricism intensifies the underlying austerity as much as Mr. Ramsay's cold appraisal of the meteorological facts sets into relief the underlying subjectivity of "The Window." The language here also intensifies the disjunction between fact and fancy, for it buries, almost, a sinister core: the fall of the house into near ruin and the deaths of Andrew and Mrs. Ramsay.

In affording a perspective on the house when no one is there, this section is the corollary to the austere kitchen table when no one is looking at it. Through virtually the whole of this short middle section no one is in the house, so this chapter is, exactly as Woolf planned it, the most impersonal of all (*Diary*, III, 36). Characters are mentioned only to indicate that they have gone on to live in the world outside that does not conform to their hopes. Andrew was killed in the war, and Mr. Ramsay

33. Schaefer, *The Three-Fold Nature of Reality*, 123–24.

had to accept his wife's death, the shock of which is here muffled under an incongruent, pleasing locution from which the following is literally bracketed: "[Mr. Ramsay, stumbling along a passage one dark morning, stretched his arms out, but Mrs. Ramsay having died rather suddenly the night before, his arms, though stretched out, remained empty.]" (L, 194). Such bracketed messages as these are the prose written in the margins of the narrator's lyrical poetry.

The only persons who have an active role in this section are the "airs," which are personifications of time and its effects on the house when no one is there. Even when there are sleepers upstairs, these airs have no power over them; they can blanch the apples and wilt the roses when no one sees these things, but they cannot disturb the sleepers (L, 191). Time has its most noticeable effects when it works on the things no one continuously observes.

"Time Passes" then is centrally concerned with that impersonal reality that Mr. Ramsay stoically searches for—the world as it really is. The view of nature advanced in this section wholly accords with this grim view of human experience. The narrator posits a wanderer who goes to the sea, hoping to find that nature will reflect his desire; but he finds no correspondence, for the mirror is broken. There exists "no image with semblance of serving and divine promptitude" that would bring to order the chaos that is the night or that would make the world "reflect the compass of the soul" (L, 193). Meaning is no longer immanent in nature, and order must be earned through man's efforts: "Did nature supplement what man advanced? Did she complete what he began? With equal complacence she saw his misery, his meanness, and his torture. That dream, of sharing, completing, of finding in solitude on the beach an answer, was then but a reflection in a mirror, and the mirror itself was but the surface glassiness which forms in quiescence when the nobler powers sleep beneath? Impatient, despairing yet loth to go (for beauty offers her lures, has her consolations), to pace the beach was impossible; contemplation was unendurable; the mirror was broken" (L, 202–203). The contemplation that this sleeper finds unendurable is the very contemplation that the narrator allows herself. The incommensurability of nature to man is analogous to the incongruence between the richly lyrical language used in this section and the austere reality which it almost succeeds in muffling.

The starkness and cold objectivity buried beneath the stylized language in "Time Passes" is the epistemological complement of the radical subjectivity in "The Window." "The Lighthouse" serves to correct both these incomplete perspectives, for it is here that we realize Mrs. Ramsay's short-sightedness.[34] Not only have the marriages she envisioned come to nothing, but the journey to the lighthouse has never taken place. Furthermore, James no longer even wants to make the journey; it becomes a chore when Mr. Ramsay insists upon it. Also in this section our view of Mr. Ramsay is corrected. Here, we come to a clearer understanding, with Lily, of his deeply felt need for sympathy and understanding—a need that in "The Window" was set forth as only the mockery of his ostensible courage. Lily is central in this last section, for she envisions the *full* implications of Mr. and Mrs. Ramsay, as separate persons and as parts of a single relationship.

Lily arrives at her vision even more gradually than Clarissa did in *Mrs. Dalloway.* She must, for one thing, learn to surmount Mrs. Ramsay's perspective, which in "The Window" she had wanted to share by *becoming* her: "What device for becoming, like waters poured into one jar, inextricably the same, one with the object one adored? Could the body achieve, or the mind, subtly mingling in the intricate passages of the brain? or the ear? Could loving, as people called it, make her and Mrs. Ramsay one? for it was not knowledge but unity that she desired, not inscriptions on tablets, nothing that could be written in any language known to men, but intimacy itself, which is knowledge, she had thought, leaning her head on Mrs. Ramsay's knee" (L, 79). She must accept that the ordinary limits of space and time do not allow such merging. Now that Mrs. Ramsay is dead, Lily must realize that not only is such merging impossible but, finally, undesirable. At this stage she recognizes the limitations to Mrs. Ramsay's perspective; then "for a moment Lily . . . triumphed over Mrs. Ramsay" (L, 260). Only after surmounting her perspective and ceasing to believe that an iden-

---

34. Freedman, *The Lyrical Novel,* 235.

tity through bodily contiguity is either possible or desirable can Lily effect the identity through analogy that her painting constitutes.[35] Like the narrator's language in *Mrs. Dalloway*, the canvas in *To the Lighthouse* merges objects and minds that cannot be fused in conventional notions of reality.

In "The Lighthouse" the distance between Lily's vision and its expression on the canvas is analogous to the distance between the lawn where she paints and the lighthouse toward which Mr. Ramsay, James, Cam, and Malcaster are journeying. The traversing of the mental space between her vision and its formulation on the canvas and of the physical space between the lawn and the lighthouse are so closely associated through the oscillating pattern in which they are described that we are invited to see them as extensions of each other. The alternating traversals of mental and physical spaces seem to synthesize mind and matter.

Until she can find a way to make her design present on canvas, Lily feels "curiously divided, as if one part of her were drawn out there" to the sea and the other part of her "had fixed itself doggedly, solidly, here on the lawn" (*L*, 234). She has yet to traverse the space that can make Mrs. Ramsay present, now that she is physically absent; similarly, she has not made the as-yet absent vision present in the line configurations on her canvas: thus, "there was all the difference in the world between this planning airily away from the canvas, and actually taking her brush and making the first mark. . . . Still the risk must be run; the mark made" (*L*, 234–35).

Her repeatedly stepping away from the canvas in order to see the design whole recalls Mrs. Ramsay's exit from the dinner table in "The Window" in order to comprehend the wholeness of life that the gathering of people represented to her. The important difference is that when Mrs. Ramsay stepped away, it was to arrest the process of living. In isolating the moment for her inspection, as in her expressed desire to preserve her children from adulthood, Mrs. Ramsay falsified the life she meant to inspect: "she was on one side, and life was on the other" (*L*, 92). Thus her perspective is false as long as she herself is living: to step out of life and inspect it is to be dead to life.

35. Love, *Worlds in Consciousness*, 174.

The epistemological significance of Lily's aesthetic perspective is that it can avoid the limitations of Mrs. Ramsay's habits of mind. When Lily recognizes the advantages of art's capacity to show life as it cannot be seen when one is in its midst, the insight comes to her in the form of a revelatory prelude to her vision:

> What is the meaning of life? That was all—a simple question; one that tended to close in one with years. The great revelation had never come. Instead there were little daily miracles, illuminations, matches struck unexpectedly in the dark; here was one. This, that, and the other; herself and Charles Tansley and the breaking wave; Mrs. Ramsay bringing them together; Mrs. Ramsay saying, "Life stand still here"; Mrs. Ramsay making of the moment something permanent (as in another sphere Lily herself tried to make something permanent)—this was of the nature of a revelation. In the midst of chaos there was shape. (*L*, 240–41)

The epistemological analogue of the reconciliation scenes of which she speaks is the synthesis of subject and object that her canvas will register. The work of art that is this novel effects the same synthesis by exacting a correspondence between the achievement of Lily's vision (subjective) and the approach to the lighthouse (objective).

As he approaches the lighthouse, James is finally able to reconcile his idea of the lighthouse with the lighthouse as it really is, beyond his imaginative grasp of it. Until this reconciliation can actually take place, however, there are, to James, two lighthouses—the subjective and the objective ones:

> "It will rain," he remembered his father saying. "You won't be able to go to the Lighthouse."
> The Lighthouse was then a silvery, misty-looking tower with a yellow eye, that opened suddenly, and softly in the evening. Now—
> James looked at the Lighthouse. He could see the whitewashed rocks; the tower, stark and straight; he could see windows in it; he could even see washing spread on the rocks to dry. So that was the Lighthouse, was it?
> No, the other was also the Lighthouse. For nothing was simply one thing. The other Lighthouse was true too. (*L*, 276–77)

Only after Lily, on the lawn, finds a way to achieve "that razor edge of balance between two opposite forces: Mr. Ramsay and the picture" (L, 287) can the synthesis of the two lighthouses be achieved for James.

Not only must Lily accommodate her view of Mr. Ramsay to her subjective biases, but she must also learn to see Mrs. Ramsay objectively and thereby overcome her biases altogether. That is why at this stage she seeks "some secret sense, fine as air, with which to steal through key-holes and surround [Mrs. Ramsay] where she sat knitting" (L, 294). This secret sense reminds us of the airs in "Time Passes" that stole through key-holes and afforded us a glimpse of the house when no mind saw it. Lily tries to see Mrs. Ramsay as objectively as the airs saw the deteriorating house, and her search is rewarded.

When someone seems to approach the window she is looking toward, Lily sees "some light stuff behind it" (L, 299) and anticipates an intrusion. But whoever it is stands inside and fortuitously throws "an odd-shaped triangular shadow over the step" (L, 299). This triangular shape recalls the tripartite structure of the novel and the triad of beams that the lighthouse would emit, representing the cycle of thesis, antithesis, and synthesis that underlies the novel's theme. The shape makes Lily feel Mrs. Ramsay's presence, yet the shadowy shape represents Mrs. Ramsay's absence: it is Lily's and the Ramsays' heart of darkness, the dark space between desire and fulfillment, imagination and knowledge, hope and reality. Precisely this patch of darkness brings Lily to her vision, because it presents her with the opportunity to imagine and thereby reconstitute Mrs. Ramsay's presence on the canvas and, imaginatively, among the living persons who knew her. In this scene we have a direct contrast to Conrad, for whom the imagination can only delay the darkness and for whom the darkness renders imagination ineffective. For Woolf, it is absence that gives the imagination its creative opportunity, and as long as the darkness fortifies the imagination, the imagination can effectively disperse it. The imagination disperses the very darkness that gives it its opportunity to exist, perhaps in order to hold the darkness off and make the rest of life seem easier to bear. When Lily links Mrs. Ramsay with the triangular shadow, she converts the accidental into the essential, absence into presence: "And then, quietly, as if she refrained, that too became part of ordinary experience, was on a level with the chair, with the table. Mrs. Ramsay—it was part of her perfect goodness—sat there quite simply, in the chair, flicked her needles to and fro, knitted her reddish-brown stocking, cast her shadow on the step. There she sat" (*L*, 300).

As if influenced by what has happened in Lily's mind, James finally reconciles what were two lighthouses—the one born of his mother's subjective idealism and the other of his father's stoical commitment to objectivity. As he approaches the real lighthouse, he jumps the gap between the idea of the lighthouse and its objective corollary: "So it was like that, James thought, the Lighthouse one had seen across the bay all these years; it was a stark tower on a bare rock. It satisfied him. It confirmed some obscure feeling of his about his own character" (*L*, 301–302). As the confirmation of some obscure feeling about himself, this reconciliation scene has the psychological effect of combining in his character the warmth of heart he associates only with his mother's subjectivity and femininity, and the unflinching confrontation with reality he associates only with his father's objectivity and masculinity. This psychological reconciliation is reinforced by his father's warm praise of his steering abilities—"Well done!"—to which James responds with a simultaneously warm inner feeling and cold exterior: "He was so pleased that he was not going to let anybody share a grain of his pleasure. His father had praised him. They must think that he was perfectly indifferent" (*L*, 306).

The epistemological analogue of the psychological reconciliation is the synthesis of subject and object, knowledge and imagination, presence and absence, which Lily's aesthetic grasp accomplishes. In real life, the novel finally implies, such a synthesis is only fleeting. For James and his father, the moment at the lighthouse must pass; for Lily on the lawn, Mrs. Ramsay's felt presence and the vision that brought it about must also pass. Reality is, at the last, a disjunctive experience. Even her vision must end, and the fight against time must be waged again: "It was done; it was finished. Yes, she thought, laying down her brush in extreme fatigue, I have had my vision" (*L*, 310). Yet there is still a permanence in the imagination—an endurance that Woolf felt but Conrad did not and Lawrence could not. The vision is as perpetual a possibility for experience as the work of art is; Lily's canvas, like Woolf's novel, can permanently register the synthesis that characterizes the momentary vision. Even more important, if the imagination can turn Mrs. Ramsay's shadow into light, absence into presence, then it does not matter whether the darkness returns. Darkness only switches the imagination back on.

The Verge of Idealism: *The Waves* and *Between the Acts*

The Waves epitomizes Woolf's experimental contribution to the English novel. It departs further from the norms of realistic fiction than any novel we have discussed so far—by Conrad, Lawrence, or Woolf herself—and advances a more decidedly monistic metatheory of knowledge and imagination. In entertaining an ideal solution to the limitations that philosophical and literary realism impose on the relationships between minds, *The Waves* finally fashions an ideal relationship between the novel and its reader. At the end that ideal is deflated, however, and the novel separates author from reader, holding each within realistic epistemological limits, and implying, as the conclusion of *To the Lighthouse* does, the distance between art and life. *Between the Acts*, Woolf's last novel, rounds out our discussion not only of Woolf but also of Conrad and Lawrence, for it takes us beyond the distinction between art and life, artist and audience, imagination and reality. It implicitly gives the mind the power that it does not have for Conrad or Lawrence—the power effectively to fill the space between art and life, imagination and reality.

The Waves, in sustaining an ideal relationship between its characters' minds, departs so far from the norms of realistic fiction that some critics have raised the question of whether it is a novel at all.[36] Its narrative technique establishes this ideal but curious relationship between the characters' minds: on its surface *The Waves* is simply a series of utterances by six distinct characters. Since there is no narrator to speak of, the plot is inferred exclusively from their speeches, which are separated from each other by quotation marks and are identified uniformly by the narrator through simple remarks such as "Bernard said" or "Susan said." There is rarely an indication that

36. Hafley, *The Glass Roof*, 127.

any of the characters can actually hear what the others are saying, and when there is, it is so indirect that we are never certain
how the characters hear each other, whether directly or by
means of the narrator's simply passing the words of one mind
into another mind. However their words are imparted to each
other, their speeches are clearly separated monologues, not the
dialogues that we normally expect in the multicharacter realistic novel. As Ralph Freedman has suggested, the characters'
isolation recalls Gottfried von Leibnitz's idealistic monadologi-
cal thesis: despite each self's radical isolation, all selves are
held together only by the grace of an overseeing preestablished
harmony. In *The Waves* the harmony is the narrator's presence.[37] Only before the end of this novel, Woolf's monads, unlike Leibnitz's, have windows.

The narrator's absorption into the characters, a logical extension of the narrator-character relationship we have followed
from *Jacob's Room* to *To the Lighthouse,* makes the narrator
seem to have disappeared altogether. The narrator's absence,
however, is merely a disguised presence. Although her ostensible voice has been reduced to the minimal task of telling us
who said what, she is so wholly absorbed in the characters that
she is, through them, more present than ever. Her position is
like that of the warder in the hills he illuminates, described in
one of the prefatory chapters. The hills seem *"smoothed into
slabs as with the back of a spade"* and to have *"a light in them
as if a warder, deep within, went from chamber to chamber
carrying a green lamp."*[38] The narrator lights up each character,
allowing us to see the character from inside as she moves from
one to the next. She smooths them into a single and collective
consciousness that at the conclusion of the novel is incarnated
into Bernard.

The narrator was gradually absorbed into the characters during the early stages of this novel's composition. J. W. Graham
has made a fruitful investigation of the available early drafts,

37. Freedman, *The Lyrical Novel,* 267.
38. Virginia Woolf, *The Waves* (New York, [1959]), 279 (in the same volume
with *Jacob's Room*). Subsequent page references to this novel (hereinafter cited
parenthetically as *W*) are to this edition.

especially of the points of view.[39] What he notices in his isolated consideration of *The Waves* becomes more apparent when
we take a broader view: the progress in Woolf's conception of
this novel, especially in regard to establishing the narrator, du-
plicates the pattern of formal innovation that we have been
tracing since *Jacob's Room*.

In the first of the novel's three forms, for example, when
Jinny kisses Louis and Susan is consumed with jealousy, the
narrator, Graham points out, steps in to defend her own observations about children's behavior. In doing this, she implies, as
the narrator of *Jacob's Room* did, that her epistemological authority must be earned through self-interrogation and that it is
open to doubt to begin with. The narrator of the earlier novel
assumed the imaginative prerogatives of the "one"—whose
perspective is as wide as the imagination can make it—and so
does the narrator of the earliest version of *The Waves* take recourse in an ideal mind: "I am not laying too great a stress upon
all this. I am not exaggerating the intensity of children's feelings! Indeed, there is nothing more certain than that children
are tortured by jealousy and love long before they know their
own names; *the mind* was certain of this."[40] At this stage "the
mind" is only ambiguously connected with the narrator's consciousness; it is spoken of as though it were someone else's. Yet
since the narrator wants to shape the epistemological authority
that she attributes to the mind, we are invited to speculate that
at some level this mind is the narrator's. The narrator claims it
so reluctantly perhaps because Woolf herself has not completely
felt her way into the characters of *The Waves*, who will collectively constitute the general mind. The narrator of the novel as
we have it drops her self-interrogation and, far from bringing
into question her authority as the knower of the characters, becomes indistinguishable from them. J. Hillis Miller's formulation of the narrator's *cogito* in *Mrs. Dalloway* is relevant here:

39. J. W. Graham, "Point of View in *The Waves*: Some Services of the Style,"
University of Toronto Quarterly, XXXIX (1970), 193–211.

40. Virginia Woolf, the ms. version of *The Waves* (MS in Berg Collection,
New York Public Library), I, 27 (italics added). As quoted in Graham, "Point of
View in *The Waves*," 198.

they think; therefore I am.[41] In the early stages of the novel's composition, though, Woolf had not yet found a way to get around the narrator's introspection.

In light of her attempts to overcome the narrator's self-consciousness, Woolf's thoughts about the status of *The Waves*—at this point called *The Moths*—make sense: "I am not trying to tell a story. . . . But there must be more unity between each scene than I can find at present. . . . I shall have two different currents—the moths flying along; the flower upright in the centre; a perpetual crumbling & renewing of the plant. In its leaves she might see things happen. But who is she? I am very anxious that she should have no name. I dont want a Lavina or a Penelope: I want 'She.' . . . Also I shall do away with exact place & time. Anything may be out of the window—a ship—a desert—London" (*Diary*, III, 229–30). In saying that anything may be seen out of the window, Woolf imparts to her novel the capaciousness that only imagination, in her previous works, is allowed to have. This capaciousness is achieved by steeping "the mind" in the consciousness of a widely diverse sample of characters, earning what Josephine O'Brien Schaefer calls "full experiencial knowledge of all potential forms of human knowledge."[42] It was only when she began to commit this mind to paper, when she began actually to write the first draft of the novel, that Woolf was able to formulate for herself the epistemological problem which lay ahead: "Yesterday morning I made another start on The Moths, but that wont be its title. & several problems cry out at once to be solved. Who thinks it? And am I outside the thinker? One wants some device which is not a trick" (*Diary*, III, 257). The question is how a capacious imagination can go on unrestrictedly knowing if it has to fall into a particular self. As the narrator's consciousness enters diverse selves, though, the question need not be raised any longer: the narrator is all the selves at once.

Thus far we have considered only the same formal innovations that we observed in the previous novels. There are important ways, however, in which the innovations of *The Waves* go well beyond what we have seen. First of all, though their utter-

41. Miller, *Fiction and Repetition*, 180–81.
42. Schaefer, *The Three-Fold Nature of Reality*, 160.

ances are all in quotation marks, the characters' speeches are not to be taken as their actual words. The narrator interpolates all the characters' thoughts by putting them into her own words.[43] Whereas in previous novels the characters' own words were set off in quotation marks, which helped us to see the distinction between interpolated and actual speeches, in *The Waves* the distance between what is thought to have been said and what is actually said has been banished. At the same time in her private speculations on *The Waves*, Graham notes, Woolf uses *speaks* and *thinks* interchangeably.[44] When the novel blurs the distinction between what is thought and what is said, it undercuts the reader's ability to doubt or verify the truth of what the characters say.

Second, the characters' use of the present tense through almost the whole novel also sets *The Waves* apart. As Graham points out, the chronic use of the present tense turns the events of the story into epitomes rather than episodes.[45] It raises menial details to a level of enigmatic significance, for the characters' words convey in the present tense what the characters would never be aware of as immediately and as consciously as their use of the present tense suggests. When Louis says, "I wear a white waistcoat now and consult a little book before I make an engagement" (*W*, 328), we are not to believe that Louis inspects himself in this much detail. Yet if the same observation were made about him by a narrator in the past tense, we would have a perfectly conventional observation. The verb tenses make an enormous difference, because they can raise even the most ordinary observations to a high level of abstraction. On this level the observations become discrete, threatening temporal continuity and the unity of selfhood, the basic premises of psychological realism.

Because every observation, however minor, seems to occur

43. Geoffrey H. Hartman, "Virginia's Web," in Thomas A. Vogler (ed.), *Twentieth Century Interpretations of "To the Lighthouse"* (Englewood Cliffs, N.J., 1970), 79; Naremore, *The World Without a Self*, 154; Jean Guiguet, *Virginia Woolf and Her Works*, trans. Jean Stewart (London, 1965), 377; Hafley, *The Glass Roof*, 107; Freedman, *The Lyrical Novel*, 256–57; Cohn, *Transparent Minds*, 263–65.

44. Graham, "Point of View in *The Waves*," 206.

45. *Ibid.*, 195–96.

right before us, in the present, each event has the same importance as all others. By virtue of its being the one occurring before us now, however, each event seems as though it should be the epitome of every other event in a temporal sequence that the narrative takes little trouble to establish. As each thing is scrutinized in the present, it is cut off from the past and the future and privileged, if only for one moment, above every other event. In the same way each character, taken alone in his monologue, is the only character we hear and seems, if only for that time, to be the only character there is. He may speak about other characters, but his thoughts and feelings about them are more important than the characters themselves.

This isolation of each character from the others introduces the issues of truth and verification. As all events seem important, so all statements seem true. Since there is no consciousness that reports the condition of an intersubjectively verifiable world—unless we consider the speaker in the prefaces to have assumed this responsibility—the extent to which the reader is allowed to verify or doubt the truth of the story's particulars is diminished. In its insistence that the reader accept certain "givens" of the fiction, *The Waves* is certainly no different from any other work of art; we cannot, if we want to continue to read sensitively, test the validity of any novel by referring to external criteria. But in another respect *The Waves* differs radically from the conventional realistic novel.

Because of the genre's complicity in the empirical philosophy that flourished when the novel did, realistic fiction characteristically invites us to doubt and constantly reexamine the validity of its world's particulars.[46] Thus the disjunction of knowledge and imagination, explored in its classic form in *Don Quixote*, is so central to the concept of the novel. A character can be illustrated as imagining things while he is in the midst of a real world against which his imagination's intensity can be measured. Similarly, in *Jacob's Room* Woolf posited the existence of a verifiable world outside her characters' subjectivities by employing devices like the escaped horse that runs through London and enters the otherwise exclusionary subjectivities of

46. Eric Rothstein, Introduction to *Systems of Order and Inquiry in Later Eighteenth-Century Fiction* (Berkeley, 1975).

isolated characters like Clara and Jacob. In *Mrs. Dalloway* the queen's car and the skywriting airplane exhibit a verifiable realm against which the validity of separate interpretations of that world can be tested. *The Waves*, by contrast, gives us no room to doubt. It presents us with a world that, if we wish imaginatively to enter there, implicitly requires, as Lawrence's novels do, that we leave skepticism behind. As an example, any passage would do: "'In this hot afternoon,' said Susan, 'here in this garden, here in this field where I walk with my son, I have reached the summit of my desires. The hinge of the gate is rusty; he heaves it open. . . . I have had peaceful, productive years. I possess all I see. I have grown trees from seed. . . . I have seen my sons and daughters, . . . taller than I am, casting shadows on the grass'" (*W*, 307–308). She mentions her son, but no other characters seem ever to have met this child. We take Susan at her word; we do not doubt that she has a son, nor do we doubt that she has grown trees from seed, has had a peaceful and productive life, has seen her children into their adulthood. There is no leverage for casting a doubt. We accept Susan's word the way we would accept a reliable omniscient narrator's if he were telling us the same facts. We must believe, because there is nothing, at this or any other point in the novel, outside Susan's purview that could give us even the faintest basis for doubting her.

By asking its reader to do everything but doubt and test the validity of what he reads, *The Waves* advances a model of direct knowledge corollary to the epistemological monism that Woolf advanced in previous novels only in restricted moments. *The Waves* is a prolongation of those moments when the mind seems no longer to fall within a self but to expand over everything. The standard philosophical criterion for direct perception is this inconceivability of doubt that *The Waves* insists upon.[47] The characters here know their surroundings as directly as any self knows its own mental processes. If I say I have a mental image of a tree, much in the fashion in which Susan says, "I am fenced in, planted here like one of my trees" (*W*, 308), my utterance is incorrigible because no one has as direct access to my mental pictures as I do myself. We are not to be-

47. Malcom, "Direct Perception," *Knowledge and Certainty*, 73–95.

lieve that Susan is literally planted like one of her own trees, of course, but we are to believe the most important part of her utterance: she thinks she is so rooted. Beyond the metaphorical validity of each character's interpretations of the world, *The Waves* has no meaning, nor does it aspire to a meaning beyond that. Incorrigible direct perception gives *The Waves* permission to do what realistic narrative resists: to plot sudden conversions of absence into presence.

I have concentrated thus far on the things the reader of *The Waves* is asked not to do. I want to finish by considering what the reader is asked to do, for it is in the peculiar relationship that the reader is asked to assume with the characters that the full implications of the monistic model of knowledge will be felt. The reader will comprehend his relationship with the characters only when he arrives at the conclusion of the novel. There, he is asked to identify with a surrogate, with the listener of the tale, whose ostensible absence from the story will have been only a covert presence.

The role of the reader in *The Waves*, based upon a model of direct perception, is linked to the structure, theme, and major events in the plot. Like *To the Lighthouse*, *The Waves* has a tripartite structure that serves, among other things, as an epistemological model of the relationship between minds. Whereas in the earlier novel we begin with discrete sections devoted respectively to subjectivity and objectivity, and considered first apart from each other and then in their synthetic wholeness, the structure of *The Waves* suggests instead that the condition of differentiation arises out of an original harmony and then subsides, returning the characters at the end to a collective wholeness.[48] Beginning their lives in a condition of paradisal unknowing, they are perpetually carried away by the small miracles of their world, which they do not distinguish from themselves. At the opening of the novel the characters are conscious neither of themselves nor of each other as distinct knowers; they are wholly caught up in their wonder:

> "I see a ring," said Bernard, "hanging above me. It quivers and hangs in a loop of light."

48. Love, *Worlds in Consciousness*, 195–96.

"I see a slab of pale yellow," said Susan, "spreading away until it meets a purple stripe."

"I hear a sound," said Rhoda, "cheep, chirp; cheep, chirp; going up and down."

"I see a globe," said Neville, "hanging down in a drop against the enormous flanks of some hill." (*W,* 180)

As they grow up and enter a more formal social structure, first by entering school, then by entering college and assuming separate careers, they become increasingly self-conscious and differentiated from one another.[49]

At the novel's midpoint, when they gather for the first dinner in honor of Percival's departure for India, the characters are most firmly established in their condition of differentiation. After Percival dies in an accident there, and when the characters are in middle age, they gather again toward the end of the novel, when their own approaches toward death encourage them to throw off their marks of individuation. By the time of the last chapter, where Bernard is the sole speaker, they have all recombined in Bernard, who thinks their thoughts in their absence, as Clarissa thought Septimus' in his absence.

Prefacing each chapter is an italicized lyrical passage that describes the sun's progress from dawn to dusk. The trajectory of the characters' progress follows the trajectory of the sun, beginning in wholeness, going to diversity, then back in wholeness once again. Just before sunrise, all is a primordial chaos in which each thing is everything: *"The sea was indistinguishable from the sky,"* and *"the fibres of the burning bonfire were fused into one blaze"* (*W,* 179). The fifth of the nine prefaces, at exactly the novel's midpoint, indicates in its images the height of differentiation that on their level the characters experience at the end of the first dinner and just before Percival's death. Here the sun *"had risen to its full height"* and was *"no longer half seen and guessed at"* (*W,* 278). In the last preface we are reacquainted with the fusion that is reproduced in the characters' incarnation into Bernard's consciousness. Once again, *"Sky and sea were indistinguishable"* (*W,* 340). At the end of

49. Madeline Moore, "Nature and Community: A Study of Cyclical Reality in *The Waves,"* in Ralph Freedman (ed.), *Virginia Woolf: Revaluation and Continuity* (Berkeley, 1980), 222.

the novel an italicized sentence appears as if to remind us of the final unity: *"The waves broke on the shore"* (*W*, 383). The progress from wholeness through differentiation and then back is suggestive of the wave itself, whose climax is its crest, its point of greatest differentiation from the sea out of which it arose and into which it will be dispersed.

In the six characters' progress through these stages, Percival has a central role. His importance is conspicuous in his silence; he is the only character, aside from the listener at the end, who says nothing throughout the novel. He is spoken of, but he never speaks himself. His role is to reestablish the characters' unity, which was lost when they entered the social arena outside their circle, and to unify them by being the common object of their adoration. As Neville puts it, "it is Percival who inspires poetry" (*W*, 202). He inspires poetry as did his legendary namesake; only this Percival's quest is to refresh their memory of another sort of covenant—their oneness. Louis says: "It is Percival . . . who makes us aware that these attempts to say, 'I am this, I am that,' which we make, coming together, like separated parts of one body and soul, are false. . . . From the desire to be separated we have laid stress upon our faults, and what is particular to us. But there is a chain whirling round, round, in a steel-blue circle beneath" (*W*, 270). If it were not for their sense of having lost their unity, these six would not be searching Percival out. Thus his physical presence is a covert reminder of their actual dispersal.

When they gather in Percival's honor at the novel's mid-point, his physical presence, which they use as only an excuse to meet, does nothing more than indicate how far apart they really are. Their gathering therefore fails to effect the coalescence of identities that they had hoped for. It is Neville's focusing on the necessity of Percival's physical presence that directs their attention all the more toward their distance from their ideal: "without Percival there is no solidity. We are silhouettes, hollow phantoms moving mistily without a background" (*W*, 259). They bicker with one another. Susan's jealousy for Jinny's having kissed Neville during their childhood is carried even further when she has to hide her hands, abused because of her rural chores. She does not want Jinny to see them, because she recognizes and is envious of Jinny's life of urban luxury. As the six assemble one by one, they are intensely conscious of how they look to each other.

After the dinner, knowing that their personalities are more distinct than ever, they despair of ever enacting the oneness that their circle of acquaintance had originally afforded. Neville's anxiety represents the feelings of the others: "What can we do to keep [Percival]? How bridge the distance between us? How fan the fire so that it blazes for ever?" (*W*, 277). Only Bernard is confident that they can regain order and unity: "We too, as we put on our hats and push open the door, stride not into chaos, but into a world that our own force can subjugate" (*W*, 276–77).

As the "phrase-maker" among them, Bernard alone can transform the episodic and random character of their separate lives into a coherent story. His unifying power differs from and exceeds Percival's. He can gather the others together after Percival's death and transform his absence into a presence that, unlike his physical presence when he was alive, will not remind them of their actual isolation. In this way Bernard takes on the roles of Clarissa Dalloway and Lily Briscoe. His phrase-making powers are all the more increased by Percival's absence. The shift in emphasis from Percival's to Bernard's unifying powers suggests that the characters' unity can be attained through a power inside, not outside, their circle. Their unity is a potential that they have carried within the circle of their acquaintance; they need only realize the power that was always there. They need not look outward to Percival.

Bernard's powers exceed those of the other six—most notably those of Louis and Rhoda. Louis is the potential rival to Bernard's unifying powers, since he aspires to be a poet, but like Septimus he is a failed poet. Unlike Bernard, Louis cannot accommodate chaos; he wants every enactment of unity to be the final one. Bernard, by contrast, is alive to the dispersal that always threatens. In this respect, Bernard and Louis are comparable to Miss La Trobe and Isa in *Between the Acts*. Isa is trapped within an artificially ordered world where she has wholly imaginary and therefore abortive romances with men other than her husband. Even her love for her husband is shaped by the clichés of fiction (*BA*, 14). She is a failed poet, registering her phrases in an account book so that no one will see them; because she never allows her imagination to meet the test of reality, she is isolated. By contrast, Miss La Trobe subjects her visions to reality—figuratively, by exposing the performance of her play to the unpredictable weather that constantly threatens it, and actually, by exposing her visions to the uncomprehending audience, many of whom attribute their confusion to Miss La Trobe's failure. For her, as for Bernard, therefore, no work of art, no phrase, no system of order is final: hence, "another play always lay behind the play she had just written" (*BA*, 63).

At the opposite end from Louis and his intolerance for disorder is Rhoda's incapacity to achieve the order required for even the minimal psychological stability:

> "One moment does not lead to another. . . . I am afraid of you all. I am afraid of the shock of sensation that leaps upon me, because I cannot deal with it as you do—I cannot make one moment merge in the next. To me they are all violent, all separate. . . . I have no end in view. . . . Because you have an end in view . . . your days and hours pass like the boughs of forest trees and the smooth green of forest rides to a hound running on the scent. But there is no single scent, no single body for me to follow. And I have no face. I am like the foam that races over the beach." (*W*, 265)

Her apparent schizophrenia, which eventually leads to her suicide, advances in philosophical terms a view of the self that subverts exactly the order Bernard can produce in the collective identity of all six.[50]

When they gather at Hampton Court after Percival's death, they approach the ideal unity they had missed at the previous gathering. Percival's absence is, in one sense, a signal that they can gather for their own benefit, and if they can, then it is because inside the circle of their acquaintance a centripetal force is at work. When they first gather here, they experience the shock that, in Woolf's portrayals of "the moment," typically precedes the instant of heightened consciousness.[51] Their initial shock comes from seeing each other transformed by age. Their gathering works here as a covert reminder of their actual individuation. They do not experience here the complete union

50. Peter Havard-Williams and Margaret Havard-Williams, "Mystical Experience in Virginia Woolf's *The Waves*," *Essays in Criticism*, IV (1954), 71–84.
51. Moore, "Nature and Community," 222.

of identities; that moment will take place only when they are physically absent from the table, in Bernard's dinner with the listener.

The characters do come closer here to attaining unity than they ever have before. They experience a sort of double vision in which they see both their similarities and their differences, and through the latter they begin to suspect their essential sameness. Thus, despite her sense of isolation from the others, Rhoda imagines that they could become a world unto themselves: "I could fancy that we might blow so vast a bubble that the sun might set and rise in it" (W, 331). Whenever he thinks about how others are perceiving him, Neville highlights his individuality, but in certain moments he comprehends that at the deepest part of himself his identity intersects the others' identities:

> "Before, when we met in a restaurant in London with Percival, all simmered and shook; we could have been anything. We have chosen now, or sometimes it seems the choice was made for us—a pair of tongs pinched us between the shoulders. I choose. . . . I am merely 'Neville' to you, who see the narrow limits of my life and the line it cannot pass. But to myself I am immeasurable; a net whose fibres pass imperceptibly beneath the world. My net is almost indistinguishable from that which it surrounds. . . . I see to the bottom; the heart—I see to the depths." (W, 324)

In seeing things this way Neville's imagination takes on the capaciousness that allows him to fill his self-image with the identities of those who are seated nearby. At the end of this gathering, the six pair off and begin thereby to approach the wholeness that Bernard's monologue in the concluding chapter completes.

In the final chapter Bernard introduces a listener into the novel, bringing the reader into the field of his own vision by employing a surrogate. The "you" whom Bernard addresses is the reader.[52] This explains why he chooses "you," the dinner guest, at random; only at random does The Waves select its reader. Bernard thinks that by addressing himself to a total stranger he will feel free to say anything. His speech can take on its capaciousness because the mind of the reader, since it is

52. Graham, "Point of View in The Waves," 209.

potentially any mind whatsoever, is the most capacious mind conceivable.

Bernard begins the dinner with the unnamed listener/reader by assuming the role of the narrator. He summarizes the main events in the plot of *The Waves*, beginning with his observation of the ring in the nursery, which turns out to be the knob of a dresser, and ending with the present moment. In retelling the story of himself and the other five, Bernard uses the past tense. This is the only section of the novel, aside from the prefaces, that is in the past tense. Since the characters' speeches are all in the present tense, we have the impression that their words are chosen by the narrator, who interpolates all their thoughts by rendering them in words the characters do not actually speak. The narrator is in all the characters at once, in a perpetual present; she does not stand apart from them and review them as though they were characters in a history, but rather epitomizes their frames of mind at each moment. Therefore, it is appropriate that she render their speeches in the present tense. But here, as he reviews his life among the other five, Bernard stands apart from himself and from the narrator. In retelling the story, he is the narrator *as a self* with wider than normal but realistic perspectival limits: these are his words, not the words of a collective consciousness.

Throughout Bernard's narrative he is thus a distinct self, detached from the other five, but the closer his story comes to the present moment, the harder it becomes for him to stand apart from himself or from the other five. His introspection can recover only the past self—the self that once existed—not the self that now exists, that now looks upon itself, just as the scope of the eye's vision never includes the eye itself. The closer Bernard approaches the present moment, the more indeterminate his selfhood becomes. When he begins describing the events immediately preceding his encounter with the listener, his sense of his self as a private arena disappears: "Thin, as a ghost, leaving no trace where I trod, perceiving merely, I walked alone in a new world, never trodden. . . . But how describe the world seen without a self? There are no words" (*W*, 376). As he approaches the present moment—the point in the narrative where he must say not what he was but what he is—it becomes impossible to predicate his existence in a moment of introspection. There are no words. He continues speaking, but now in the present tense as all characters did earlier, by striking an identity with the narrator, who can give him the words that complete the chapter. We know he becomes the narrator because he enters the mind of the other five characters and thinks their thoughts as only the narrator has been able to do in her status as a collective mind.

In becoming the collective mind, Bernard is the narrator's word made flesh. Sitting before his unnamed dinner guest, he is, in Joyce's phrase, an ideal mind speaking to an ideal listener. The climax of his narrative, and the climax of the whole novel, is his moment of identity with the other five. He is no longer a separate self; he assumes the identity that all six have been trying throughout the novel to share:

> "And now I ask, 'Who am I?' I have been talking of Bernard, Neville, Jinny, Susan, Rhoda and Louis. Am I all of them? Am I one and distinct? I do not know. We sat here together. But now Percival is dead, and Rhoda is dead; we are divided; we are not here. Yet I cannot find any obstacle separating us. There is no division between me and them. . . . Here on my brow is the blow I got when Percival fell. Here on the nape of my neck is the kiss Jinny gave Louis. My eyes fill with Susan's tears. I see far away, quivering like a gold thread, the pillar Rhoda saw, and feel the rush of the wind of her flight when she leapt." (W, 377)

Bernard thinks their thoughts.

At the end of his monologue Bernard takes upon himself the realistically conceived boundaries of selfhood. The signal of this, as it is for the narrator of *Jacob's Room*, is his self-consciousness. The collective mind, like the narrators of *Mrs. Dalloway* and *To the Lighthouse*, is not a self even if it is made up of selves, so it cannot inspect its own cognition. But when Bernard sees himself in the mirror that is situated near the listener, he registers his awareness of himself as a self and not as a collective mind any longer. He immediately passes his self-consciousness over to the listener/reader: "Oh, but there is your face. I catch your eye. I, who had been thinking myself so vast, . . . am now nothing but what you see—an elderly man, rather heavy, grey above the ears, who (I see myself in the glass) leans one elbow on the table, and holds in his left hand a glass of old brandy. That is the blow you have dealt me" (W, 380).

Self-awareness is the blow, because it forces him to recall the boundaries of his selfhood. Bernard accuses the listener/reader of dealing him this blow, because as soon as he recognizes the listener/reader for what he is—that is, recognizes him as a self, apart from the narrator and from the circle of six—Bernard must at that moment recognize himself as a self apart from the listener/reader. Bernard is no longer the ideal mind speaking to the ideal listener, but a self with perspectival boundaries. Ideally, the narrator and the listener would never part: his narration would be endless because his power to give order to chaos, to render in phrases the random events of life, would be unchallenged by anything or anyone outside himself in his relationship to the listener. His imagination would be reality; his silence would be his speech. Although the novel leads up to this ideal, the moment ends before the novel does, as Lily's vision does in *To the Lighthouse*. The listener and the narrator part from each other at the table, just as the author and the reader part at the end of this novel. *The Waves* finally stands back from itself to critique its own ideal of knowledge. It admits the inevitable distance between art and life, artist and audience, imagination and reality. *The Waves*, for all its departures from the norms of literary realism, is finally conceptually rooted in the tradition that insists that texts cannot adequately embody reality.

In *Between the Acts*, Woolf also maintains the distinction between art and life, imagination and reality. Although she sustains a polar opposition between the terms of subjectivity and objectivity, mind and world, art and life, and inspects the relationships between them throughout the novel, here the polarities are reversible. Art and life exchange positions so fast that we are brought closer than in any other of Woolf's novels to discovering they are indistinguishable.

Between the Acts embodies two parallel and at times intersecting plots: the performance of Miss La Trobe's pageant on one June day in 1939 in an English rural town as a part of an annual celebration, and the lives of a few members of the audience. Although it also considers the question of whether time is circular or linear—whether in moving forward we are not at the same moment moving backward—it concentrates on the relationship of art to life, artist to audience, imagination to reality. At the point in the novel where the pageant becomes indistinguishable from the real world where it is performed, art and life intersect; it becomes impossible to tell whether art imitates nature or nature imitates art. This intersection is suggested throughout the novel, even in the most minor details, which are among the novel's most brilliant moments: "Certainly Miss La Trobe had spoken the truth when she said: 'The very place for a pageant!' The lawn was as flat as the floor of a theatre. The terrace, rising, made a natural stage. The trees barred the stage like pillars" (*BA*, 75–76). At one point, when the clothing and stage props lie on the grass, nature seems to absorb art: "Red Admirals gluttonously absorbed richness from dish cloths, cabbage whites drank icy coolness from silver paper" (*BA*, 63). At various times nature participates in the pageant. The cows sound off as though on cue; and in one particularly dramatic moment the rain falls, but instead of disrupting the play, as everyone supposed it would, it shapes the audience's emotional response: "Isa murmured. Looking up she received two great blots of rain full in her face. They trickled down her cheeks as if they were her own tears. But they were all people's tears, weeping for all people. . . . Nature once more had done her part. The risk [Miss La Trobe] had run acting in the open air was justified. She brandished her script" (*BA*, 180–81).

Where art and nature intersect, imagination is indistinguishable from the knowledge of reality. In these moments the novel expresses the same ideal relationship between the actors (the exponents of the artist's vision) and the audience that we had between the narrator and the listener/reader in *The Waves*. This intersection, however, is constantly fractured throughout the novel, and the distance between art and life takes up the space between the acts—a space that is richly ambiguous: it at once displays the distance between life and art and provides the opportunity for their intersection, as Mrs. Ramsay's shadowy absence is Lily Briscoe's opportunity to exert the powers of imagination in making her present once again. The interval between the acts is disruptively filled with the real adventures of members of the audience. Their adventures are also the subject of this novel—we could almost say the *real* focus—so that the pageant, whenever it resumes, constitutes the interruption between the acts in the audience's lives. This space between the acts is thus ambiguous: depending on which perspective we choose, it is either real life or the artistry of the pageant itself.[53] Seated as it is in the treacherous void separating imagination from reality (the distance that the artist must span), that ambiguity is Miss La Trobe's opportunity to synthesize the two, to disperse that heart of darkness.

In an effort to exact this mingling of imagination and reality, Miss La Trobe plays a trick on her audience. As the culmination of her dramatic presentation of the history of Western civilization, she presents "ourselves"—the pageant's audience: the actors proceed across the stage with mirrors held up to the spectators. She turns her spectacle into its spectators. Just before the mirror-bearers emerge, she designates "'ten mins. of present time. Swallows, cows, etc.' She wanted to expose them, as it were, to douche them, with present-time reality" (BA, 179). The audience, though, is galled by Miss La Trobe's presumption to know them well enough to present them at all: "'Ourselves. . . .' They returned to the programme. But what could she know about ourselves? Elizabethans, yes; the Victorians, perhaps; but ourselves; sitting here on a June day in 1939—it was ridiculous. 'Myself'—it was impossible" (BA, 178–79). They cannot believe Miss La Trobe can present the spectators who are right in front of her nearly as well as the remote figures from history because, to their minds, the presentation must be kept apart from those who are presenting, just as an actor cannot be said to act except insofar as he is not the person whose part he acts. There must be artifice. So Miss La Trobe confronts them with their own unsuspected demands for art and imagination. They cannot be the spectacle they observe as long as they insist upon a division between the seer and the seen, the acting and the real self—the conventional distinction that allows knowledge's independence from imagination but not imagination's independence from knowledge.

Miss La Trobe, in effecting a seamless unity of her spectators with her spectacle, ultimately reveals the dependence of her vision on reality. First, however, she tries to write the ultimate play, the one within which all plays would be subtexts.

53. Miller, *Fiction and Repetition*, 212; Hartman, "Virginia's Web," 78.

She tries to blow a bubble and make everyone live in it, to make them see themselves inside it while they are outside it—as if their reflection on the bubble's surface put them inside. She wants her play to internalize its own internalizing powers, to reflect its own reflection. Her imagination attempts the ultimate embrace, the final inclusiveness within which all reality, and all other imaginations, would have subordinate places; her imagination would then constitute reality. Such an all-inclusive embrace, though, if it were possible, would banish imagination, because there would be nothing pushing against it from the outside to indicate or necessitate its activity. Miss La Trobe's attempt to write the ultimate play, assigning parts even to its audience, also covertly banishes the audience. There would be no watchers, only actors:

> "Reality too strong," [Miss La Trobe] muttered. "Curse 'em!" She felt everything they felt. Audiences were the devil. O to write a play without an audience—*the* play. But here she was fronting her audience. Every second they were slipping the noose. Her little game had gone wrong. If only she'd had a back-cloth to hang between the trees—to shut out cows, swallows, present time! But she had nothing. She had forbidden music. Grating her fingers in the bark, she damned the audience. Panic seized her. Blood seemed to pour from her shoes. This is death, death, death, she noted in the margin of her mind; when illusion fails. Unable to lift her hand, she stood facing the audience. (*BA*, 179–80)

To rid herself of her audience would be to abolish at once her spectacle. As long as Miss La Trobe feels the anguish of struggle, she can know, at least, that the death she seems to undergo here only assures us that her imagination has something more to do. It lives.

Apparently only one member of the audience comprehends the ambition of Miss La Trobe's vision—Mrs. Swithin. This seems appropriate, for Mrs. Swithin has, at least, a capacious mind as broad as Miss La Trobe's imagination and a religious apprehension of the world that the others deride. She is open enough to tolerate William, whose homosexuality makes him an outcast. Her vision approximates Miss La Trobe's and, by extension, Woolf's, for she intuits a harmony in life that she cannot hear by virtue of her condition within the flux of life, just as Miss La Trobe hears a harmony in art that she cannot hear in life, least of all in the unaccommodating arena where her vision is staged. During one of the several interruptions in the pageant, Mrs. Swithin betrays the novel's focal interest in enacting unity, the same wish Miss La Trobe expresses through her pageant: "Mrs. Swithin caressed her cross. She gazed vaguely at the view. She was off, they guessed, on a circular tour of the imagination—one-making. Sheep, cows, grass, trees, ourselves—all are one. If discordant, producing harmony—if not to us, to a gigantic ear attached to a gigantic head. And thus—she was smiling benignly—the agony of the particular sheep, cow, or human being is necessary; and so—she was beaming seraphically at the gilt vane in the distance—we reach the conclusion that *all* is harmony, could we hear it. And we shall" (*BA*, 174–75). This circular tour is reproduced in the pageant, which is designed to take the audience back through history and into the present again. The past is in the present; the beginning is in the end.

To this circular tour there is no ending. In the novel's concluding scene, where we see Giles and Isa alone for the first time, the pageant has ended. Yet it has not and cannot, for upon this final scene of the novel, "the curtain rose. They spoke" (*BA*, 219). Here the author herself seems to attempt Miss La Trobe's ultimately impossible embrace, to make her imagination constitute reality: the curtain rises on this final scene, ironically at the end of the novel, in order to suggest a continuation of Miss La Trobe's play, the one she had the idea for when the last play was in performance, and to suggest its continuation outside the confines of this novel, where the real life of Giles and Isa is indistinguishable from Miss La Trobe's play.

The trick that Miss La Trobe plays on her audience is the same trick that Woolf plays on the genre to which she made her distinct contributions. By making the categories of knowledge and imagination reversible, Woolf does something to reduce the boundaries between life and art that are upheld more insistently in *To the Lighthouse* and *The Waves*. In her last novel, by closing in on the distance between art and life, Woolf makes a distinct contribution to the ongoing attempt that has always given the novel its life. She takes the novel into new territory by asking the imagination to embrace more than it ever had before. If her fiction cannot finish this task of taking in everything, as *Between the Acts* tries to do at its conclusion, that failure indicates only that the realistic novel has further to go. It has not achieved closure, and it will not until the unfinished phrases of the life it tries to incorporate stop generating subsequent attempts to achieve wider embraces.

CONCLUSION

REALISM AND THE FUTURE OF AN ANALOGY

> Realism is always realism *in a certain respect*. . . . What is realistic is after all not relative to the ease with which information is conveyed.
>
> —Roger Scruton
> *Art and Imagination: A Study in the Philosophy of Mind*

> An axiomatic system cannot be made to generate a description of the world which matches it fully, point for point; either at some points there will be holes which cannot be filled in by deduction, or at other points two opposite deductions will turn up. And when a contradiction does turn up, the system becomes capable of proving *anything*, and no longer distinguishes true from false. That is, only an axiom which introduces a contradiction can make a system complete, by making it completely useless.
>
> —J. Bronowski
> "The Logic of the Mind"

At the outset we noticed that conventional literary realism advances a dualistic model of knowledge that sets up an opposition between the imaginary and the real, and we subsequently defined the conventional attributes of Conrad's, Lawrence's, and Woolf's fiction according to that epistemological model. Such a theory of knowledge, as Ian Watt and others have demonstrated, has been transmitted through the mainstream of eighteenth- and nineteenth-century realistic fiction. But the experimental features in Conrad, Lawrence, and Woolf seem to challenge the analogy between literary and philosophical realism. Although there are important points of differentiation between them, their innovations have in common a tendency to place the imagination at the very center of their models of knowledge. The dualism of subjectivity and objectivity is then transformed into a monistic vision of knowledge that, in specific aspects of their fiction, points toward a kind of literary realism in which the imaginary and the real are finally indistinguishable.

In Conrad, perception collapses into imagination. He disparages the powers of cognition and holds to his intuition of an external reality that cannot be brought into the subject's experience by the powers of imagination or perception. It remains outside, a constant threat to the mind's ordering powers, for to think one knows reality is only to continue in the illusion that the mind can control the real, and to order it would be to pretend that the chaos beyond does not exist. In the face of that ineffable reality, the subject is dualistically related to its surroundings, but the mind retreats into imagination. Perception, when Conrad recognizes its inability to penetrate to the inner reality, merges with the imagination, and perception and imagination then become equal and indistinguishable powers in the apprehension of our *accustomed* world, the reality that our cognitive powers order and where we find asylum from the diabolical character of reality's vacant core. Though he disparages the imagination, which serves only to remind him of cognition's inefficacy in apprehending the real nature of our world, Conrad sees it as the only hope. In his fictional representation of our accustomed view of reality, Conrad makes perception a creative act, and merging perception with imagination, he posits a model of knowledge that challenges our ordinary sense of the analogy between literary and philosophical realism.

Lawrence similarly proposes that our mental powers, as dualistic epistemology formulates them, cannot comprehend the reality that grounds human experience. But he proposes an alternative, "blood-knowledge," which reconciles the dualism that distances the knower from the known and that partly accounts for the failed human relationships he depicts. In the comprehension of reality that only blood-knowledge can effect, ego-bound knowledge and imagination are cast out; they are seen as the indistinguishable powers of a single debilitating force. Despite Lawrence's deliberate attempts wholly to extract it from blood-knowledge, however, the imagination remains at the center of his own vision. It is an inextricable part of his alternative model of knowledge for two main reasons: first, because he invents the fictional landscape that communicates his vision, and second, because a full appreciation of his innovations and considerable literary merits requires no clear distinction in the experience of his novels between what is imaginary and what is real.

The persistently chaotic and unaccommodating reality that Conrad flees by withdrawing into the orderly world perpetuated by language and fiction Lawrence brings directly into his novels by proposing a monistic model of knowledge that, instead of averting our attention from the core of reality, brings the self into direct contact with it. Woolf's fiction reconciles these two responses to the distance between knower and known that Conrad and Lawrence represent. Although her fiction implies a distinction between the imaginary and the real whenever it models art's distance from life, this distinction does not amount to a dualism. She bridges the distance, as the realistic novel has always tried to do, but she does so on the basis of a different model of knowledge. For Woolf the moment of vision that initiates the construction of fictions also constitutes our apprehension of reality. To see reality as it truly is, she urges, is to call upon the powers of the artistic imagination and, most importantly, to direct our attention not only outward to the world of objects but also inward to the world of the subject, which is no less valid. She revolts against conventional realism's inventory of externality because it respects the relationship of objects to each other more than their relationship to the apprehending subject. Her revolt converts these inventories of reality into epitomes that infuse the external world with the subject's imaginative powers.

In *The Waves*, this conversion ultimately renders the idea of a thing the covert reminder of its absence; for example, Bernard's ideas of the persons who sit around him at the table become most definite precisely when the persons themselves are absent, and Percival's presence earlier in the novel covertly reminds the others of his absence. I recall this here because in *The Waves* we see one important logical conclusion toward which Conrad's, Lawrence's, and Woolf's experimentation leads—the potentially total break between the idea and thing. Meaning is no longer immanent, but some hope for correspondence must remain for the same reason that, even though in literary realism appearances are often disjointed from reality, if there were an absolute disjunction, then the appearances would point to nothing unless it be to other appearances. The word *appearance* would lose its meaning. *The Waves* moves us toward the extinction of realism or, at best, back to scholastic realism, against which eighteenth-century literary realism rebelled. George Levine lucidly describes this state of affairs: "The idea is reified again, but phenomenally, as an idea, not as a prior reality or a means to reality. By virtue, then, of the very 'realistic' discourse that marks the connection between idea and thing, we are, in the modernist predicament, cut off from things. The idea becomes the clearest indication of the thing's absence."[1]

This brings us to a question that I need to address but obviously cannot settle in these last few pages: is there any point in extending our sense of literary realism beyond the place where it begins to lose its affinities—as it does in Conrad, Lawrence, and Woolf—with seventeenth- and eighteenth-century philosophical realism, whose broad outlines have been amenable to analogies to literary realism? One implication of my study is that the philosophical realism that serves as the closest analogy to these three novelists' fiction lends itself to increasingly specialized understanding, so that by comparison with the broad outlines of Lockean epistemology, for example, the experimental realism we have been discussing pertains to issues that fewer and fewer even critical readers ordinarily confront. I cannot help taking seriously J. P. Stern's observation that "only of 'realism' can it be said that its meaning as a literary term has its parallel in 'life' rather than in one or more specialized pursuits (as 'baroque' has in architecture and music)."[2] Thus, even if we want to refine our sense of literary realism so that it goes beyond defining the realistic novel as fiction that corresponds to the way we experience our lives right now (a definition with limitations too obvious to be specified), and if we want instead to refine our definition through reference to what is realistic in philosophical discourse, we still must recognize that the more refined, abstract, and inaccessible discussions of philosophical realism become, the less meaningful the analogy between literary and philosophical realism might be-

---

1. George Levine, *The Realistic Imagination: English Fiction from Frankenstein to Lady Chatterley* (Chicago, 1981), 9.
2. J. P. Stern, *On Realism* (London, 1973), 37.

come. We face the danger that Levine described in connection with ideas: just as an idea can be reified to the point where it loses its referentiality to things, so might the term literary realism be refined to the point where it ceases to describe the way we experience either literature or life. This problem must be addressed at the outset of any further investigation of this analogy, especially in the study of the more radically experimental novelists in the last few decades, novelists whose philosophical sophistication invites us to expand on the analogy so far that literary realism loses its usefulness as a descriptive term.

In the historical moment when Conrad, Lawrence, and Woolf steered the novel's course, I maintain, the analogy is both recoverable and useful. Their fiction asks us to interrogate the conventional realism it simultaneously embodies. Even in cases where their realism collapses under the burden of their self-interrogation, our speculating on the questions their fiction raises can only add to our understanding of their fiction and its place in the realistic tradition of the novel.

Our speculation may also add to our understanding of some of the more radical novelistic experimentation in recent fiction. In a novelist like Thomas Pynchon, for example, we see certain implications of psychological realism's deterioration. In *V.* (1963) we have a main figure rather than a character. He is more strictly a figure, as his name, Stencil, implies, because there is no attempt to assign ordinary motives for his purpose either in life or in the design of the novel. He is simply a stencil in search of the figure "V," whatever that may be. If his character is psychologically realistic at all, it is according to some pattern of identity or of verification that most of us are unacquainted with. He is not far from the outer limits of characterization that Conrad reaches in *Nostromo* and *Under Western Eyes* especially, where characters threaten to dissolve into sets of randomly assembled self-images with no certain connection and where the self becomes a series of stories about the self rather than a coherent center of experience. Nor is Stencil far beyond the outer limits of characterization Lawrence and Woolf offer, since in Lawrence the self is a collection of internal gods with no imperative for consistency and in Woolf the self is a compendium of other selves. Taken along with Pynchon's other experimental techniques for making his characters knowable to us, Stencil's habit of referring to himself in the third person may presage the disappearance of the interiority so important to psychological realism and to Cartesian epistemology, which privileges introspection.

This is only one of a number of possible strands traceable to later experimental fiction and would require another study to explore its full implications. The most important point is that so much of the last few decades' experimentation betrays a pervasive attitude so thoroughly infusing knowledge with imagination that we are no longer certain that knowledge can effectively cast doubt on and thereby correct our imaginative projections. Knowledge is so completely bonded to imagination that doubt can no longer bring us either to affirm the doubter as an inviolate center of his own experience or to affirm a real world discernibly external to the doubter.

In connection with this attitude toward knowledge and imagination, we could more profitably address an issue I raised at the very beginning of this study—the question of the death of the novel. When critics and novelists speak of the death of the novel, they usually mean that the novel no longer represents the world we live in. But in the midst of such criticism there lingers a naïve assumption that conventional realism invites—the assumption that what we mean by reality is prior to and independent of its fictional representation. Here Alain Robbe-Grillet's comment illuminates matters: "Academic criticism . . . employs the word 'realism' as if reality were already entirely constituted . . . when the writer comes on the scene." In the fiction of Conrad, Lawrence, and Woolf, this assumption he speaks against becomes increasingly difficult to maintain. The novels we have discussed insist that they represent a world bonded to the imaginative media that present it. In contrast to academic critics, Robbe-Grillet believes that "the novel is precisely what creates [reality]. The style of the novel . . . *constitutes* reality."[3]

With this wider view of the novel's powers of representation, we find it easier to see why the question of the death of the novel does not signal its demise. If it does anything, it indicates

---

3. Alain Robbe-Grillet, *For a New Novel: Essays on Fiction*, trans. Richard Howard (New York, 1965), 160, 161.

the novel's continuing viability; the longer the question is raised, the more one must wonder why it was ever raised in the first place. As Jerome Klinkowitz eloquently puts it, "Of everything that died in the years from 1967 through 1969, only one obituary now seems to be false: the death of the novel."[4] What is evident, though, is that its epistemological foundations are shifting.

A better question than whether the novel has died is why the question was ever seriously considered. One reason is that in its more than two-hundred-year history the realistic novel has always invited the question in one form or another because it inherently subverts its own literary qualities. The realistic novel has characteristically taken the literary imagination to the edge of its powers by demanding that the novel seem both to move us outside of the imagination's ordering propensities and to put us in the midst of life. It invents its own crises by seeming to transcend its literary attributes in order to present reality as it is, by wanting to step out of literature and into life. Such a step is ultimately impossible; no novel is the whole of life even if it claims to be part of it. By subverting past novelistic achievements, each novel tries to lay claim to special powers of originality. Such a grasp for both originality and finality in representing reality holds the novel's shaping literary attributes hostage in the anticipation of logically impossible demands. The question of the death of the novel is a very old one, and it serves only to indicate and generate subsequent novelistic achievements.

Other grounds for raising the question of the death of the realistic novel are based on the criterion of generic homogeneity. The novel has tended to move, especially in the last twenty years, in two seemingly irreconcilable directions: in one direction, nonfiction; in the other, fabulation. This bifurcation threatens the nexus that grounds the novel's continuity. But this is not a new problem either, because just as individual novels suppress their literariness, so has the novel historically defied literary critics' expectations for generic homogeneity. On the face of it, this bifurcation, requiring us to ignore for the

4. Jerome Klinkowitz, *Literary Disruptions: The Making of a Post-Contemporary American Fiction* (2nd ed.; Urbana, 1980), 32.

moment the wide middle ground represented by figures no less than John Updike and Saul Bellow, threatens what David Lodge calls the "stable synthesis of the realistic novel," its power to balance the claims of fabulation and mimesis.[5] But in fact it does not, for although, as one critic has pointed out, fabulist and nonfiction novels lend to credibility different meanings and obligations, even they have in common the implicit assumption that there is no final distinction between our imaginative grasp of the world and the supposedly disinterested representation of it.[6] For Conrad, Lawrence, and Woolf this indistinguishability points up the failure of dualistic models of knowledge to describe how we know reality. One implication of many nonfiction and fabulist novels may be that our knowledge does not fail simply because our imaginative, subjective powers are bonded to the world that we deem to await perception.

Conrad, Lawrence, and Woolf were all in their own time accused of writing either poor novels or works that in their experimental features hardly resembled novels at all. No critics today would think of suggesting that their works are not recognizable parts of an ongoing tradition. Nor should our present concept of what it is possible for literary realism to encompass move us to pronounce the death of the novel on the grounds of what at present seems to be its dispersal in heterogeneous disarray, or on the grounds that it has departed from its mimetic imperatives. Especially on the grounds of mimetic imperatives, the experimentation of Conrad, Lawrence, and Woolf urges us toward a more comprehensive view of the genre's enterprise. If their innovations foretell the more recent forays into experimentation, their doing so does not forecast the end of the realistic tradition of the novel. Their innovations widen its horizons.

5. David Lodge, *The Novelist at the Crossroads and Other Essays on Fiction and Criticism* (London, 1971), 7.
6. John Hellmann, *Fables of Fact: The New Journalism as New Fiction* (Urbana, 1981), 11.

SELECTED
BIBLIOGRAPHY

Literary Criticism

GENERAL

Alter, Robert. *Fielding and the Nature of the Novel*. Cambridge, Mass., 1957.

———. *Partial Magic: The Novel as a Self-Conscious Genre*. Berkeley, 1975.

Auerbach, Erich. *Mimesis: The Representation of Reality in Western Literature*. Translated by Willard R. Trask. Princeton, 1953.

Bakhtin, M. M. *The Dialogic Imagination: Four Essays*. Edited by Michael Holquist. Translated by Caryl Emerson and Michael Holquist. Austin, 1981.

Beach, Joseph Warren. *The Twentieth Century Novel: Studies in Technique*. New York, 1932.

Cohn, Dorrit. *Transparent Minds: Narrative Modes for Presenting Consciousness in Fiction*. Princeton, 1978.

Donoghue, Denis. *The Sovereign Ghost: Studies in Imagination*. Berkeley, 1976.

Eliot, T. S. "*Ulysses*, Order, and Myth." Rpr. in *Critiques and Essays on Modern Fiction 1920–1951*, edited by John W. Aldridge. New York, 1952.

Ermarth, Elizabeth Deeds. *Realism and Consensus in the English Novel*. Princeton, 1983.

Humphrey, Robert. *Stream of Consciousness in the Modern Novel*. Berkeley, 1954.

Hunter, Jefferson. *Edwardian Fiction*. Cambridge, Mass., 1982.

Kaplan, Harold. *The Passive Voice: An Approach to Modern Fiction*. Athens, Ohio, 1966.

Kawin, Bruce. *The Mind of the Novel: Reflexive Fiction and the Ineffable*. Princeton, 1982.

Kermode, Frank. *Romantic Image*. London, 1957.

Kiely, Robert. *Beyond Egotism: The Fiction of James Joyce, Virginia Woolf, and D. H. Lawrence*. Cambridge, Mass., 1980.

Lester, John A., Jr. *Journey Through Despair 1880–1914: Transformations in British Literary Culture*. Princeton, 1968.

Levin, Harry. *Contexts of Criticism*. Cambridge, Mass., 1957.

Levine, George. *The Realistic Imagination: English Fiction from Frankenstein to Lady Chatterley*. Chicago, 1981.

Lukács, Georg. *The Theory of the Novel: A Historico-Philosophical*

Essay on Great Epic Literature (1920). Translated by Anna Bostock. Cambridge, Mass., 1971.

MacLean, Kenneth. *John Locke and English Literature of the Eighteenth Century.* 1936; rpr. New York, 1962.

Miller, J. Hillis. *The Form of Victorian Fiction: Thackeray, Dickens, Trollope, George Eliot, Meredith, and Hardy.* Notre Dame, 1968.

Pearce, Richard. "Enter the Frame." In *Surfiction: Fiction Now . . . and Tomorrow,* edited by Raymond Federman. Chicago, 1975.

Robbe-Grillet, Alain. *For a New Novel: Essays on Fiction.* Translated by Richard Howard. New York, 1965.

Schneider, Daniel J. *Symbolism: The Manichean Vision: A Study in the Art of James, Conrad, Woolf, and Stevens.* Lincoln, 1975.

Scholes, Robert, and Robert Kellogg. *The Nature of Narrative.* London, 1981.

Stevens, Wallace. *The Necessary Angel: Essays on Reality and the Imagination.* New York, 1951.

Sypher, Wylie. *Loss of the Self in Modern Literature and Art.* New York, 1962.

Todorov, Tzvetan. *Theories of the Symbol.* Translated by Catherine Porter. Ithaca, N.Y., 1982.

Tuveson, Ernest Lee. *Imagination as a Means of Grace: Locke and the Aesthetics of Romanticism.* Berkeley, 1960.

Watt, Ian. "Realism and the Novel." *Essays in Criticism,* II (1952), 376–96.

———. *The Rise of the Novel: Studies in Defoe, Richardson and Fielding.* Berkeley, 1957.

Winters, Yvor. "Problems for the Modern Critic of Literature." *Hudson Review,* IX (1956), 325–86.

JOSEPH CONRAD

Baines, Joycelyn. *Joseph Conrad: A Critical Biography.* London, 1960.

Burstein, Janet. "On Ways of Knowing in *Lord Jim.*" *Nineteenth-Century Fiction,* XXVI (1971), 456–68.

Cox, C. B. *Joseph Conrad: The Modern Imagination.* Totowa, N.J., 1974.

Crankshaw, Edward. *Joseph Conrad: Some Aspects of the Art of the Novel.* 1936; rpr. New York, 1963.

Daleski, H. M. *Joseph Conrad: The Way of Dispossession.* London, 1977.

Dowden, Wilfred S. *Joseph Conrad: The Imaged Style.* Nashville, 1970.

Garnett, Edward, ed. *Letters from Joseph Conrad 1895–1924.* Indianapolis, 1928.

Glassman, Peter J. *Language and Being: Joseph Conrad and the Literature of Personality.* New York, 1976.

Guerard, Albert J. *Conrad the Novelist.* Cambridge, Mass., 1958.

Guetti, James. *The Limits of Metaphor: A Study of Melville, Conrad, and Faulkner*. Ithaca, N.Y., 1967.

Gurko, Leo. *Joseph Conrad: Giant in Exile*. New York, 1962.

Hawthorn, Jeremy. *Joseph Conrad: Language and Fictional Self-Consciousness*. London, 1979.

Hay, Eloise Knapp. "Conrad Between Sartre and Socrates." *Modern Language Quarterly*, XXXIV (1973), 85–97.

Jean-Aubry, G[eorges]. *Joseph Conrad: Life and Letters*. 2 vols. Garden City, N.Y., 1927.

———, ed. *Lettres Françaises*. Paris, 1930.

Johnson, Bruce. *Conrad's Models of Mind*. Minneapolis, 1971.

Karl, Frederick R. "The Significance of the Revisions in the Early Versions of 'Nostromo.'" *Modern Fiction Studies*, V (1959), 129–44.

———. *Joseph Conrad: The Three Lives*. New York, 1979.

Karl, Frederick R., and Laurence Davies (eds.). *The Collected Letters of Joseph Conrad*. New York, 1983–

Land, Stephen K. *Paradox and Polarity in the Fiction of Joseph Conrad*. New York, 1984.

Leavis, F. R. *The Great Tradition*. London, 1948.

Miller, J. Hillis. *Poets of Reality: Six Twentieth-Century Writers*. Cambridge, Mass., 1965.

Roussel, Royal. *The Metaphysics of Darkness: A Study in the Unity and Development of Conrad's Fiction*. Baltimore, 1971.

Said, Edward W. *Joseph Conrad and the Fiction of Autobiography*. Cambridge, Mass., 1966.

———. "Record and Reality." In *Approaches to the Twentieth-Century Novel*, edited by John Unterecker. New York, 1965.

Schwartz, Daniel R. *Conrad: "Almayer's Folly" to "Under Western Eyes."* Ithaca, N.Y., 1980.

Senn, Werner. *Conrad's Narrative Voice: Stylistic Aspects of His Fiction*. N.p., 1980.

Stewart, J. I. M. *Joseph Conrad*. New York, 1968.

Warren, Robert Penn. Introduction to *Nostromo*, by Joseph Conrad. New York, 1951.

Wasserman, Jerry. "Narrative Presence: The Illusion of Language in *Heart of Darkness*." *Studies in the Novel*, VI (1974), 327–38.

Watt, Ian. *Conrad in the Nineteenth Century*. Berkeley, 1979.

Wiley, Paul L. *Conrad's Measure of Man*. New York, 1966.

Zabel, Morton Dauwen. *Craft and Character: Texts, Methods, and Vocation in Modern Fiction*. New York, 1957.

D. H. LAWRENCE

Balbert, Peter. *D. H. Lawrence and the Psychology of Rhythm: The Meaning and Form in "The Rainbow."* The Hague, 1974.

Bedient, Calvin. *Architects of the Self: George Eliot, D. H. Lawrence, and E. M. Forster.* Berkeley, 1972.

Bertocci, Angelo P. "Symbolism in *Women in Love.*" In *D. H. Lawrence: A Critical Survey,* edited by Harry T. Moore. Toronto, 1969.

Black, Michael. *D. H. Lawrence: The Early Fiction.* Cambridge, England, 1986.

Daleski, H. M. *The Forked Flame: A Study of D. H. Lawrence.* Evanston, 1965.

Delavenay, Emile. *D. H. Lawrence: The Man and His Work: The Formative Years 1885–1919.* Translated by Katharine M. Delavenay. London, 1972.

Ford, George H. *Double Measure: A Study in the Novels and Stories of D. H. Lawrence.* New York, 1965.

Fraiberg, Louis. "The Unattainable Self." In *D. H. Lawrence and "Sons and Lovers": Sources and Criticism,* edited by E. W. Tedlock, Jr. New York, 1965.

Hochman, Baruch. *Another Ego: The Changing View of Self and Society in the Work of D. H. Lawrence.* Columbia, S.C., 1970.

Hoffman, Frederick J. *Freudianism and the Literary Mind.* 2nd ed.; Baton Rouge, 1957.

Hough, Graham. *The Dark Sun: A Study of D. H. Lawrence.* London, 1956.

Howe, Marguerite Beede. *The Art of the Self in D. H. Lawrence.* Athens, Ohio, 1977.

Jarrett, James L. "D. H. Lawrence and Bertrand Russell." In *D. H. Lawrence: A Critical Survey,* eidted by Harry T. Moore. Toronto, 1969.

Kermode, Frank. *Lawrence.* N.p., 1973.

Leavis, F. R. *D. H. Lawrence: Novelist.* New York, 1956.

Lindenberger, Herbert. "Lawrence and the Romantic Tradition." In *D. H. Lawrence: A Critical Survey,* edited by Harry T. Moore. Toronto, 1969.

Miko, Stephen J. *Toward "Women in Love": The Emergence of a Lawrentian Aesthetic.* New Haven, 1971.

Moore, Harry T., ed. *The Collected Letters of D. H. Lawrence.* 2 vols. New York, 1962.

——. *D. H. Lawrence: His Life and Works.* Rev. ed.; New York, 1964.

——, ed. *D. H. Lawrence's Letters to Bertrand Russell.* New York, 1948.

Moynahan, Julian. *The Deed of Life: The Novels and Tales of D. H. Lawrence.* Princeton, 1963.

Mudrick, Marvin. "The Originality of *The Rainbow.*" In *D. H. Lawrence: A Critical Survey,* edited by Harry T. Moore. Toronto, 1969.

Sagar, Keith M. *D. H. Lawrence: Life into Art.* New York, 1985.

——. *The Art of D. H. Lawrence.* Cambridge, England, 1966.

————. *The Life of D. H. Lawrence.* London, 1980.

Sale, Roger. "The Narrative Technique of 'The Rainbow.'" *Modern Fiction Studies*, V (1959–60), 29–38.

Sanders, Scott. *D. H. Lawrence: The World of the Five Major Novels.* New York, 1973.

Schneider, Daniel J. *D. H. Lawrence: The Artist as Psychologist.* Lawrence, Kans., 1984.

Schorer, Mark. "Technique as Discovery." In *D. H. Lawrence and "Sons and Lovers": Sources and Criticism*, edited by E. W. Tedlock, Jr. New York, 1965.

Spilka, Mark. *The Love Ethic of D. H. Lawrence.* Bloomington, 1955.

Tindall, William York. *D. H. Lawrence and Susan His Cow.* New York, 1939.

Tiverton, Father William. *D. H. Lawrence and Human Existence.* New York, 1951.

Van Ghent, Dorothy. "[*Sons and Lovers*]." In *D. H. Lawrence and "Sons and Lovers": Sources and Criticism*, edited by E. W. Tedlock, Jr. New York, 1965.

Vivas, Eliseo. *D. H. Lawrence: The Failure and the Triumph of Art.* Evanston, 1960.

Weiss, Daniel A. *Oedipus in Nottingham: D. H. Lawrence.* Seattle, 1962.

VIRGINIA WOOLF

Apter, T. E. *Virginia Woolf: A Study of Her Novels.* New York, 1979.

Bell, Anne Olivier, ed. *The Diary of Virginia Woolf.* 5 vols. London, 1977–84.

Bell, Quentin. *Virginia Woolf: A Biography.* New York, 1972.

Blackstone, Bernard. *Virginia Woolf: A Commentary.* London, 1949.

Fleishman, Avrom. "Woolf and McTaggart." *ELH*, XXXVI (1969), 719–38.

Franks, Gabriel. "Virginia Woolf and the Philosophy of G. E. Moore." *Personalist*, L (1969), 222–40.

Freedman, Ralph. *The Lyrical Novel: Studies in Hermann Hesse, André Gide, and Virginia Woolf.* Princeton, 1963.

Friedman, Norman. "The Waters of Annihilation: Double Vision in *To the Lighthouse*." *ELH*, XXII (1955), 61–79.

Gorsky, Susan. "'The Central Shadow': Characterization in *The Waves*." *Modern Fiction Studies*, XVIII (1972), 449–66.

Graham, J. W. "A Negative Note on Bergson and Virginia Woolf." *Essays in Criticism*, VI (1956), 70–74.

————. "Point of View in *The Waves*: Some Services of the Style." *University of Toronto Quarterly*, XXXIX (1970), 193–211.

Guiguet, Jean. *Virginia Woolf and Her Works.* Translated by Jean Stewart. London, 1965.

Hafley, James. *The Glass Roof: Virginia Woolf as Novelist.* Berkeley, 1954.

Hartman, Geoffrey H. "Virginia's Web." In *Twentieth Century Interpretations of "To the Lighthouse,"* edited by Thomas A. Vogler. Englewood Cliffs, N.J., 1970.

Havard-Williams, Peter, and Margaret Havard-Williams. "Mystical Experience in Virginia Woolf's *The Waves.*" *Essays in Criticism,* IV (1954), 71–84.

Hungerford, Edward A. "'My Tunnelling Process': The Method of 'Mrs. Dalloway.'" *Modern Fiction Studies,* III (1957), 164–67.

Kapur, Vijay. *Virginia Woolf's Vision of Life and Her Search for Significant Form: A Study in the Shaping Vision.* Atlantic Highlands, N.J., 1980.

Kelley, Alice van Buren. *The Novels of Virginia Woolf: Fact and Vision.* Chicago, 1973.

Leaska, Mitchell. *Virginia Woolf's Lighthouse: A Study in Critical Method.* New York, 1970.

Love, Jean O. *Worlds in Consciousness: Mythopoetic Thought in the Novels of Virginia Woolf.* Berkeley, 1970.

Miller, J. Hillis. *Fiction and Repetition.* Cambridge, Mass., 1982.

Moore, Madeline. "Nature and Community: A Study of Cyclical Reality in *The Waves.*" In *Virginia Woolf: Revaluation and Continuity,* edited by Ralph Freedman. Berkeley, 1980.

Morgenstern, Barry. "The Self-Conscious Narrator in *Jacob's Room.*" *Modern Fiction Studies,* XVIII (1972), 351–61.

Naremore, James. *The World Without a Self: Virginia Woolf and the Novel.* New Haven, 1973.

Roberts, John Hanley. "'Vision and Design' in Virginia Woolf." *PMLA,* LXI (1946), 835–47.

Rosenbaum, S. P. "The Philosophical Realism of Virginia Woolf." In *English Literature and British Philosophy,* edited by S. P. Rosenbaum. Chicago, 1971.

Schaefer, Josephine O'Brien. *The Three-Fold Nature of Reality in the Novels of Virginia Woolf.* Folcroft, Penn., 1969.

Philosophy and Psychology

Ayer, A. J. *Philosophy in the Twentieth Century.* New York, 1982.

Bergson, Henri. *Time and Free Will: An Essay on the Immediate Data of Consciousness.* Translated by F. L. Pogson. London, 1910.

———. *The Two Sources of Morality and Religion.* Translated by

R. Ashley Audra, Cloudesley Brereton, and W. Horsfall Carter. New York, 1935.

Bradley, F. H. *Appearance and Reality: A Metaphysical Essay.* 1893; rpr. London, 1966.

Brentano, Franz. *Psychology from the Empirical Standpoint* (1874). Translated by Antos C. Rancurello, D. B. Terrell, and Linda McAlister. New York, 1973.

Burrow, Trigant. *The Social Basis of Consciousness: A Study in Organic Psychology Based upon a Synthetic and Societal Concept of the Neuroses.* New York, 1927.

Casey, Edward S. *Imagining: A Phenomenological Study.* Bloomington, 1976.

Chisolm, Roderick M., ed. *Realism and the Background of Phenomenology.* Glencoe, Ill., 1960.

Descartes, René. *The Philosophical Works of Descartes.* Translated by Elizabeth S. Haldane and G. R. T. Ross. 2 vols. 1911; rpr. Cambridge, England, 1969.

Ehman, Robert R. "Imagination, Dream and the World of Perception." *Journal of Existentialism,* V (1965), 389–402.

Engell, James. *The Creative Imagination: Enlightenment to Romanticism.* Cambridge, Mass., 1981.

Freud, Sigmund. *The Standard Edition of the Complete Psychological Works of Sigmund Freud.* Edited and translated by James Strachey. 24 vols. London, 1953–74.

Fry, Roger. *Vision and Design* (1920). New York, 1937.

Goffman, Erving. *Frame Analysis: An Essay on the Organization of Experience.* San Francisco, 1974.

Hasan, Syed Zafurul. *Realism: An Attempt to Trace Its Origins and Development in Its Chief Representatives.* 1928; rpr. New York, 1971.

Hicks, G. Dawes. *Critical Realism: Studies in the Philosophy of Mind and Nature.* London, 1938.

Holt, Edwin B. *The Concept of Consciousness.* 1914; rpr. New York, 1973.

James, William. "Does 'Consciousness' Exist?" *Journal of Philosophy, Psychology, and Scientific Methods,* I (1904), 477–91.

———. *The Principles of Psychology.* 1890; rpr. New York, 1950.

Koch, Sigmund. "Psychology as Science." In *Philosophy of Psychology,* edited by S. C. Brown. New York, 1974.

Laird, John. *A Study in Realism.* Cambridge, England, 1920.

Malcom, Norman. *Knowledge and Certainty: Essays and Lectures.* Ithaca, N.Y., 1975.

McTaggart, John. *The Nature of Existence.* 2 vols. Cambridge, England, 1921.

Merleau-Ponty, M. *Phenomenology of Perception* (1945). Translated by Colin Smith. London, 1962.

Mill, John Stuart. *Collected Works of John Stuart Mill.* 21 vols. Toronto, 1963–85.

Moore, G. E. *Philosophical Studies.* London, 1922.

——. *Principia Ethica.* 1903; rpr. Cambridge, 1968.

Morick, Harold, ed. *Wittgenstein and the Problem of Other Minds.* New York, 1967.

Pitcher, George. *The Philosophy of Wittgenstein.* Englewood Cliffs, N.J., 1964.

Russell, Bertrand. *The Analysis of Mind.* 1921; rpr. New York, 1922.

Ryle, Gilbert. *The Concept of Mind.* London, 1952.

Santayana, George. *Interpretations of Poetry and Religion.* New York, 1900.

——. *Winds of Doctrine.* New York, 1913.

Schlick, Moritz. "Meaning and Verification." In *Readings in Philosophical Analysis,* edited by Herbert Feigl and Wilfrid Sellars. New York, 1949.

Schopenhauer, Arthur. *The World as Will and Idea.* Translated by R. B. Haldane. 3 vols. 1883; rpr. London, 1950.

Scruton, Roger. *Art and Imagination: A Study in the Philosophy of Mind.* London, 1982.

Shaffer, Jerome A. *Philosophy of Mind.* Englewood Cliffs, N.J., 1968.

Strawson, P. F. "Imagination and Perception." In *Experience and Theory,* edited by Lawrence Foster and J. W. Strawson. N.p., 1970.

——. *Individuals: An Essay in Descriptive Metaphysics.* London, 1959.

Wild, John. *Introduction to Realistic Philosophy.* New York, 1948.

Wittgenstein, Ludwig. *Philosophical Investigations.* Translated by G. E. M. Anscombe. New York, 1953.

INDEX